Inside Tunisia's al-Nahda

In the wake of the Arab uprisings, the Tunisian Islamist movement al-Nahda voted to transform itself into a political party that would for the first time withdraw from a preaching project built around religious, social, and cultural activism. This turn to the political was not a Tunisian exception, but reflects an urgent debate within Islamist movements as they struggle to adjust to a rapidly changing political environment. This book reorientates how we think about Islamist movements. Drawing on extensive fieldwork with grassroots activists of Tunisia's al-Nahda, Rory McCarthy focuses on the lived experience of activism to offer a challenging new perspective on one of the Middle East's most successful Islamist projects. Original evidence explains how al-Nahda survived two decades of brutal repression in prison and in social exclusion, and reveals what price the movement paid for a new strategy of pragmatism and reform during the Tunisian transition away from authoritarianism.

RORY MCCARTHY is a fellow of Magdalen College, Oxford, where he specializes in social movements, contentious politics, and Islamism in the Middle East and North Africa. He is the author of *Nobody Told Us We Are Defeated: Stories from the New Iraq* (2006) and co-editor of *Civil Resistance in the Arab Spring: Triumphs and Disasters* (2016). He spent a decade as a foreign correspondent for The Guardian, with postings in Islamabad, Baghdad, Beirut, and Jerusalem. He has a BA in History from the University of Cambridge and an MPhil and DPhil in Oriental Studies from the University of Oxford.

T0349194

Cambridge Middle East Studies

Editorial Board

Charles Tripp (general editor)
Julia Clancy-Smith
F. Gregory Gause
Yezid Sayigh
Avi Shlaim
Judith E. Tucker

Cambridge Middle East Studies has been established to publish books on the nineteenth- to twenty-first-century Middle East and North Africa. The series offers new and original interpretations of aspects of Middle Eastern societies and their histories. To achieve disciplinary diversity, books are solicited from authors writing in a wide range of fields including history, sociology, anthropology, political science, and political economy. The emphasis is on producing books affording an original approach along theoretical and empirical lines. The series is intended for students and academics, but the more accessible and wide-ranging studies will also appeal to the interested general reader.

A list of books in the series can be found after the index.

Inside Tunisia's al-Nahda

Between Politics and Preaching

Rory McCarthy

University of Oxford

CAMBRIDGE
UNIVERSITY PRESS

University Printing House, Cambridge CB2 8BS, United Kingdom

One Liberty Plaza, 20th Floor, New York, NY 10006, USA

477 Williamstown Road, Port Melbourne, VIC 3207, Australia

314–321, 3rd Floor, Plot 3, Splendor Forum, Jasola District Centre, New Delhi – 110025, India

79 Anson Road, #06–04/06, Singapore 079906

Cambridge University Press is part of the University of Cambridge.

It furthers the University's mission by disseminating knowledge in the pursuit of education, learning, and research at the highest international levels of excellence.

www.cambridge.org
Information on this title: www.cambridge.org/9781108472517
DOI: 10.1017/9781108560511

First published 2018

Printed and bound in Great Britain by Clays Ltd, Elcograf S.p.A

A catalogue record for this publication is available from the British Library.

Library of Congress Cataloging-in-Publication Data
Names: McCarthy, Rory, 1971– author.
Title: Inside Tunisia's al-Nahda : between politics and preaching / Rory McCarthy.
Other titles: Cambridge Middle East studies.
Description: Cambridge, United Kingdom : Cambridge University Press, 2018. | Series: Cambridge Middle East studies | Includes bibliographical references and index.
Identifiers: LCCN 2018021300 | ISBN 9781108472517 (hardback : alk. paper) | ISBN 9781108459938 (pbk. : alk. paper)
Subjects: LCSH: Ḥarakat al-Nahḍah (Tunisia) | Islam and politics–Tunisia. | Tunisia–Politics and government–1987-2011. | Tunisia–Politics and government–2011–
Classification: LCC JQ3339.A529 M38 2018 | DDC 961.105/3–dc23
LC record available at https://lccn.loc.gov/2018021300

ISBN 978-1-108-47251-7 Hardback
ISBN 978-1-108-45993-8 Paperback

For Juliette

For Jillian.

Contents

Acknowledgements

This book would not have been possible without the many Tunisians who gave their time to answer endless questions from this frequently puzzled researcher. I spent many hours in homes, offices, and coffee shops talking with people of all political backgrounds and none, but especially with current and former members of al-Nahda, who told me about their activism and their many years of exclusion, including distressing stories of hard times spent in prison. Most of these men and women remain unnamed in this text, but their stories inhabit every page. I am very grateful for their participation, and especially so to Abdedayem Noumi, who encouraged me to start my research in Sousse, found me somewhere to live, frequently fed me and took me out for tea, and who graciously introduced me to the Nahdawi community in the city.

Michael Willis helped shape this project from the outset as my doctoral supervisor and has been endlessly encouraging ever since. In Tunisia, many people gave practical and intellectual help, including Fethi el-Mehri, Gsouma Gsouma, Chokri Zoghlami, Mohamed Chemli, Sayyid Ferjani, Oussama Homri, Sadok Ayari, Carlotta Gall, Fabio Merone, Eileen Byrne, Fadil Aliriza, Joel Rozen, and Michaël Ayari. I also owe much to the many friends and colleagues who gave generous guidance during my research and writing, including Francesco Cavatorta, Sami Zemni, Faisal Devji, Mohamed-Salah Omri, Walter Armbrust, Tariq Ramadan, George Joffé, Hussein Omar, Anne Wolf, Charles Tripp, the late John Shipman, and my anonymous reviewers. Thank you to Maria Marsh of Cambridge University Press for taking on this project with such enthusiasm. I would like to thank *The Middle East Journal* for allowing me to reproduce in this book parts of my article 'When Islamists Lose: The Politicization of Tunisia's Ennahda Movement', published in 2018. The interpretations I make in this book and any mistakes are my own responsibility.

I began this project for a doctoral thesis at St Antony's College, Oxford, and finished the book while a Fellow by Examination at Magdalen College, Oxford. Portions of this research were funded by grants and awards, and I am grateful for their support. These include: an Ali Pachachi Doctoral Studentship, Dahrendorf Scholarship, McCone Fund Grant, and Writing Up Bursary, all from St Antony's College; and a Travel, Research, and Engagement Grant from the Project on Middle East Political Science, run by Marc Lynch at George Washington University. I am especially grateful to the president and fellows of Magdalen College, particularly Marilyn Booth, who gave me the time and encouragement to complete this book in such a welcoming academic community.

My deepest thanks go to Juliette Seibold, patient reader of many drafts, who has spent years travelling around the world with me and who brings joy to every new encounter.

Note on Transliteration

In transliterating from Arabic, I follow the guidelines of the *International Journal of Middle East Studies* (IJMES). Thus, ʿ denotes the letter *ʿayn* and ʾ denotes the *hamza* glottal stop. I do not use diacritics for personal names, place names, names of political parties and organizations, or titles of books and articles. Therefore, the movement I write about is al-Nahda and its members are Nahdawis, rather than *al-nahḍa*, An-Nahda, Ennahda, Ennahdha, or Nahdaouis. For words that are more common in English I keep to the simplified IJMES version, thus the shariʿa, not *al-sharīʿa*. I do, however, stray from these stylings to use commonly accepted Tunisian spellings for personal and place names (which are often themselves derived from French transliteration conventions) so that those public figures and places I write about may be more easily recognizable. That means I write about Rachid Ghannouchi rather than Rashid al-Ghannushi, and, for example, the district of Kalaa Kebira rather than the more formal al-Qalʿa al-Kubra.

Abbreviations

AISPP	International Association for the Support of Political Prisoners
AKP	Justice and Development Party (of Turkey)
CPR	Congress for the Republic
FJP	Freedom and Justice Party (of Egypt)
GEAST	Group of Studies and Socialist Action in Tunisia
IAF	Islamic Action Front (of Jordan)
ISIE	Independent High Authority for the Elections
ISIS	Islamic State of Iraq and Syria
LTDH	Tunisian Human Rights League
MDS	Movement of Socialist Democrats
MOUPAD	Movement of Democratic Patriots; also known as WATAD
MPDC	Popular Democratic and Constitutional Movement (of Morocco)
MTI	Islamic Tendency Movement
MUR	Movement of Unity and Reform (of Morocco)
PCOT	Tunisian Workers' Communist Party
PDP	Progressive Democratic Party (previously the RSP)
PJD	Party of Justice and Development (of Morocco)
PSD	Destourian (Constitutional) Socialist Party
PSP	Social Party for Progress
PUP	Popular Unity Party
RCD	Democratic Constitutional Rally
RSP	Progressive Socialist Rally (later the PDP)
UDU	Unionist Democratic Union
UGET	General Union of Students of Tunisia
UGTE	Tunisian General Union of Students (associated with al-Nahda)

UGTT	Tunisian General Labour Union
UTICA	Tunisian Confederation of Industry, Trade and Handicrafts
WATAD	Movement of Democratic Patriots; also known as MOUPAD

1 Introduction

In a crowded hotel ballroom in the beach resort of Hammamet, hundreds of delegates from the Islamist al-Nahda movement gathered for their tenth congress. It was a moment not just to assess how they had fared since the fall of Tunisia's authoritarian regime five years earlier, but to agree a decisive new strategy for the future. After many hours of debate, the culmination of months of nationwide workshops and discussions, the delegates voted by a large majority to transform al-Nahda into a political party that would for the first time formally separate itself from religious, social, and cultural activism. Rachid Ghannouchi, al-Nahda's charismatic 74-year-old co-founder and leader, presented this decision to the outside world in bold terms. 'We are leaving political Islam to enter into Muslim democracy,' he said. 'We are Muslim democrats who no longer call for political Islam.'[1] At the congress in May 2016, Ghannouchi took to the stage beneath a vast Tunisian flag to defend this strategic reorientation before his supporters:

The al-Nahda movement has not stopped evolving throughout its long journey ... The functional specialization between the political and other social fields is not a sudden decision or a submission to temporary pressures, but rather the culmination of an historical path in which the political work was distinct from the social, cultural, and preaching work in our movement.[2]

The 'functional specialization' that transformed a religious social movement into a political party was not merely a structural decision about how best to allocate resources or how to be seen to comply with electoral regulations in the new Tunisia. Instead, it was the product of a long, strategic, and intellectual debate driven by growing disquiet among many Nahdawis about the identity of their movement after decades of repression and political exclusion. Thirty-five years earlier, Ghannouchi and five of his colleagues had sat at a simple wooden table in a lawyer's office in Tunis for a press conference to propose an audacious new political project based on a 'comprehensive conception of Islam' (al-taṣawwur al-shumūlī li-l-islām), which combined the political and the religious in one vision.[3] Yet here in 2016 was a rare public admission that it was no longer possible to fuse political and religious ambitions as one, and that what the movement called political work (al-'amal al-siyāsī) should now be distinct from what it called preaching work (al-'amal al-da'wī). What had happened to that first comprehensive vision? Why was there such internal disagreement about the true character of al-Nahda? What did it mean to be an Islamist movement in a nascent democracy? Who really spoke for the movement?

In all that is written about Islamists across the Arab world, fuelled by a security-led fascination with violent groups and the blossoming of jihadology as the new Kremlinology, movements like al-Nahda are often overlooked as merely peripheral. Yet this organization offers an intriguing study into the way an Islamist movement transforms over time as it interacts with both authoritarian regimes and democratic political institutions. Here was a movement that began with ideas and a model borrowed from the Egyptian Muslim Brotherhood, but which soon branched out along a path so shaped by the Tunisian environment that the Nahdawis came to be regarded as a rather special case, as 'Islamists unlike any others'.[4] However, although al-Nahda has followed a particular historical path, it is by no means unique. The movement has encountered many challenges familiar to Islamists elsewhere. The recent claim to have departed from political Islam was Ghannouchi's own articulation of a debate under way within many such movements as they scramble to adapt to a rapidly changing political environment. Al-Nahda has played a central role in the modern history of a small nation that stands out for its pioneering uprising against the regime of Zine El Abidine Ben Ali in 2010–11 and, amid a region-wide descent into civil war and counterrevolution, for its hopeful transition away from authoritarianism in the years that followed. This transition is neither the unalloyed success that many observers imagine, nor is it an anomalous model that holds no value for comparative research.[5] Instead, Tunisia's political, social, and cultural forces deserve our sustained consideration and interrogation, and not only when Western tourists die on Tunisian beaches.[6] Islamist movements across the region have closely followed the historical experience of al-Nahda and the writings of Ghannouchi when deciding their own strategies and intellectual positions. We would do well to pay similarly close attention.

There are many ways to examine the workings of an Islamist movement like al-Nahda, but one remark has stayed with me throughout my research. Two decades ago, the French scholar François Burgat made the case for 'involved empathy' in the often-fraught study of Islamism, even at the risk of appearing too sympathetic to those we observe.[7]

A reminder is unfortunately necessary: if there has been a methodological error, it has not been made by those who have taken the trouble to meet with Islamists before discussing Islamist issues, but by those who for so long thought that they could forego such an enterprise.[8]

This book draws on hundreds of hours of formal and informal discussions with current and former members of the al-Nahda movement during several months of fieldwork in Tunisia. While I am sensitive to the difficulties of perspective this approach entails, I draw on Burgat's reminder to present an immersive, fine-grained micro-study of the shifting trajectories of an Islamist movement in one Tunisian city.

The primary question of this book is how best to explain the transformation of al-Nahda's Islamist project over time. One way to approach this problem is to consider the lived experience of Islamist activism: how individuals came to the movement, what meanings they gave to their actions, and how and why these meanings changed over time. I trace the genealogy of meaning-making within the movement from its origins to the present day to explain the contest and negotiation between political and preaching ambitions. My research operates in an explicit geography of the local and privileges the experiences of non-elite members of the movement. I explore how Islamist activism operates offstage, beyond the most visible, formal politics of movements and their leaders.

I make three arguments. First, the relationship between the political and the religious within the movement has been conflicting and ultimately irreconcilable, rather than interdependent and cohesive. For a movement that, like other Islamist groups in the region, proposed a 'comprehensive' vision of Islam, there was a striking historic tension at the heart of this project. Until 2011 this vision was an untested, utopian proposition, but its ambiguity and plasticity served a purpose as the movement grew. Second, at the local level we find the sources of the movement's resilience inside Tunisia during the decades of repression. The paradox of al-Nahda is that the movement re-emerged quickly following the popular uprising against Ben Ali, despite two decades of repression and without being able to call on those elements understood from research elsewhere to be so crucial to Islamist resilience, like a deep movement structure and grassroots social welfare activities. Instead, from 2011 al-Nahda rebuilt itself rapidly because of sources of resilience I identify here, including deep informal networks, an individual reimagining of the Islamist project, and activism on the movement's intellectual and structural periphery. Third, al-Nahda has undergone a series of strategic and intellectual adaptations to the changing political context of Tunisia. In 2016 al-Nahda underwent its most significant adaptation yet as it made an irrevocable strategic commitment to politicization and sought an intellectual justification for its new approach. Movements like al-Nahda are highly adaptive to their environment, yet adaptation comes at a cost, both organizational and intellectual. Adapting the movement this time has brought fragmentation and demobilization.

Party and Movement

It might be tempting to take an Islamist leader at his word when he talks of the 'evolution' of his movement from 'social, cultural, and preaching work' towards an exclusive focus on 'political work'. But simply transcribing a linear narrative like this does nothing to explain what is being said or to uncover its sociopolitical location. Nor can the views of a leader expressed in a speech at a congress be taken as the uncontested view of all within the movement. These words were a careful act of framing, designed to legitimate a particular set of decisions and to inspire a certain course of action.

The greater danger, though, is that this stereotyped dichotomy, the political versus the religious, makes Islamist activism appear to be merely an instrumental politicization of religious ideas. Paying attention to the political nature of Islamist movements has done much to move the debate beyond older Orientalist notions of an essential, unchanging Islam as the primary explanatory factor for Muslim behaviour. The assumption, for example, that this religion produces exceptional politics because in the historic experience of Muslim societies there has been an indivisibility of religion and state, *dīn wa-dawla*, has by now been persuasively discredited.[9] However, in presenting a corrective, some scholars emphasize Islamism as highly politicized behaviour, as 'a religionized political agenda, not a spiritual one'.[10] This leaves little space for the mobilizing forces of faith and identity, of shared values, and new solidarities. And it focuses attention on formal politics at the state level. For Olivier Roy, Islamists are 'obsessed with the state' and seek 'to re-create a true Islamic society, not simply by imposing sharia, but by establishing first an Islamic state through political action'.[11] But in identifying the goal of this political action as state power, so capturing state power is made the sole criterion of success against which to judge Islamist activism. When Islamists fall short of this goal they fail to 'pass the test of power'.[12] As Frédéric Volpi reminds us, this focus on formal state institutions alone assumes a Western political science notion of 'politics' that is just as essential and unchanging as previous Orientalist notions of Islam.[13]

Distinctions between political and religious activities have tended to shape the way different Islamist formations are defined. Some are considered 'vanguard' movements, which seek political power to effect top-down reforms; others, by contrast, are 'grassroots' movements, which work to build a bottom-up, counter-hegemonic community.[14] Similarly, some, like groups based on the Muslim Brotherhood model, are seen as 'statist', participating in the politics of the nation-state; others, like quietist Salafis or transnational violent jihadis, are 'non-statist' and give primacy to their relationship to the community.[15] For Roy, the entire Islamist project has exhausted its revolutionary zeal and Islamist groups have split into nationalist political parties, which advocate democracy, elections, and coalitions but which have no model for a different society, and 'neofundamentalism' or morality-focused activism in the private domain.[16] Such analytical distinctions help explain the remarkable diversity within the spectrum of Islamist behaviour. However, a valuable insight is lost in the process. These rival tendencies can coexist within the same organization for many years, where they become the subject of negotiation and competition. Therefore, in this book I approach Islamism in an inclusive fashion, defining it as a project that seeks to be active in the political, social, and cultural spheres by drawing on the Islamic scriptural tradition and reinterpreting it for the present day.[17] I set out to explore the overlaps and ambiguities between ideas of political ambition and religious outreach. And I find debates, tensions, and meaning-making that complicate these analytical distinctions between political parties and religious movements, between top-down and grassroots projects.

There are two reasons why such overlaps and ambiguities should not be a surprise. First, the Islamist project which is today seen as so highly politicized actually has non-political intellectual origins. This was a project that favoured divine sovereignty over rule by the people, for fear that the people would pronounce against scripture or that a ruler would seek to control Islam.[18] It pushed back against the intrusions of the colonial and post-colonial state to privilege instead social self-management through the shari'a under the guidance of religious experts. This is why there is so little detail in Sunni Islamist programmes about how political institutions should be fashioned, because it is not the institutions that must be virtuous or moral, but the individuals themselves. Hence the problem of circular logic identified by Roy: an Islamic state would promote virtue, but it could not exist without first a society of virtuous individuals.[19] There was, in other words, an intellectual ambiguity ingrained in the Islamist project from the beginning.

A second, connected reason for these overlaps is that 'politics' for Islamist movements constitutes more than the capture of state power. In the context of the intrusive colonial and post-colonial state, religious, social, and cultural activism become a political act in the endeavour to forge an ideal society. Such activism does not merely pay attention to superficialities of style and dress, but challenges the state's regulation of quotidian practices which shape the public sphere.[20] Islamist movements are engaged in a dual effort to transform not just the state, but also their society, what has been called 'the politics of everyday practice'.[21] As Salwa Ismail argues, 'Islamist interventions raise questions about the basis of the frames of references of public morality, the boundaries of the private and public, and, ultimately, about who controls the public sphere.'[22] Where Islamists are indeed preoccupied with state power it is surely not only to produce a virtuous community, but because the modern state seeks to transform and control all aspects of life. Even in their social and cultural activism Islamists cannot ignore the state's pervasive reach. As Talal Asad puts it, social activity requires legal consent and therefore state approval: 'Because the modern nation-state seeks to regulate all aspects of individual life – even the most intimate, such as birth and death – no one, whether religious or otherwise, can avoid encountering its ambitious powers.'[23] That in turn, Asad argues, makes social spaces, and their definition, ordering, and regulation, 'political'. As a result, we see Islamists in competition with many actors including, but not limited to, the state 'over both the interpretation of symbols and the control of the institutions, both formal and informal, that produce and sustain them'.[24]

Islamist movements like al-Nahda do target state power. Later in this book when I talk about politicization I refer specifically to the process of engaging with formal political institutions. This means adopting a set of behaviours focused on party structures, elections, appealing to new constituencies, and taking part in formal institutions.[25] But that is not all the political work these movements do. Al-Nahda's repertoire of political acts included religious, social, and cultural activism.

Making Islamist Meanings

Studies of Islamism are prone to a self-conscious fascination with the perspectives of leaders, as if they as individuals embody the thoughts and ambitions of monolithic movements. This produces a static reading of the 'language of the ideologues', which overlooks the possibility that Islamist organizations are more fragmented than they appear.[26] Scholars interview leaders, read their statements, and listen to their public performances, but they pay much less attention to considering how such words are received and understood by their own supporters and how these perceptions vary over time.[27] This tendency is pronounced with al-Nahda because of the enduring role of Ghannouchi as founder–leader and intellectual reference.[28] Historical accounts of the movement concentrated on leadership debates; analyses of al-Nahda's activism after 2011 once again centred on the leadership's strategic choices. Scholars identified the importance of mutual ideological tolerance as explaining the success of the initial transition away from authoritarian rule, or they emphasized how the constraints of pluralist politics pushed the leadership to compromise in drafting the constitution and in negotiating with former regime elites.[29] This is often a broader problem. Studies of democratization since 2011 continued to focus largely on the role of the state, ruling elites, and the leadership of major political parties.[30] Perhaps such a tight focus on the elite-level politics of al-Nahda was inevitable given the remarkable political opportunities in the new Tunisia. But stressing the political behaviour of the leadership reinforces a historical view of al-Nahda, and one perpetuated by some of the leaders themselves, as a unified movement pursuing primarily a political project aimed at state power. It does not ask how this came to be the priority, whether that path to politicization was seamless, and whether ordinary members of the movement perceived it in the same way as their leaders. Obscuring these internal dynamics misses much about the complex trajectory of this Islamist movement, how it built informal networks and why it survived two decades of severe repression. The transmission of ideas from the leadership to the grassroots of the movement and the contest and negotiation over these ideas is easily occluded.

I offer an alternative approach in this book by taking as my starting point the activists of the movement themselves, their offstage mobilizations, and the way they understood what it meant to be an Islamist. My intention is to reorient our understanding of an Islamist movement. I do not mean to imply that the informal activities of men and women are more important than those of their leaders, but instead I offer a corrective to the 'systematic overlooking of the role of nonelite actors' that others have already warned against.[31] A focus on top-down politics, which looks at Islamist rhetoric, publications, and organizational activities from above, tends to miss the solidarities that emerge from informal, value-centred, grassroots politics.[32] The challenge in explaining the transformations of Islamist movements is to capture the little-noticed collective actions at the local level and to map how they unfold over time.

I treat al-Nahda and its precursors as a social movement because it presents a collective challenge based on shared purpose and solidarities and is engaged in a sustained interaction with authorities, elites, and opponents.[33] The standard framework for researching such groups is social movement theory, which seeks explanations for how people mobilize support, create solidarities, and make collective challenges. In its classic articulation, this theory drew on concepts developed in studies of social movements in the West: political opportunities, how shifting constraints and opportunities shape movements; mobilizing structures, the formal and informal 'collective vehicles' through which people mobilize; framing processes, the way a group makes conscious strategic efforts to create meanings of the world; and the idea of repertoires of contention, in which past actions are shown to shape the choice of future forms of mobilization.[34] But this approach is limited by what are often stretchable concepts, as well as a reliance on structural explanations, rational-actor assumptions, and Western contexts. I find more useful subsequent work, which argued for the creative role played by such factors as emotions, behaviour, meaning-making, and informal networks.[35]

A prominent Egyptian Islamist recently argued that the primary drivers of his movement's behaviour were 'moral and religious', and could not be explained away by theories of rational choice.[36] His movement, he said, privileged 'faith over utility'. How can we make sense of this? I am interested here in how an Islamist movement draws on a particular supply of religious resources. These might provide organizational opportunities, shared identities, motivations, and legitimacy, all of which can be found in other social movements. But religion also has what Christian Smith identifies as a 'disruptive, defiant, and unruly face' because it offers a sacred transcendence that acts to judge the mundane earthly reality.[37] It thereby provides 'the seeds of radical social criticism and disruption'.[38] This disruptive social criticism emerges through a series of social processes, which this book draws out in the context of one Islamist community in Tunisia. A combination of study groups, new spoken and written discourses, and a set of behaviours were used to construct new interests and values within the early preaching community. One behavioural element was the act of preaching or *da'wa*, the call to Islam. This began with training to acquire an individual ethical conduct, but then reached out to the goal of an Islamic reform of the community and then society. This behaviour reflects Asef Bayat's concept of an 'imagined solidarity', which is 'forged spontaneously among different actors who come to a consensus by imagining, subjectively constructing, common interests and shared values between themselves'.[39] By building this imagined solidarity, so these activists created a new social action which in turn constructed informal networks and subcultural communities. These networks provided the resilience that later helped the movement survive two decades of intense repression.

Social movements, however, are not unified actors and might be better thought of as comprising 'sets of competing discourses'.[40] The meanings formed in these imagined solidarities are contested when they emerge and are subject to negotiation and change over time.[41] If a social movement is not a unified actor at any one moment, then how diverse too might it look when considered from a historical perspective? Are the meanings and behaviours which demonstrate belonging to the movement in the 1970s the same as those relied on in the post-2011 era? A movement's collective identity is continually formed and reformed by people operating in different sites at different times.[42] These negotiations over meanings provide a framework through which to study how the sinews of political and religious orientations might pull in different directions within al-Nahda at different moments in its development. This book takes a historical approach to cover a period of more than forty years in the life of a movement in motion. It is a perspective that demonstrates, first, that bonds formed by early networks are remarkably resilient and flexible but, second, that the need to adapt a collective identity to changing contexts can prove profoundly disruptive.

Meeting Islamists

One hot day in June I rode in a *louage*, a shared minibus, from Tunis down the highway for two hours to the coastal city of Sousse, Tunisia's third largest city. There I met a former political prisoner from al-Nahda. Abdedayem was fifty-five years old and married with three children. He volunteered with a small prisoner support association and had begun compiling a list of the hundreds of Nahdawi former prisoners from Sousse, with details of their convictions and the length of time they had spent in jail, 'before they are forgotten', he said. Over lunch on his patio he described how he had first become involved with the Islamist movement as a schoolboy, when he led religious study groups. He told me about his eight hard years in prison in the 1990s, during which the regime forced his wife to divorce him, and then how after jail he had come home, remarried his wife, and worked discreetly to support other prisoners and their families. Now he was employed in the local administration under an amnesty issued after 2011, and spent his free time visiting former prisoners compiling details for his list.

Abdedayem found me a small apartment to rent in a block not far from his home off the Street of the Date Palms, in al-Khezama al-Sharqiyya, a lower middle-class area of the city. On my first night in Sousse, he took me to a local al-Nahda meeting, where activists were discussing how to train their supporters and where I was asked to give an impromptu talk on the relative merits of the British educational system over the French. From then on, Abdedayem introduced me to his friends within the movement and so I began my research by meeting older activists who, like him, had been present in the founding years. Each of them directed me to others and I gradually found my way into the community through suggestions and connections.

Until 2011 it was difficult and dangerous for both researcher and activist to ask detailed questions about Islamism in the semi-authoritarian police state that was Tunisia, which explains the relative dearth of recent detailed studies of al-Nahda.[43] The French scholar Béatrice Hibou, who visited Tunisia during the 2000s, described how her interviewees were often harassed and how she too was systematically intimidated by 'police men in civvies, straight out of bad cop films, with leather jackets, dark glasses and faces like gangsters, hurrying to keep up with me'.[44] But after January 2011 such intimidation, at least as far as foreign researchers were concerned, became no more than a bad memory. The uprising threw open the door to scholars and presented a wealth of new opportunities for immersive study.[45]

This book is a political ethnography of the al-Nahda movement in Sousse which explores the texture of lived experiences and how individuals made sense of their world. I use ethnographic techniques in my research, but I also adopt ethnography as a way of understanding my work, as a 'way of seeing' what I found.[46] After several visits to Tunisia from 2011 onwards, I spent fourteen months living in Sousse from late 2013. I interviewed eight-five current or former members of al-Nahda asking about their life histories and their involvement in the movement, often going back to see people several times to finish half-told stories or to clarify earlier comments. I met as many members as possible from the dozen or so who had been elected to al-Nahda's Sousse regional bureau, and from those who led the sixteen local bureaux, which operated in each of the governorate's administrative districts. I met the senior Sousse activists who had been elected to the movement's national Consultative Council (*majlis al-shūrā*), a 150-member body which meets every three months and functions as an internal parliament, and I interviewed dozens of other non-Islamist politicians, human rights activists, and academics.

Our discussions were nearly always in Arabic and I recorded our conversations when people agreed, as well as making notes during and after discussions and observations. I translated and transcribed these words, which became the primary sources for this book. I offered all of those I interviewed the right to anonymity and have respected that throughout the text, except when individuals explicitly asked to be named or when referring to senior public figures. For those anonymous participants, I use a single pseudonym to represent their identities and I denote their position in the movement in broad terms: local al-Nahda member, meaning an ordinary low-level member; local leader, meaning one of the dozen or so individuals elected to a local bureau; regional leader, meaning one of the dozen or so individuals elected to the Sousse regional bureau, some of whom may also have been elected to the Consultative Council; and senior leader, meaning a high-ranking member of the movement usually based in Tunis and often not represented in their home regional bureau, but perhaps holding an administrative office within the movement or sitting in the Consultative Council or the smaller and more senior Executive Bureau (*al-maktab al-tanfidhi*). I also spent my time observing at al-Nahda offices, and wherever possible attending rallies, celebrations, meetings, and family weddings, as well as watching the October 2014 legislative election campaign, when I followed door-to-door campaign efforts and small-scale political events. To put these discussions into context I call on written archival sources, including historic al-Nahda documents, published memoirs, court transcripts, reports by human rights associations, and newspaper articles, including from the Islamist journals *Al-Ma'rifa* (The Knowledge) and *Al-Fajr* (The Dawn).

This system of chain referral, or snowball sampling, as a way to find people to talk to can be problematic because it risks producing biased samples: individuals might only introduce me to others who think like they do.[47] And it can limit generalizable conclusions because this is not a randomized control sample but one selected in what may seem at times a haphazard manner. However, al-Nahda was an organization emerging from two decades as a repressed underground movement into a polarized public sphere, where Islamists were routinely vilified in the national media. It was difficult to convince people to talk to me without first demonstrating who else I had met in the movement, and Nahdawis I met for the first time would usually consult with fellow activists first. In these circumstances, a snowball approach is often the only way to make access into the community.[48] There was always the danger, too, that their narratives slipped into retrospective rationalizations of an idealized past or that individuals only told me what they wanted me to hear. My answer to this problem was to ask many people about the same events, themes, and processes over many months, until I gathered multiple, overlapping accounts from different perspectives. It is harder for people to put on an act for you the more time you spend among them. Surviving party documents and other written sources allowed me to compare oral narratives with historical accounts. In the end, these spoken histories were imperfect, as written sources can be too. Yet they have significant value as evidence, given that so many of the movement's own documents from the early years of activism were destroyed by the Tunisian intelligence agencies and police.

As much as I have tried to be comprehensive in my ambition, this project is bound by the idiosyncrasies of ethnographic research. But a close study like this can bring to light problems and variations that get missed in broader research. This means studying a movement at a smaller scale to understand what it meant to individuals to be an Islamist. The informal workings of power relations capture micro-mechanisms of change and resistance operating outside institutional political life.[49] A focus on insider meanings and perspectives offers many benefits. It gives agency to social and political actors by asking how they view political situations, rather than relying on overly structural explanations. It offers insights into self-perception and identity politics, showing how collective meanings are formed, how they influence political processes, and how individuals understand them.[50] It demonstrates the powerful role of informal networks in producing meanings, shaping mobilization, and providing organizational resilience. Insider perspectives also reveal the process of adaptation, which is often uneven and improvised. I decipher fragments of history and memory, because those habits formed in an individual's early experience of activism provided a repertoire from which to craft ways of acting, thinking, and feeling in the years that followed. And this was a movement in constant motion. This book, therefore, considers the movement from its origins as a preaching circle, which in the mid-1970s became al-Jamaʿa al-Islamiyya (the Islamic Group), through the period of 1981–88 when it operated under the name Harakat al-Ittijah al-Islami (the Islamic Tendency Movement, MTI), and then its subsequent development as Harakat al-Nahda (the Movement of the Renaissance). The period under study begins in the early 1970s, when the preaching circle first emerged, and reaches until 2016, when al-Nahda responded to an election defeat by opting for a deep, hard-to-reverse commitment to politicization. I hope not to generalize about the al-Nahda movement as a whole, and even less about 'Islamism' as a unified concept. Instead, this book engages with scholars who have used different techniques to study similar movements elsewhere in a dialogue about diverse, changing Islamisms.

I did not always agree with the views of those I met, but this book is not about making yet another moral judgement as to whether al-Nahda or any other Islamist group meets some definition of 'democratic' or 'liberal'. Instead, it is my effort to understand what this movement meant for those within it, and how they transformed their project over time. These were people who suffered years in prison and in social exclusion for their political beliefs and yet willingly told me their stories in often painful detail. I could not have pursued this project without their remarkable generosity, and the rare gift of their memories, experiences, and narratives.

The book is structured chronologically. Chapter 2 introduces the city of Sousse and addresses the origins of the movement to ask why it first emerged in the city and what mechanisms of mobilization it employed. Chapter 3 rethinks the politicization of the movement in the 1980s to challenge those previous assumptions that suggest the movement grew more distant from its preaching origins during this period. The effect of two decades of repression is considered in Chapter 4, which excavates the prison experience, with its intellectual evaluations and physical acts of resistance, and in Chapter 5, which argues that social exclusion disaggregated the movement into its constituent parts. Chapter 6 asks why the movement so quickly began to fragment and demobilize after 2011, even as activists rebuilt and redefined their project. In conclusion, Chapter 7 asks what lessons similar Islamist experiences in the region might offer al-Nahda and then assesses the tension between politics and preaching within the movement, explains al-Nahda's resilience under repression, and interrogates the politicization of the movement.

2 Morality, Behaviour, and Networks

> We started preaching and it was about bringing people back to the mosque and back to prayers. There were meetings open to everyone in the style of da 'wa, about how Islam means doing good to others, to help others follow the correct path ... We did little trips to villages, going into the mosques and explaining to people their religion, how to pray, how to do ablutions. It started like that ... And people followed me because they knew my family, and they had confidence in me and recognized that what I said was the right path.
>
> *Abdallah, a former medical student from a prominent Sousse family, who was one of the first of a new wave of preachers in the city in the early 1970s.*[1]

There is a tendency in accounts of al-Nahda to hasten through its early years, disregarding them as some form of intellectually and organizationally discrete 'religious' stage, which was soon replaced by a more mature and important 'political' formation. This occurs just as much in the movement's own accounts of its history as when scholars observe from outside. This chapter, however, argues that the ideas and actions first established in the 1970s remained central to the way al-Nahda's members conceived of their movement. By these ideas and actions, I mean mosque preaching (as led by men like Abdallah), discussions of morality, faith, and behaviour, and the informal networks these inspired. Of course, I do not mean to argue that religion was the sole motivational factor, because clearly the socioeconomic context, political aspirations, cultural contests, and opportunities for action also shaped mobilization. Rather, I mean to suggest that even from its earliest days the collective action represented by a new preaching movement in the 1970s was about more than merely using religious vocabulary to express political, economic, social, or structural grievances. It was about faith and belief as pillars in themselves. Here I draw on those who argue that ideas, in this case religious faith, can matter as much as interests in forging mobilization within social movements or in shaping interests and identities.[2]

From the early 1970s large groups of young people began to gather regularly at a handful of mosques in Tunis to listen to a new generation of preachers, including Rachid Ghannouchi, a philosophy graduate and former Arab nationalist born in the southern town of El Hamma, in Gabes governorate, in 1941;[3] Abdelfattah Mourou, a charismatic lawyer from Tunis born in 1948 who had studied at Sadiki College, the elite bilingual Tunis secondary school; and Hmida Ennaifer, a theologian born in Tunis in 1942 who had studied at the historic Zaytuna mosque-university and the Sorbonne in Paris. These preachers offered an energizing reassessment of their faith, giving classes explaining Qur'anic passages, elaborating methods of prayer, and presenting Islam as a comprehensive guide for life. Though most of their work was in Tunis, these men also travelled through the country, spreading their ideas. In Sousse several sympathizers built their own branch of this movement, forged again around mosque classes, a new search for morality, and what proved to be robust informal networks in schools, universities, mosques, and villages. These networks established a new religious community, even in a city long considered a stronghold of the secular elite of the new Tunisian nation.

This chapter begins by exploring the political and economic context of Sousse in the early 1970s before analysing the nature of the first religious activism in the city through preaching and mosque classes. It explains the deep personal relationships built through networks at schools, universities, and mosques to show the interconnectedness that bound together members of a shared project. In this way I track the organizational development of the movement as it matured towards the end of the decade.

Pearl of the Sahel

The city of Sousse conjures up a particular fascination in the Tunisian political imagination. Its allure derives not just from its history as a Phoenician colony founded ahead of Carthage, or as a military port used by Hannibal and later for the Aghlabid conquest of Sicily in the early ninth century. It is the modern period that has established the city's particular reputation.

At the moment of Tunisia's independence in 1956, the Sahel, a prosperous coastal strip running from just north of Sousse down to the smaller cities of Monastir and Mahdia to the south, was the political and economic mainspring of the new nation.[4] It was a region which divided the rainy climate of the north from the desert of the south and where the income from dense olive groves funded the emergence of a new middle class. During France's colonization of Tunisia as a protectorate between 1881 and 1956, Sahelian village solidarity and a high concentration of population made it harder for European settlers to buy land. Most settlement was concentrated in the north, while in the Sahel the few European settlers tended to be schoolteachers or civil servants.[5] Where French rule had often weakened traditional elites, the Sahel maintained a demographic and economic base. Wealthier parents sent their sons to schools in the capital. In 1939 Sahelians made up half of the entry class to Sadiki College, the elite school founded in 1875 by the reformist prime minister Khayr al-Din.[6] From there, many went on to study in universities in France. They returned to forge the nationalist movement and then to become the administrative elite of the new nation, even though they were still considered the provincial outsider (*āfāqī*) by the Tunis-born elite (*beldī*). In the early days of independence the sociologist Jacques Berque was taken by the 'vigour' and 'energies' of the Sahelians; for Clement Henry Moore the Sahel was 'the axis of a modern integrated nation emerging from the impact of a colonial situation'.[7] It was in the town of Ksar Hellal, halfway between Sousse and Mahdia, that the nationalist Neo-Destour held its founding congress in March 1934, not far from Monastir, home to the party's co-founder and Tunisia's first president, Habib Bourguiba, who had studied at the Sadiki College and later in Paris. From Hammam Sousse came Ben Ali, the ambitious security officer who overthrew the ageing Bourguiba in 1987, along with many of the ministers who served under Bourguiba and Ben Ali. After 2011, many government ministers were drawn from the Sahelian elite, often from Sousse itself.

In a country riven by deep regional inequalities, Sousse was one of the more privileged regions. Under Ben Ali, two-thirds of public investment were directed to the coastal regions.[8] More than half of Tunisia's 11 million citizens lived within an hour's drive of Tunis, Sousse, and Sfax, the industrial city further to the south, and these three cities alone accounted for 85 per cent of Tunisia's gross domestic product.[9] Poverty rates along the coast were the lowest nationwide and the official unemployment rate in Sousse stood at 11.5 per cent in 2014, well below the national average of 14.8 per cent.[10] By 2013 Sousse had a population of 220,000 in a mostly urbanized governorate covering 650,000 people.[11] The Pearl of the Sahel (*jawharat al-sāḥil*), as it is marketed, is also a centre of the tourism industry and boasts a string of Orientalist-kitsch hotels with names like Scheherazade, Orient Palace, Marhaba Club, Le Marabout, and Dreams Beach, which ran from the Old City up five long miles of sandy beach to Port El Kantaoui. In late 2013 music still blared from hotel beach bars and tourists in swimsuits floated above the Mediterranean on parasails. Their *zone touristique* was geographically isolated from the rest of the city by a long straight road, formerly Boulevard 7 novembre, marking the date of Ben Ali's coup in 1987, hurriedly renamed

Boulevard 14 janvier, marking the date of his fall in 2011. The only sites of confluence with Tunisians were either in the corridors of tourist hotels, where low-paid staff worked in financial precarity, or in the Old City, where tourists in shorts and sandals buying overpriced trinkets passed Tunisian families shopping at the market for fresh vegetables, second-hand clothes (*fripes*), and sweet doughnut treats (*bāmbālūnī*). However, a short walk inland from anywhere else along the beachfront and there were no more tourists to be seen. Here Sousse spread out from the relatively wealthy middle-class areas north of the Old City, to the industrial zone of Sidi Abdelhamid to the south and the poor student suburb of Hai Riadh to the west, home to many of the migrants who came to the coast over the previous five decades looking for work. The geographical segregation of this mass-market, low-cost tourism served to reproduce an impression of a Tunisia that was stable, tolerant, and by nature quiescent, what Hibou identified as 'this form of *culturalisme* that is in line with the *imaginaire touristique* which confuses the professional obsequiousness of the lift boy with a quasi-natural preference for conciliation over conflict'.[12]

Fragments of evidence, however, suggest there are transgressive microhistories of Sousse to be written. That it drew so many economic migrants from the rural interior in the decades after independence meant the city became a complex urban mix of wealth, poverty, and aspiration. From the mid-1970s onwards, new university campuses attracted a large student population, which today stands at nearly 30,000, and with it the student politics of a new middle class. New subcultures soon emerged, including the Islamist movement which became al-Nahda and, in later years when al-Nahda was heavily repressed, Sousse became a source of recruitment for Salafist groups. Many of the hundreds of young men arrested under a new anti-terrorism law in 2003 were from the city, as were several of those involved in an armed confrontation with security forces in the northern town of Suleiman in 2006–07.[13] Sousse's tourism industry was itself the target of terrorist attack. First, in August 1987, when hotels in Monastir and Sousse were bombed by a fringe Islamic cell, then again in October 2013, in a failed suicide bombing on the beach of the Riadh Palms hotel, and once more in June 2015 in the deadly shooting at the Imperial Marhaba Hotel in Port El Kantaoui, where thirty-eight people, including thirty British tourists, were killed by a lone gunman. The hotels promptly emptied as the already debt-laden tourist industry sank.[14] The *imaginaire touristique* was exposed in all its superficiality.

My study begins in the 1970s, a moment when Sousse still had the outward signs of a successful city. It attracted financial firms, with nine banks, eight insurance companies and several private lenders, and had a growing service sector, according to a contemporary study by a Tunisian academic.[15] Most secondary schools in the Sahel region were in Sousse, and drew in more than two-thirds of their students from the surrounding rural areas or from further north up the coast, which would become a significant factor in the early days of Islamist activism. Primary state school enrolment stood at 74.8 per cent in 1972–73, the third best performing region in the country, and more than 27,800 attended state secondary schools, making Sousse the region with the second highest number of pupils in the country.[16] The city also hosted the main food markets for the region, and the most important transport hub outside Tunis.

However, despite a political importance disproportionate to its small size, the city was socially and economically dislocated. Agriculture was in decline. Farming and fishing employed only 6.5 per cent of the city's working population in 1963, and by the late 1960s the olive forests were neglected and ageing. Large landowners were disappearing as they divided up their land for heirs or sold it off in small parcels, and Sousse in general seemed to show a 'lack of interest' in agricultural issues.[17] The port, which should have been a vibrant source of trade, was ranked only fourth in the country because repairs had been slow after it had been badly damaged in the Second World War. Sousse continued to export halfa grass, used in the manufacture of paper, as well as salt, grain, and olive oil. But Tunisia's primary natural resource, phosphate from the southern mines of Gafsa, was exported out of Sfax, further down the coast. To add to the challenge the population of Sousse was growing rapidly, reaching 56,000 in 1966 according to the government census, a 14 per cent increase in the previous decade fuelled by a rural exodus of jobseekers who filled new suburbs on the edges of the city.[18] Yet Sousse appeared to be losing its national influence as the cities of Tunis and Sfax grew more economically powerful. In Sousse, rapid population growth and a faltering agricultural sector had brought 'the economic decline of the city'.[19] Industry was seen by local party officials and business interests as in urgent need of expansion – Sousse represented only 9 per cent of national industrial activity, and ranked far behind Sfax and Tunis, because of poorer infrastructure, lesser trade at the port, an unfavourable tax environment, and a lack of skilled labour.[20] In March 1973 the governor of Sousse, Mohamed Ennaceur, was already warning of growing unemployment, which he said stood at 5,000 in the Sahel but which was expected to rise to 15,000 by the end of the decade, especially affecting young people.[21] That year the Sousse governorate identified the nascent tourist industry as the target for most inward job-creating investment, including the new 1,200-bed el-Hana Beach hotel on the seafront, followed by agriculture and an emerging industrial sector, which included textile exporters, food producers, small clothing manufacturers, and mechanics firms.[22]

Indeed, nationwide the early 1970s were a time of malaise. Over the previous decade the regime had dramatically shifted economic development towards a planned economy, with import-substituting industrialization and the creation of 1,500 mostly agricultural cooperatives under Ahmed Ben Salah, a former leader of the Tunisian General Labour Union (UGTT) and now minister of planning, finance, and economy, and himself a Sahelian from Moknine. Yet, rather than reform and modernize agriculture as intended, this 'Tunisian socialism' brought a significant decline in agricultural production and a series of strikes. In early 1969 Ben Salah announced he would expand his cooperatives into the politically influential olive farms of the Sahel. This was too much for farmers and for the ruling party, by now renamed the Destourian Socialist Party (PSD).[23] The PSD turned against Ben Salah; Bourguiba sacked him and he was jailed for treason. From 1970, under the new prime minister, Hedi Nouira, a former central bank governor from Monastir, the government began a policy of economic liberalism, *infitāh* (literally: opening up), shifting the economy to export-oriented development, focused on phosphate, petroleum, olive oil, and textiles.[24] One of the key pieces of legislation behind *infitāh* had a significant impact in Sousse with its sweeping concessions to businesses. Law 72–38 of April 1972 gave foreign-owned export-oriented industries a ten-year tax break, fee and duty waivers, and the right to repatriate their profits.[25] This encouraged foreign-owned exporters to set up in Sousse and the Sahel, and in 1973 the Sousse governorate already forecast it would bring in 2,100 new jobs that year alone.[26] This law would go on to offer unanticipated opportunities for Sousse's al-Nahda activists during the hard years of repression under Ben Ali. Good weather in the early 1970s helped grain and olive oil harvests but regional competition soon began to weaken olive oil and phosphate prices. Recession in Europe and new European tariffs on textiles contributed to a decline in Tunisian exports in the second half of the 1970s and through the 1980s. Restoring economic growth remained an ongoing challenge.

The failure of Ben Salah's cooperative experiment left Bourguiba vulnerable. He was weak both politically and physically, after a heart attack in 1967. His illness and his poor judgement over Ben Salah set off a bout of political jockeying within the party. Ahmed Mestiri was expelled in 1971 for pressing for reform and set up his own party, the Movement of Socialist Democrats (MDS), while the self-absorbed Bourguiba, who had once said of the new state: 'The system? What system? I am the system!', tried to drown out the increasingly urgent succession debate by appointing himself president-for-life in 1974.[27] The left now presented the most acute political challenge. Its influence was growing within the UGTT, on university campuses, and particularly through the Group of Studies and Socialist Action in Tunisia (GEAST), a student group known by its influential journal *Perspectives*, many of whose members were jailed for protests against the regime. Industrial unrest culminated in a UGTT strike on 26 January 1978, Black Thursday, the first general strike since independence, which triggered clashes that left hundreds dead. The violence reached Sousse, where armed pro-regime militias were sent to attack the local UGTT headquarters in the city centre.[28] As many as 101 trade unionists were brought before the Criminal Chamber of the Court of Appeal in Sousse on charges connected to the January protests, including incitement and calling for armed demonstrations, and they were eventually sent to the State Security Court for trial.[29]

Much less obvious amid this industrial protest from the left was a gradual wave of religiosity which began to spread through Tunisia from the late 1960s. This was part of a broader Islamic revival across the Arab world: a new religious ethos marked by increased mosque attendance, new Qur'anic classes, the consumption of religious literature and the wearing of the hijab.[30] One Tunisian sociologist identified this new period of Islamic revival as early as 1973 but saw it in terms of a power struggle within the party elite in which modernist intellectuals were using a 'reactivation of tradition' to win the support of old party activists and peasants.[31] Others, however, pointed at more structural causes that suggested this was a modern, not traditional, phenomenon. John Entelis used an attitudinal survey to observe a growing disaffection among young Tunisians and the emergence of a 'counterculture' based on an awareness of and pride in being Arab and a 'strong emotional attachment to Islam', though one that stressed cultural over strictly religious heritage.[32] Another attitudinal survey suggested there was a marked increase in personal religious attachments between the late 1960s and early 1970s, with an increase in prayer and in attention to morality and faith, particularly among Tunisians disadvantaged by modernization.[33] In February 1976 the magazine *Jeune Afrique* reported a new dress code on the streets of Tunis: young women wearing long dresses and a veil covering their head and shoulders.[34]

Of course, not all those who were rediscovering Islam during this period were part of the new preaching movement that eventually developed into al-Nahda. Many were merely looking for an individual reconnection with their religion. Others among the preachers disagreed at an early stage with the direction this new movement was taking: in the late 1970s they split off to form their own apolitical intellectual trend, the Progressive Islamists.[35] However, a small but influential group, led by a handful of charismatic preachers, came to stand out amid this broader religious revival. A report in 1979 described a consciously chosen way of life, in which individuals spoke Arabic and shunned French, showed growing interest in Egyptian Islamist literature, and circulated cassettes of mosque preaching.[36] Large crowds gathered in the capital Tunis to attend classes led by the preachers, Ghannouchi, Mourou, Ennaifer, and Hassen Ghodhbani. These men were briefly part of the Association for the Preservation of the Qur'an (al-Jam'iyya li-l-Muhafaza 'ala al-Qur'an al-Karim), formed in 1967 as a state-sanctioned organization to spread Qur'anic teaching and which served as a rare meeting place for more religiously inclined figures within the regime and the new generation of preachers.[37] Some sympathetic Zaytunian shaykhs, who favoured Arabization and Arab–Islamic cultural patrimony, tried to draw these preachers into the ruling party in order to change it from within, but the preachers rejected these overtures and soon the government grew wary and expelled them from the association.[38] The preachers focused on their own movement, and in the mid-1970s they came together as the loosely organized Islamic Group, the first organizational precursor of what later became al-Nahda.

It was in this context of political and economic uncertainty in the early 1970s that the preaching movement spread to Sousse and began to establish itself rapidly throughout the city and the wider governorate. Soon the movement generated its own momentum independently of the leading preachers in Tunis.

Origins of Islamist Activism

The earliest years of the Islamic revival were marked by techniques adopted from the early twentieth-century South Asian preaching movement, the Tablighi Jamaat. This group emerged in Mewat, near Delhi, in 1926 and used a direct *da'wa* appeal to revive the faith and identity of Indian Muslims. For the Tablighi Jamaat, *da'wa* was not just about renewing faith in Islam; the very act of *da'wa* itself was 'a mechanism of reform', meaning that a preacher need not be a scholar or even a model practising Muslim before starting his work.[39] It was the performative act of *da'wa* itself that embodied the reform of the individual. The movement's founder, Maulana Mohammad Ilyas, was neither a charismatic leader nor a religious scholar, but was nonetheless remarkably successful in his missionary zeal, building a communal structure forged around close personal ties. In the following decades, under the leadership of his son, Maulana Mohammad Yusuf, the Tablighi Jamaat grew into a mass movement that reached well beyond the subcontinent. Ghannouchi, who was among the co-founders of the Islamic Group, had encountered Tablighi preachers while a student in Paris, as had other Tunisian Islamists.[40] Even those who had not been students abroad had met Tablighi preachers travelling through Tunisia in the late 1960s, who invited people to join them for sessions at local mosques, including in Sousse, where they spoke of rediscovering Islam. Theirs was not a conception of Islam as a political ideology, but an intent to reform the moral character of the individual.[41] Such transnational influences brought an innovative repertoire of faith-based activism. The Tunisian preachers adopted their approach, travelling through the country, from mosques to beaches to coffee shops to market stalls, calling believers to Islam through preaching.[42]

Among the first preachers in Sousse were a pair of teenagers. One, Yahya, was born in 1952 in Sidi Bou Ali, a village north of the city, and was training to become a teacher. He had been profoundly moved by meeting Tablighis in Sousse in the late 1960s, when he was a pupil at a boarding school in the city.[43] His friend Habib was born in 1951 to a family in the Old City. Habib dropped out of school and spent several months in Italy looking for work. The pair met at a Qur'anic discussion class and then began travelling from Sousse to neighbouring small towns, holding meetings to identify and train like-minded young believers. Their work drew heavily on the Tablighi da'wa: how to pray correctly, how to behave, how to dress. From there they grew the community by encouraging believers to attend classes and by recruiting and training new preachers to teach them. This was a young generation speaking to and drawing in its peers. The preachers, with their auto-didactic revivalism, intentionally subverted the traditional power structure of state-approved, state-approving clerics. Habib, who by 2014 was retired and volunteering in an association working on local governance, explained:

We moved from place to place. We trained people and we nominated people to be responsible for lessons there every day between *maghrib* and *'ishā'* prayers. There were no shaykhs to do the studies, it was us who led the classes. We were training ourselves at the time ... Our enthusiasm pushed us to make the first core (*nawāat*) of the Islamic movement.[44]

Their target was young people of their own age to whom they were careful to offer a vigorous programme far removed from the clerics in the mosque with their staid traditional sermons. As Habib said:

You should give the youth in the mosque some fun, give them a good climate in order to attract them. Most young people love football, so after morning prayers we played football with the sunrise. And we directed the young people. For example, we sat them in a circle and told them: 'You are playing with your brothers and you should not harm them, you should not shout at them, you shouldn't speak nonsense or harm your brother with hurtful words.' Through football we were bringing them up.

The priority at this stage was the creation of a community formed around shared beliefs and teachings. It enveloped these young men and women in a new solidarity of belonging.

From the earliest moments there were important connections of ideas and individuals between Sousse and Tunis, 80 miles away. One Sunday in 1973 a group of several dozen young men and women gathered for a weekly discussion meeting in Sousse's Great Mosque, a handsome ninth-century twin-domed sandstone structure inside the crenelated walls of the Old City. These meetings, known as circles (*ḥalaqāt*), were held regularly between afternoon and sunset prayers as the religious revival gained ground. Abdallah, a young medical student born in 1952 into a wealthy Sousse family, was another of the new preachers to lead the discussions in the city. While studying in the capital Tunis he had been inspired by well-attended mosque classes given by the charismatic preachers in the capital. At weekends, Abdallah would come home to Sousse and try to replicate their classes. On that Sunday Ghannouchi, Mourou, and Ennaifer drove down to the coastal city to join Abdallah's group at the Great Mosque for the first time. They sat, prayed, and discussed religious questions together – as many as ninety attended, by one count.[45] However, as they emerged into the Old City after their discussions, the political police were waiting for them. Abdallah described the scene:

The policemen said: 'What are you doing?' I explained what we were doing, that we were preaching in the mosque, and he said: 'No! It's completely forbidden.' I told him I didn't know it was forbidden and he took us to the police station.[46]

Eventually they were released after several hours of interrogation because one policeman knew Abdallah's father, who had rented him some land. The three preachers from Tunis were ordered to return home. It was the movement's first emergence in public in Sousse and its first encounter with the police, who were yet to see this religious revival as a political threat.[47] It became a story often retold within the movement, particularly during the prison years. Even 41 years later, during the October 2014 election campaign, Ghannouchi invoked his memory of the police encounter as he addressed a large crowd of al-Nahda supporters at the

Sousse port, a few hundred yards from the Great Mosque: 'It was the first meeting of the Islamic movement! And despite the fact that the meeting resulted in us being taken to the police station and spending most of the night in the police station, that was the start of the Islamic movement!'[48]

The first leaders of this community in Sousse came from different social and educational backgrounds, which stretched beyond the assumption that Islamic activism originated in a marginalized lower middle class.[49] Yahya had been a pupil in Sousse and then went to a teacher-training college in Tunis, returning home at weekends and in the summer. He was a pro-Palestinian, pro-Fatah nationalist activist within the leftist-dominated student union, the General Union of Students of Tunisia (UGET). In later decades he remained on the intellectual periphery of the Islamist movement, even joining a centre-left political party in the 2000s, despite his strong and enduring personal relationships with fellow Islamists. Habib, his colleague, left school before completing his studies and worked in a bookshop in Sousse. Both came from modest social backgrounds. However, others came from much wealthier families. Abdallah, who was present at the 1973 meeting in the Great Mosque, was from a well-known Sousse family: his father owned a large area of land in the centre of the city and later helped fund the construction of a nearby mosque. Abdallah himself had gone to Tunis to study medicine, a prestigious, high-achieving degree. One of the young men attending at these early mosque discussions in the 1970s was Mohamed Chemli, who was born in 1960 into a wealthy trading family which still ran a fabric business after 2011 and maintained its original store in the Old City. His father had been a supporter of Bourguiba's Neo-Destour.[50] Chemli became the leader of the Sousse region for the movement in the late 1980s and was reappointed to the post after the 2011 uprising. Though the movement was largely made up of lower middle-class young people, most of whom were the first in their family to attend university, it also included some who were wealthier and some who were not among the student community. As one activist from the 1970s said:

We gathered all this flock, from the rich to the poor to the middle class, all types of people, and all social levels. The idea that it began only with the oppressed (al-mustaḍ 'afīn) is not correct. The movement was a movement of pupils and some were from the countryside and were oppressed but in mixing with other pupils from the cities it gathered all this flock together, this mixed texture.[51]

While some were born into families from central Sousse itself, others came from nearby towns or villages, where one inspirational figure could produce significant pockets of Islamist support. Mahmoud, a young medical student who was an early preacher in Sousse, came from the village of Beni Hassan, south of Monastir, which was home to several activists, including a future leader of the Monastir region. Another prominent earlier leader, Ali Nouir, came from Chorbane, a village near El-Jem. Nouir, who was born in 1949, was a mathematics teacher who taught locally and who inspired several others from his extended family and from Chorbane to join the movement. Nouir served as the movement's leader in the Sahel for a period.[52]

This group of activists from divergent backgrounds were bound together by Bayat's 'imagined solidarity', common interests and shared values subjectively constructed by actors between themselves.[53] The shared value most frequently cited by the Sousse activists was a reassertion of Islam's place in the modern world, and thus the building of an alternate modernity. This both challenged the marginalization of religious knowledge and rebutted a modernization thesis that suggested scientific advances had rendered religion outmoded. It was not merely to argue that Islam was compatible with science, but that Islam had been a source of science. For example, the young preacher Yahya was influenced by an Islamic scholar and former member of the Jamaat-e-Islami of India, Wahiduddin Khan, who wrote a book entitled *al-Islam Yatahadda* (Islam Defies), which was originally published in Urdu in 1966, then translated into Arabic in 1974 (and later published in English as *God Arises*). In this book Khan challenged the prevailing view that scientific empiricism had eclipsed man's need for religion. Instead, he proposed that Qur'anic verses anticipated modern scientific discoveries, and that materialism was the cause of a 'deep-rooted malaise' in modern society: 'While man's body receives more and more nourishment, his soul is gradually being killed. Materially, he is pampered; spiritually, he is starved.'[54] Similarly, activists read *La Bible, le Coran et la Science*, published in 1976 by the French doctor Maurice Bucaille, a convert to Islam who argued that the Qur'an accurately predicted modern scientific discoveries and that therefore Islam still had an important role to play in the modern world. These ideas had a particular resonance in Tunisia where Bourguiba sought to supersede religious faith with modernism. One early activist in Sousse had taken part as a schoolboy in a demonstration in Kairouan in the mid-1960s in protest at Bourguiba's efforts to discourage Tunisians from observing the Ramadan fast. Several activists came from families where a father, uncle, or grandfather had studied at some level at the Zaytuna mosque-university, one of the first targets of Bourguiba's secularizing policies.[55] Given the symbolism of the attack on Zaytuna, it is not surprising that many scholars adopt a cultural explanation for this Islamic revival, as if this was a 'counter-elite in search of a more culturally authentic alternative', or 'the rocket of decolonization's third stage' after the political and economic.[56] But it was not just cultural: there was a sense too of personal humiliation at the banishment of Islam from the public sphere. Their shared hostility to Bourguibist secularizing was not primarily political, but moral. The resistance against a state-led civilizational project was a personal crafting of an alternative modernity, in which science and Islam, for example, were closely intertwined.

For the young adherents to this new trend, faith and morality were the most important binding elements in their imagined solidarity. This was forged through 'educational work' (al-ʿamal al-tarbawī) and 'raising awareness' (al-tawʿiyya): a focus on renewing the precepts of the faith and the manner of belief through memorization of the Qurʾan and the hadith (accounts of the Prophet's words and actions), and reform of the individual, though notably not, at this stage, reform of the state. This was described as an 'ethical reform' (al-iṣlāḥ al-akhlāqī), in which faith was renewed by the ritual of practice through regular meetings of believers in mosque classes, study groups, sports events, or on day trips. The preoccupation was with living a good life on earth and using Islam as a solution to daily dilemmas, hence the focus on morality and ethical behaviour in a period when many sensed a spiritual vacuum. 'It was an Islam which was linked to your ordinary everyday life, not an Islam that's a bit utopian and about waiting for paradise. This was about someone who did good deeds,' said Abdallah, the medical student preacher. He quoted a Qurʾanic verse that was popular among them at that time: 'As for those who believe and perform righteous deeds, theirs shall be Gardens of refuge, as a welcome for that which they used to do', which highlights how the declaration of faith is not in itself sufficient unless put into practice.[57]

Perhaps these individuals wanted in hindsight to present a particular faith-driven account of their early experiences as cover for sensitive or material explanatory factors, whether psychological or economic. Yet it is striking how frequently dozens of people gave similar, detailed descriptions of the role of faith and morality in explaining these early years of activism. It is this extra dimension of morality through activism that carries us beyond once-popular psychological explanations for the Islamic revival, in which it was proposed that structural strains triggered 'psychosocial alienation' and 'a quest for positive self-identity'.[58] This rather determinant and structural approach always fell short in explaining why these young Tunisians chose a religious course of participation over other movements, whether leftist, unionist, or Arab nationalist, and why their activism endured beyond moments of socioeconomic crisis. The transcendent motivation and the embrace of a new community offered by religious faith and morality offers an answer.

Embedded in the Islamic revival was an ethic of action, which soon became a collective mobilization. 'Our religion imposes on us to be active and to help others and to be productive,' as Abdallah, the medical student, said. Another described it as a 'way of life' (*manhaj ḥayāt*): 'Islam must guide all our life not just our prayer, but all our behaviour'.[59] This echoes the social activism identified in later years in the parallel Egyptian Islamic revival, what Janine Clark calls the reinvention of the concept of *da 'wa* to become 'the very act of "activating" Islam through deed in all spheres of life'.[60] In Sousse activism grew during the 1970s from mosque classes open to all, to informal networks and private study groups at home, and eventually into an organized semi-formal movement structure. At the heart, though, was a particular understanding of faith that bound believers together and shaped their behaviours, individually and collectively.

Here was a new generation of young Tunisians who challenged the tired clerical structures of their mosques and bound themselves together in a new, youthful imagined solidarity, forged around the transcendent motivation of faith and morality. They searched for an alternative modernity, shaped by religious faith and the ethic of action. Their shared religious teachings also began to produce a series of resilient informal networks.

School and University Networks

The development of the Islamic Group throughout Sousse and the Sahel in the second half of the 1970s relied on a remarkable process of inspiration and recruitment conducted through schools and university faculties. This created a firm web of relationships that proved resilient. The most important secondary schools in the Sahel were in Sousse and they drew in pupils not just from the city but from villages and small towns across the region. Pupils would live together in shared dormitories during term-time and this communal environment far from home provided fertile ground to recruit new adherents. An unexpected repercussion of Bourguiba's marginalization of Zaytuna was that many of its graduates who might otherwise have become clerics instead qualified as teachers of Arabic or of religious and civics education in the public school system, and were employed in both primary and secondary schools.[61] By the late 1980s this was, belatedly, considered by the state to have been one factor behind the rapid spread of Islamist ideology in schools and universities and eventually led to a new effort to curtail Zaytuna's influence on the education system.[62]

The influence of individual teachers could be striking. In Sousse, two teachers at the prominent Lycée de Garçons from 1962 were Zaytuna-educated shaykhs who had been highly critical of Bourguiba: Abderrahman Khelif and Taieb Ouertani. Khelif had led anti-Bourguiba demonstrations in Kairouan and in his sermons criticized the president's attempt to curb the observance of Ramadan; his removal as imam in the city in January 1961 had sparked more protests.[63] One of their pupils was Salah Karkar, a future al-Nahda leader and hardliner who was born in Bodheur, near Monastir, and who took his baccalaureate in 1968. Karkar described their hostility to Bourguiba and their efforts to have a prayer room set aside in the school, to have the school respect timings for the Ramadan fast, and to have an imam attached to the school. 'It was in some way the core of moral identity that lay at the origin of the Tunisian Islamist movement,' he said.[64] Mahmoud, a young medical student and preacher, had also been a pupil during this period at the Lycée de Garçons, and remembered Ouertani describing his experience in jail and some of the brutality he had faced. At medical school in Tunis, Mahmoud studied alongside two of Khelif's sons. Khelif went on to become an inspector of religious and civics education, which meant he travelled through the Sahel from school to school assessing teachers, among them an activist preacher from Akouda who by then was teaching Islamic studies at a school in Enfidha, in the north of the Sousse governorate and who fondly remembered Khelif for his inspirational preaching. Neither Khelif nor Ouertani joined the Islamic Group in the 1970s or the Islamic Tendency Movement (MTI) in the 1980s. Instead, they crossed between the realms of an official Islam and an anti-establishment Islam as intellectual 'couriers', transferring ideas between the two.[65] From this liminal position they inspired a new generation of activists.

A similar network developed in the other main boys' school in Sousse, the Lycée Technique. There a group of boys encouraged a sympathetic teacher to invite Ghannouchi to visit for a lecture in 1977. As one of the pupils, Abdedayem Noumi, who soon joined the Islamic Group himself, remembered:

Shaykh Ghannouchi talked about development from the basis of Islam and how the real values of Islam were liberty and science and he proved this with verses of the Qur'an, the verses that call on us to read and to read. And many pupils came to this talk and we had small books that we handed out, especially from the Muslim Brothers in Egypt, books of Hassan al-Banna, al-Hudaybi, Mohammed al-Ghazali, books that talked about how to behave with others.[66]

Several teachers at the Lycée Technique were directly or indirectly linked to the Islamic Group. One teacher of religious education in the 1970s was Mansour Bennour, a Zaytuna-educated cleric who was the imam at the main mosque in Akouda, to the north-west of Sousse. His son went on to become a prominent activist within the movement and the head of the Akouda bureau after 2011. In 1979, another newly qualified teacher recruited to the Lycée Technique was Nejib Khediri, a preacher from Chorbane, the village to the south of Sousse, who was a graduate of the small Faculty of Shari'a and Theology in Tunis (the replacement to the Zaytuna mosque-university) and who would be among the first founding members of the MTI. By the end of the decade the Lycée Technique pupils had earned a reputation for piety and had persuaded the administration to begin building them a mosque. According to a report in one Tunisian newspaper, a crowd of two- or three-hundred pupils chanting '*Allahu Akbar!*' staged a protest in January 1980 against a French teacher accused of accidentally tearing pages of the Qur'an.[67] Here then was an informal network of connections under construction, involving charismatic teachers and intellectual guides from within and without the movement. The network not only bound the nascent community together but also transmitted ideas to a new and eager generation of young pupils in Sousse. The bonds formed in this period were remarkably resilient.

Schools also provided an opportunity for pupils to organize themselves and to become active. Noumi, the schoolboy at the Lycée Technique, was by the late 1970s in a group of pupils who gathered together not only in school and in the mosque, but outside as well. Again, the emphasis was on self-improvement as individuals through acquiring skills and self-confidence and the forging of a new community that stood apart from contemporary Tunisian society.

We practised sport in the morning and swam, and we did scientific and spiritual studies about the Qur'an and hadith, and even about important personalities in the world and how they worked, people like Nelson Mandela, Indira Gandhi, Malcolm X, and others. We talked about a lot of personalities, even people not from the Islamic movement, about what they give to the world in terms of values. We also joked with each other, and we did poetry, we learnt some martial arts even. It taught us how to communicate with each other and with other pupils and our families. We learnt how to behave with friends and families, how to speak to our families about Islam.[68]

This newly forged community offered a sanctuary to pupils boarding in school dormitories far from their family homes. Pupils from nearby villages who had been among the best students in their primary school could go on to board at a secondary school in Monastir or Sousse, spending at least two or three weeks at a stretch away from home. The pupils boarding in the dormitories were free on Sundays, allowing them to attend the *ḥalaqāt* at the Great Mosque. One of those who went on to lead the Islamic Group in the Sahel in the late 1970s, Khairi, began his activism while boarding at a secondary school in Monastir. He was one of several activists from Chorbane. For Khairi the school environment in the city was an escape from what he called the 'forgotten' and 'neglected' life in the countryside. It was here in the school dormitory that they forged a new network of belonging.

We shared the dormitories, and we shared our food, our drink, and our studies. There were many ways in which we gathered and it shaped very specific relations between us and people became for each other another father or mother or brother because of our isolation and distance from our families ... And this was a benefit for us in calling people to prayer, to Islam, to good morals (*al-akhlāq al-ḥamīda*), and in reminding people of their history and glory, and so it began to spread.[69]

This reflects a stark social transformation, in which a wave of literate young people found themselves newly resident in cities, struggling with the excitement and inequalities of their new environment, far from the narrower experience of their villages and less well-educated parents. Here began the generational 'social and cultural chasm' identified among Islamists elsewhere.[70]

The pupils of the Islamic Group insulated themselves from this cultural shock by building an alternative world. In Khairi's school, classes could elect representatives who would lead cultural and sports activities, even running small cafes selling food and drinks to other children. From the mid-1970s at this Monastir school the religious pupils began to win the elections and to start running cooperative cafes, which proved small financial successes. They were mocked by their fellow pupils as '*khouanjiyya* ', the derogatory epithet that came to be widely applied to the Tunisian Islamist movement and which suggested they were merely another branch of the Egyptian Muslim Brotherhood. However, for the pupils themselves the experience was formative.

Our cooperatives made profits and the headmaster appreciated what we did ... That left an indelible impression on the pupils, that we were clever and had values and morals and belief. And that encouraged us to be a model to others and we attracted people and the group became larger and larger. What happened in Monastir was the same in Sousse and Mahdia. And we did some sports activities and we did other week-long activities, like a week of fasting, a week of praying, a week about the hijab, when we distributed headscarves, and a week of *da 'wa*. Each week focused on one subject, and we distributed leaflets and small booklets.[71]

The group also encouraged pupils to do well in school: they awarded each other small prizes for those with the best marks, or the hardest working, or the girls who were most 'modest' (*muhtashima*). They arranged discussions among themselves on subjects ranging from religious belief, to history and geography. Outside term the groups held meetings or went on camping holidays together by the beach. By the time these pupils were finishing their baccalaureate exams they were already part of an organized network, which had connections on university campuses. Pupils were passed on to new contacts when they entered university so that they were immediately absorbed into the Islamist student collective and assigned responsibilities according to their past experience in school. In this respect Khairi was unusual: he was expelled from school at sixteen because he had become such a prominent Islamic Group figure (he went on to lead the Group in the Sahel in 1978–81). Rather than attend university, he left the country in 1981 to avoid a conviction for his activities. He later returned and was jailed for seventeen years in a subsequent crackdown. After 2011 he was appointed to a senior administrative position within al-Nahda in Tunis.

In the 1970s most students who left schools in Sousse heading for university went to a faculty of Tunis University in the capital. A strong and organized group of Islamists emerged at the Faculty of Science in Tunis.[72] However, as the education system expanded several faculties were established in Sousse, eventually becoming Sousse University. The first to open, in December 1974, was the Faculty of Medicine, which became an important centre of Islamic Group activism not just for medical students but for others who came to join in the activities on campus. One of al-Nahda's regional leaders in the Sahel after 2011, Fethi, was a medical student in Sousse in the first year that the faculty opened, when the initial intake was only around 100 students. He attended the weekly *halaqāt* at the Great Mosque and took part in the religious activities that began to spread within the faculty. They made claims on the faculty administration, persuading them, for example, to set aside space for a prayer room. This instilled a sense of particularity, of being apart from their fellow students. In 1978 the students invited Maurice Bucaille, the French Muslim doctor and author, to come to speak in the lecture theatre. Fethi, the medical student, explained:

This was important because he linked the past and the present, and especially when someone is highly cultivated, educated, and Western it gives you another image, it adds another dimension to those Muslims in the country. It was like a breath of air that gave you some hope that at least you are not alone and there are other people with you, enlightened, cultivated, educated ... We felt we were not living like ordinary people but that we held a certain idea and that we were living for it, defending it, believing in it.[73]

Nor was the faculty solely a domain for male activism. Souad Ladhari entered the faculty in 1978, aged 18, and faced a more confrontational experience. It was a period of student strikes and demonstrations, and a moment that had a profound impact on her as a young student. One cousin, a unionist activist, had been arrested during the UGTT demonstrations of January 1978, and was jailed and tortured to death. Ladhari and her friends were engaged in constant debates on campus between different political factions: leftists, Islamists, Communists, and Destourians, those loyal to Bourguiba's ruling party. In her first year she was one of just five female students in the faculty who decided to start wearing the hijab.

We were really persecuted for it, eventually by the administration, but also by our colleagues who didn't share our opinion and who hit us with stones when we went to the university restaurant, and they sang songs at us to annoy us ... but for us the hijab signified a religious conviction, no more than that and nothing else. It was a conviction dictated by the Qur'an. It came from within our own faith. We were convinced and we are convinced that we are more respected, more protected against the vices of society, but also responding to an obligation dictated by the Qur'an.[74]

An important influence at the time was Hind Chelbi, a young veiled philosophy lecturer who took part in a televised evening talk during Ramadan in Tunis in October 1975 which was attended by Bourguiba. In her lecture on 'Women in Islam' she criticized those Tunisian women who dressed as Westerners or 'mimicked' other societies in the way they dressed, and she insisted that choice of clothing was as vital an element of a nation as its language. She criticized the condition of Tunisian women, arguing for equal civil rights and economic independence and dismissing those interpretations of Islam that saw it as patriarchal.[75] Not only did she challenge the regime's ideal of womanhood, she dared refuse a paternalistic kiss from Bourguiba in public.[76] Many women who later became members of al-Nahda spoke of Chelbi's deep influence on them. She came to talk in their schools and Ladhari remained in contact with her in later years.

The strength of the Islamic Group was not just its morality-based educational programme but also this informal, local-level network, which bridged different age groups and class backgrounds and which bound together this new community of faith. As the student population grew in the years ahead, so this Sousse network expanded. The deep relationships formed between these young men and women were vital in building an organizational structure and they survived into the post-2011 period.

Mosques and Study Cells

By the late 1970s the religious revival across Tunisia was visible and organized, both in schools and universities, and around particular mosques. The first approach of the regime was to co-opt this revivalism, in the hope it might fend off the challenge from the left and simultaneously shore up its own failing legitimacy. Bourguiba's approach to the role of religion in public life had always been more instrumental than ideological. His secularizing ambition did not separate religious institutions from the state, or separate religion from politics, or even propose a new relationship of tolerance between religious individuals and the state. Rather, seen through Asad's conception of the modernizing state's interference in and remaking of religion, Bourguiba's approach represented a regulation of religious affairs and an appropriation of religious symbols in order to monopolize religious activity.[77] His approach was flexible. Whereas in the 1950s and 1960s Bourguiba had stripped Zaytuna of its independence and proposed abandoning the Ramadan fast in the name of urgent development needs, by the 1970s the regime began to embrace Islam again, now as a moral guide at a time of social and economic dislocation. The regime was inserting itself into a competition over religious symbols. It reinforced its religious rhetoric with administrative changes, adjusting working hours in the state administration to accommodate the Ramadan fast, restoring Arab-Islamic architecture, and introducing religious education in schools as a subject of its own.[78]

This official co-option of the Islamic revival was visible even in Sousse. In August 1977, for example, more than 500 boys and girls took part in the city's eleventh annual competition of Qur'anic commentary and recital in the Great Mosque, which included cash prizes, and had official endorsement: it was reported in the party newspaper and organized by the regional cultural committee of the governorate and the regional council of the Association for the Preservation of the Qur'an.[79] In January 1978 the governorate's regional cultural committee also arranged a screening of the Moustapha Akkad film, *The Message*, about the life of the Prophet.[80] By 1979 the Qur'anic recitation competition had become well established, with increasing prize money and entrants as young as twelve taking part and doing so 'not with extremism but a diligence worthy of respect', according to one semi-official newspaper.[81]

Regime efforts at co-option, however, did little to curb the revivalist movement. From around the time of the 1973 police encounter in

Sousse and perhaps in part because of it, the young preachers turned away from the Tablighi Jamaat style of preaching towards the semi-structured movement which came to be the Islamic Group. The travelling and public call to Islam involved in the Tablighi style was beginning to arouse the interest of the state. But some of the new preachers also felt this approach was unsuited to Tunisian society; later they also argued it was limited by its avoidance of political questions.[82] In September 1972 the group began issuing a new monthly magazine, *Al-Ma'rifa*, using a publishing licence owned by Abdul Qadir Slama, a 64-year-old Zaytunian shaykh originally from Qusaybat al-Madyun, a village just south of Monastir. This magazine brought the group new reach and a curated arena for discussion. The moment coincided with the first Tunisian Book Fair in 1973, which offered the young preachers new access to a wave of literature being published by the newly released from jail Egyptian Muslim Brothers. Habib, the preacher who worked in a bookshop, brought many of these books back to Sousse to share with the group. Among the leaders of the Islamic Group in Tunis, the transnational influence of the Egyptian literature marked the start of an intellectual shift. As one of the co-founders, Ennaifer, said in 1985:

It is this current which was to influence us and push us to engage more directly in political action, as well as in a certain underground formation. We began at that time to form secret groups to give them training, but always with a spiritual dimension that specified it.[83]

Mohamed Elhachmi Hamdi, who was himself a member of the movement during this period, argues that from 1973 'the influence of the Muslim Brotherhood would prove to be decisive on almost all levels'.[84]

This influence was quickly apparent in the new magazine *Al-Ma'rifa*. 'We will study together the absence of Islam among its followers in the present era,' wrote Abdul Qadir Slama, introducing the new project in his first editor's preface.[85] Early issues were dominated by moral and spiritual discussions on questions like the challenges for young people of applying the real 'Islamic approach', the importance of rediscovering Islamic history, and the perils of gender mixing. The magazine discussed important issues for the new preaching community, including Hind Chelbi's speech and books like Maurice Bucaille's *La Bible, le Coran et la Science* and Wahiduddin Khan's *al-Islam Yatahadda*, as well as praising a rare government decision in 1972–73 to halt the sale of alcohol in the evenings during Ramadan. By 1975 as many as 6,000 copies of the magazine were being printed every month, with distribution across the Arab world and into Europe. From its earliest issues the magazine also drew on writings by figures from outside Tunisia, who were usually from the Egyptian Muslim Brotherhood or closely linked to it, including the Brotherhood's founder Hassan al-Banna, as well as the Egyptian writers Yusuf al-Qaradawi, Mohammed al-Ghazali, Sayyid Qutb, whose Qur'anic commentary *In the Shade of the Qur'an* (written in 1951–65) was regularly excerpted, and his brother Muhammed Qutb, whose guide to performing *da'wa* was printed at length.[86] Rachid Ghannouchi was a frequent contributor, and later editor of the magazine, with a succession of articles in the early to mid-1970s which prioritized the civilizational challenge presented by the West. In one article, entitled 'Colonialism left the land to infiltrate the head', he criticized the Tunisian education system for drawing on Western but not Islamic sources.[87] In another, entitled, 'What is backwardness?', he argued that the Arabs should develop solutions to their problems through their own 'civilizational will' rather than borrowing ideas from the United States or the Soviet Union. 'We must know: Who are we? And what is the culture to which we belong?', he wrote.[88] The magazine paid detailed attention to the apparent moral decline of the West, with assessments of the bankruptcy of capitalism and socialism and even one long account of the phenomenon of the hippy generation in the United States, interpreted as 'a decisive refusal to comply with so-called "development" and the obligations it prescribes'.[89]

As the movement grew in Sousse, the most important organizational nodes were the mosques. As well as the weekly classes at the Great Mosque, there were four other mosques in central Sousse that became organizing centres for the new movement. In each mosque there was at least one activist chosen for his charisma and religious commitment. Closest to the Great Mosque, and still within the Old City, was the small Jami' al-Suq, where Yahya and Habib were active from the early 1970s. This was close to the Chemli family fabric shop, which soon became a meeting point for young activists. Another was the small Corniche mosque, up from the seafront just north of the Old City. The first preacher here was Abdallah, the medical student who had been present at the Great Mosque in 1973. He said of this experience:

There were people who followed the preaching and they cried. They cried! And even today sometimes I meet people in the street who say hello, and I don't know them but they say: 'I attended prayers with you in the Corniche and we cried!' Many people say that.[90]

By the late 1970s Abdallah was replaced at the Corniche mosque by Nejib Khediri, the teacher of religious and civic education at the Lycée Technique. Khediri studied in a religious secondary school in Kairouan, then attended the Faculty of Shari'a and Theology in Tunis and became active within the Islamic Group from 1977 onwards. In 1979 he became the Friday imam at the Corniche mosque, meaning he had the right to lead the main weekly prayers. The third key mosque, Jami ' al-Turabi in Trocadero, was newly built nearby, with funding from Abdallah's family, and it was here that Abdallah went from the Corniche mosque.

Some of the clerics were controlled by the state and were corrupted a bit. But there were mosques where there were no imams, they were abandoned, and we took them. And especially in the new districts we built mosques. So here [in Trocadero] it was a new mosque, for example. The owner of the land built it, and we helped in the construction. It was extraordinary this movement of young people. We took part in the building and the owner asked me to take charge of the mosque and so I led the mosque as the imam.[91]

Another important preacher from the movement at this mosque was Mokhtar al-Mehri, a Zaytuna-educated scholar, one of whose sons later went on to lead a local al-Nahda bureau after 2011. The fourth important mosque, Jami ' al-Nur, was in a different area, to the west of the Old City, on the main road leading to a large football stadium built in 1973 that was home to the Sousse team Étoile Sportive du Sahel. The imam at this mosque was Ali Nouir, the mathematics teacher from Chorbane, who was one of the regional leaders of the Islamic Group at this time. These four mosques became central poles of influence and activism for the movement. In other towns and villages in the Sousse region and across the country, activists preached from mosques and formed their own local sections within the Islamic Group.

The mosque sessions were an opportunity to educate a new generation of activists in the details of religious belief and practices. One activist from Hammam Sousse started attending the sessions at his local mosque at the age of 16 in 1978 and described them as a 'social incubator' (al-ḥaḍāna al-ijtimā'iyya).[92] Sympathetic clerics provided protection for these study sessions. In Akouda, then a village northwest of Sousse, Mansour Bennour, the Islamic studies teacher at the Lycée Technique, was the imam of the district's main mosque where he allowed his son to lead the study circles. In this case, the imam acted as a 'cover' to protect the young activists, as one member of the study group described it. The mosques were also places of selection: some of those attending the mosque were then invited back to additional study sessions in the privacy of individuals' homes. Again, not all of those attracted by the religious revival were part of the distinct Islamic Group. Such a private meeting was known as a 'cell' (khaliyya) or a 'circle' (dā'ira) and gathered around eight to ten activists together. These cells, which emerged in the late 1970s, incorporated religious training but added a political and intellectual dimension derived from the Muslim

Brotherhood literature that the movement's leaders were now reading. As one activist described it:

There were sentences from the hadith of the Prophet, and memorizing of the Qur'an, and a commitment to Islamic behaviour, and the requirements were more educational than anything. We were young, around sixteen or seventeen, and it was required to have an educational direction to internalize the values of Islam. In addition, there were some other indications—the questions of freedom in the country, of oppression, dictatorship, the one-party system. And that was the beginning of the understanding of the political framework in the country.[93]

Others described having to memorize parts of the Qur'an and hadith, as well as reading Islamist literature and simpler short texts with explanations of Islamic principles. One activist from M'saken, Riadh, whose father was a Zaytuna scholar and an imam in one of the city's mosques, had been brought up in a religious environment and led weekly *halaqāt* for young activists himself. However, he found a new direction in the cell he attended weekly from 1979 in Sousse, where he was by now a student at the medical faculty. His reading led him to a new path that conflicted with the traditional Zaytuna education of his father.

We were speaking another language that was different to that of Zaytuna, it was the language of Islamist writers like Sayyid Qutb, Mohammed al-Ghazali, Abul Ala Maududi, Yusuf al-Qaradawi, and then we had a wave after the Iranian revolution of writings like Baqir al-Sadr, Khomeini himself. The Shiite writings were revolutionary and they had an influence on the young people and that irritated the Zaytunians a lot. They didn't like that and even my father was a bit irritated.[94]

The relationships formed in these private meetings were particularly robust. They required greater attention to the programme of study and a clearer leadership structure. They also tended to attract the better-educated followers of the movement, particularly university students who went on to become doctors, lawyers, engineers, and teachers. By the late 1970s, the influence of Islamist thought from outside Tunisia had become more pronounced. In the pages of *Al-Ma'rifa* there was an increasingly explicit engagement with an Islamist political vision. Championing the 1979 revolution in Iran, Ghannouchi wrote: 'Islam is not just spiritual *da'wa* but creed, and worship, and a comprehensive political and social system which does not differentiate between the material and the spiritual.'[95] Later that year the magazine put a triptych on its cover of 'the leaders of the modern Islamic movement', al-Banna, Maududi, and Khomeini, and Ghannouchi wrote at length about the 'idea of comprehensiveness' (*fikrat al-shumūl*) in which 'there is no room to differentiate between religion and politics, and religion and the state'.[96] For some within the Group, this transnational Islamist influence was discomforting. In a series of articles published in early 1977 and entitled 'Where do we begin?', Ennaifer, one of the co-founders, argued that the Tunisian movement needed to develop a specifically Tunisian project; shortly afterwards he broke with the Group to establish the Progressive Islamists, with a more intellectual and less political project.[97] On the ground, it was apparent to all those taking part that what they were now doing made them a target in the eyes of the regime. Student activists were becoming increasingly vocal and critical of the Bourguiba regime.[98] Arrests soon followed in the early 1980s. As one activist from Akouda said:

Most of the individuals of these educational cells received training in belief and education, and this enabled the movement's steadfastness and fixedness. Their models were the Companions of the Prophet, and they expected trials and prison at any moment. We can say that the Islamic movement continued and was steadfast because of the secret educational cells. The public studies were in front of people and gathered the old and the new, those who were deeply rooted in religious culture and the beginners who were weak in belief and you didn't rely on them a lot. But you did rely on the culture that was received by that person in the secret cell.[99]

The national leadership held a first secret congress in August 1979 in Manouba, in Tunis, to organize a formal structure and to recast the Islamic Group as a more political organization, Harakat al-Ittijah al-Islami (the MTI), with an organizational hierarchy that reached down from the national level to a regional leader ('āmil), with a regional bureau, district leaders, and smaller cells beneath. However, even as the discussions assumed a more structured, political form, strong religious belief remained central to this project at the local level.

Despite regime efforts at co-option, the movement became well organized, taking advantage of a relative freedom in the mosques, sometimes under the cover of sympathetic clerics, to develop poles of mobilization. From these congregations grew a committed Islamic movement, which would soon come to express political ambitions in parallel with its moral convictions.

*

The cumulative effect of these accounts is to privilege the role of faith and morality. It was these factors rather than a cultural clash or a psychosocial upheaval which best explain what drew these young men and women together into a movement of imagined solidarity. The socioeconomic context of Sousse and Tunisia in general in the early 1970s was one of malaise, a time of social change that precipitated an array of political mobilizations across the country. However, it was a particular, often personal, sense of humiliation at the repudiation of religion in the public sphere which brought a young generation to seek sanctuary in the new morality of the preacher-led Islamic revival. Soon an informal network sprang up in schools and universities, drawing on transnational Islamist literature and reinforcing these shared values and common interests. Even as the regime grasped the religious revival underway and tried to co-opt it, the movement was organizing and taking its activities beyond the public spaces of the mosques into the privacy of the home.

What is striking in the accounts of Sousse activists is how these ideas and networks endured well beyond the 1970s. This was not a passing phase on the path to becoming a formal political party; this training and these friendships, often crossing geographical and class boundaries, retained their collective mobilizing power for many decades. In the 1980s, while the movement at the elite level in Tunis adopted a distinctly political turn, the local activists in Sousse instead enacted this new morality through a vanguard community built around an imagined solidarity.

3   Rethinking Politicization

> We always looked for a way to change the reality of the country by
> changing ourselves. If we change ourselves, we can change others ...
> It was always in my mind that I was a representative of the movement
> wherever I was. It was a test of all our actions.
>
> *Hassan, a former student activist and then teacher at the Lycée*
> *Technique in Sousse, arrested in 1986 and again in 1991.*[1]

On 6 June 1981 the Islamist leadership staged its first formal political act.
At a press conference in a lawyer's office in Tunis, the Islamists
announced their intention to enter political life with the formation of
the Islamic Tendency Movement (MTI). It was this turn to the political
and the early embrace of pluralist politics, and soon afterwards democracy as an explicit concept, that has come to define the movement's
history. Scholarly attention has focused on the visible formal contest
between the MTI and the regime, as it developed through arrests and
negotiations to a brief moment of political freedom in 1989, before
culminating in a repressive crackdown in the early 1990s.[2] Burgat, for
example, frames his analysis by noting that 'by the start of the 1980s the
Islamists and the Bourguibists started identifying themselves as politically opposed forces on the national scene'.[3] Likewise, Alaya Allani positions his account as an analysis of 'the shifting relations between
Tunisia's Islamist Movement and the Tunisian government'.[4] Such
studies explain how the movement tried, and ultimately failed, to enter
the political process in an authoritarian system. However, in this chapter
I argue that a focus on formal politics overlooks a rich territory of offstage
activism, which encompassed a variety of social practices. Negotiations
for entry into the formal political process were conducted through a
discourse determined by the regime, but this was not the only arena of
struggle.

In public, al-Nahda's leaders continue to conceive of their movement
in deference to a state-centred political system. They emphasized how it
adopted democratic political goals and worked for inclusion in the political process, despite facing a closed one-party system. As Ghannouchi

said in an interview just after the fall of the Ben Ali regime: 'We drank the cup of democracy in one gulp back in the 1980s while other Islamists have taken it sip by sip.'[5] This was not merely a presentation for Western readers; it recurred in writings intended for a Tunisian and wider Arab audience. In an interview with his movement's own newspaper *Al-Fajr* in 2012, Ghannouchi framed the history of al-Nahda as coming in 'important and distinctive stages', moving from a *da'wa* association in the 1970s to a political opposition party in the 1980s to a 'civil party with an Islamic reference' in the post-2011 era.[6] He presented the movement as seeking a role within the system, and often used the analogy of a stallholder wanting to sell his wares in the marketplace.

This official framing masks multiple alternative narratives. The project's plasticity allowed the movement to maximize its mobilizing potential, engaging an array of interests including identity and religion as well as democratic, social, economic, and class aspirations. A focus on formal political discourse risks giving the false impression that the political struggle was fought for state-level political power alone. Although the first MTI press conference in June 1981 seemed to mark the politicization of the movement, a closer reading suggests that formal political work was not the primary goal. The movement's transcript of the press conference reads:

> For us, political work is not aimed just at obtaining a seat in parliament or among the ministers. We go deeper than that, for at this stage political work aims to provide a climate of freedom in which we can establish the roots of our main goal. Political work essentially starts from intellectual and cultural freedom. And we as an Islamist movement consider that the essential struggle is foremost a struggle in the cultural, social, and intellectual arena before the political level as generally understood.[7]

There were sharp debates at this point between those who wanted to seek immediate legal recognition as a political party (an approach favoured by Ghannouchi and Mourou) and those who wanted to remain a sociocultural movement (an idea favoured by Karkar).[8] Only by a close vote did those in favour of pursuing legal authorization as a party win out. The image of the movement as merely a political party occludes these differences and obscures the fact that it remained simultaneously a political party and a social movement. It aspired both to compete in elections and to forge a dissident subculture built around identity, morality, and *da'wa*. The ambiguity and tension of this duality is what shapes the movement's development.

Here I look beyond the formal political relations between the MTI and the regime to address how the movement operated at a local level when its national leadership embarked on a political project. After addressing the impact of the first repression on the movement in Sousse, this chapter excavates previously overlooked terrains of activism in two social sites: on university campuses and as a discrete community-building project. I argue that it was this activism which better defined the movement at a local level rather than the formal political negotiations and competition with the regime. These social activities began in the late 1970s, before the regime started repressing the movement, and therefore appear to have been the result of conscious choice rather than a mere response to oppression. Yet, by the mid- to late-1980s it is clear that such offstage work offered an outlet at a time when public political activities were highly constrained. The chapter then addresses the moment when political ambition and offstage activism collided in confrontation with the regime.

The First Repression

A series of events encouraged the leaders of the Islamic Group to reach beyond their initial *da'wa* project. The January 1978 protests led by the Tunisian General Labour Union (UGTT) turned the Group towards the pressing social and political questions Tunisia was now facing. The student movement on university campuses, the scene of an intellectual and physical contest between the Islamic Group and the left, accelerated the new political vision. It was the Iranian revolution of January 1979, however, that offered a model of what might be achieved, as well as a new vocabulary of contention. The magazine *Al-Ma'rifa* put Khomeini on its cover at least four times from late 1978 and Ghannouchi himself hailed the Iranian revolution as part of the same Islamic project as his own movement despite its sectarian difference. He described Islam as 'the only ideology capable of leading the deprived and oppressed peoples'.[9] As he explained later:

The most important thing the Iranian revolution gave us was the idea of the conflict between the oppressed and the oppressors (*bayn al-mustad'afin wa-l-mustakbirin*), and that's another translation of the conflict between the poor and the rich, the class struggle, but in an Islamic framework using Islamic terminology.[10]

Here was the diffusion of a new vocabulary and analytic framing, from revolutionary Shia Iran to a nascent Sunni Islamist movement thousands of miles away.

In Tunisia, there was a climate of mistrust developing towards the movement, particularly after the beginning of the hostage crisis in Iran in December 1979 and a failed Libyan-sponsored uprising in Gafsa in

January 1980. Police intervened after clashes on Tunis university campuses in February 1980 between Islamic Group students, who opposed the Gafsa uprising, and leftist groups calling themselves Democratic Patriots, who favoured what they considered a 'popular revolt'.[11] Difficult economic conditions contributed to a febrile atmosphere: in 1980 unemployment stood at 11.9 per cent, with more than half of those looking for work under 25, and prices rose more than 10 per cent.[12] In February 1981 students again held days of protests against curbs on freedom of expression on campus.[13] It was Islamic Group students who the regime immediately identified as the culprits. Other incidents followed, including protests at the Club Méditerranée resort in Korba when the Israeli national anthem was played, after which 200 Islamists were arrested, and scuffles in M'saken, south of Sousse, on 11 July when a crowd forced out a state-appointed imam from a mosque and put in place one of their own.[14] Police uncovered an archive of Islamic Group names and organizational structures in December 1980, pushing the movement to act quickly ahead of an expected crackdown.

The leaders of the new MTI announced themselves at a press conference in Tunis on 6 June 1981, only weeks after Bourguiba had promised a new opening for opposition political parties. The MTI would awaken the 'Islamic personality', reject a one-party state in favour of pluralist political competition, side with the oppressed (*al-mustaḍ 'afīn*) against the oppressors (*al-mustakbirīn*), and restore the mosque as the centre of mobilization.[15] The movement's programme included an ambition to establish an Islamic state in that it proposed the 'crystallization and embodiment of a contemporary image of the Islamic system of government' (*balwara wa-tajsīm al-ṣūra al-mu 'āṣira li-niẓām al-ḥukm al-islāmī*), though this was always more aspirational than detailed.[16] The movement was to be self-financed, with mandatory contributions from its members, a system which continued after 2011. The programme explicitly described the activists not merely as Muslims but as 'Islamists' (*al-islāmiyyūn*) and adherents to an 'Islamic tendency' (*al-ittjāh al-islāmī*).

There was a significant Sahel representation in the first tier of leadership. The Group held a secret second congress in Sousse in April 1981, and among the twenty-five men and women selected weeks later as the founding core of the MTI, five were from the Sahel: Abdul Qadir Slama, then aged 73, the cleric who owned the *Al-Ma 'rifa* newspaper; Ali Nouir, 33, the mathematics teacher and preacher from Chorbane; Zouhair Mahjoubi, 29, a professor of engineering from Beni Hassen, near Monastir; Nejib Khediri, 28, the teacher of civics at the Lycée Technique, also from Chorbane; and Habib Mokni, 26, a senior journalist at *Al-Ma 'rifa*, from Jemmal, near Monastir.[17] Other prominent Sousse figures at this point included Afifa Makhlouf, a teacher and daughter of an imam whose family came to be prominent in the movement in Sousse and who herself in 1981 was one of two women to attend a meeting of the movement's central committee. There she successfully argued against a colleague who had insisted on an all-male gathering.[18] At the time, the Tunisian scholar Mohamed Elbaki Hermassi identified more than a third of the MTI's members in the early 1980s as coming from the Sahel and Sfax, which were by far the most represented regions within the movement.[19]

The regime response to the growing Islamist phenomenon was rapid. First, from the late 1970s onwards it appropriated religious symbols to co-opt the religious revival. In April 1979 Prime Minister Hedi Nouira insisted it was the ruling party that had been behind the reawakening of Islam and the preservation of Tunisian 'Islamité'.[20] In July 1981, a month after the MTI's first press conference, the interior ministry announced new regulations to enforce the Ramadan fast including restricted working hours, the closure of cafes and restaurants during the day, a ban on the sale of alcohol, and an encouragement to shop-keepers to prevent passers-by from drinking or eating in public during the day.[21] It was a striking reversal of Bourguiba's dismissal of the fast in the 1960s as an impediment to national development, but it was also a miscalculation. The ministry's circular was rapidly annulled after public criticism; it was clear there was a limit to the claims the state could make on religious discourse.[22]

Second, in an effort to ease a broader sense of crisis, Bourguiba promised a new pluralist political future at a party congress in April 1981. However, any party that wanted authorization needed to sign a new National Pact, which set limits on formal political action and legit-imized Bourguiba as president.[23] Only the Tunisian Communist Party was initially authorized, although Ahmed Mestiri's Movement of Social-ist Democrats (MDS) was formally approved in November 1983, together with the Arab Nationalist Popular Unity Party (PUP).[24] It made little difference: the ruling party (in alliance with the UGTT) won the November 1981 elections with more than 94 per cent of the vote and took all the seats in the Chamber of Deputies.

The most important regime response was to punish the Islamists for the intellectual challenge they presented. They were denigrated as deceitful, retrograde, and as embodying 'obscurantism and intolerance' and 'anarchy and intellectual terrorism'.[25] Police began arresting MTI leaders from mid-July 1981: 107 were charged with belonging to an unauthorized association, defamation of the head of state, and spread-ing false information, according to a transcript of the judge's verdict.[26]

The accusation of 'belonging to an unauthorized association' (*intima' li-jam 'iyya ghayr murakhkhaṣ fīhā*) was one of the most common levelled against members of the MTI, and later al-Nahda, during the 1980s and 1990s. It derived from Law 59–154 of 7 November 1959 relating to associations, which, under article 30, set a punishment of up to five years for anyone taking part in any association that was not authorized by the interior ministry.[27] Most of the charges in the case blamed the MTI for the student violence earlier that year. The judge identified several of the movement's pamphlets, including one entitled simply *What Happened in Tunisia in February and March 1981*, which called for a front against 'oppression and dictatorship' and against 'the traitor Bourguiba'.[28] The accused were given sentences ranging from six months to eleven years in jail, but this was merely the first in a series of trials. The senior leadership was jailed in 1981 and released in mid-1984, then jailed again in early 1987 and released later that year, and then jailed again from late 1990 or forced into exile in the final crackdown. For much of the 1980s the movement's leaders were either in jail or in hiding from arrest. That alone suggests a focus on formal state-level political interactions might offer only limited insight into the movement.

The immediate impact of the 1981 court case was to remove the first generation of leaders, not just at a central level but in the regions too. Among those jailed were all five of the Sahelians who had been founders of the MTI, as well as some of the early Sousse preachers, including Abdallah, the medical student who had been present at the 1973 meeting, and Mahmoud, the preacher from Beni Hassan, who was caught in a second round of arrests targeting students in 1983. For both, this prison experience dissuaded them from further Islamist activism. After two years in jail, Abdallah was dismissed from his position as an inspector at the ministry of health and set up a small private medical clinic in central Sousse, where he still worked in 2014. He distanced himself from the MTI, uncomfortable with its new direction. Likewise, Mahmoud, spent several months in prison in 1983 but was shocked by the younger student Islamists he met:

It was a very aggressive activism with protests and insults, and calling the regime a government of the depraved. It was an extremist, radical political discourse. After six months in prison I went back to my normal life in Tunisia and to do that of course you have to make concessions and I think al-Nahda didn't forgive me those concessions.[29]

This prison experience illustrated the cost of dissent but also brought him into contact with a more radical element within his own movement. It drove him away from the MTI altogether. Mahmoud went on to join the ruling party after Ben Ali's 1987 coup, in the hope of reforming it from within.[30] He too set up a small medical clinic in central Sousse, where he continued to work in 2014. Elsewhere in Tunisia others also turned away from the MTI, put off by the new radical tendency. In the view of Kamel Ben Younes, a student Islamist activist from Djerba who was jailed in 1981, the campaign of arrests and court cases created an ideological fault line and 'froze the contradictions' between those proposing intellectual revision and a legalistic political project on the one hand, and a more radical, activist youth who favoured a sociocultural movement.[31]

In place of the first rank leaders a new, younger generation stepped forward. At a national level the leadership of the movement was taken up by Hamadi Jebali, an engineer from Sousse born in 1949 who had spent several years while a student with the Tablighi Jamaat in France and who returned to Tunisia in the autumn of 1981.[32] Several other young activists were propelled into local positions of responsibility. Jaleleddine Rouis, a medical student born in 1957 who came from a religious family in M'saken, was contacted by Jebali and asked to fill the 'serious vacuum' of leadership.[33] Rouis led the MTI in the Sahel in 1981–83 as the regional leader or 'āmil. In his memoir of this time, Rouis writes:

We studied, we made plans, we discussed reports, we took decisions, we practised leading meetings, and guiding discussions. And it was really a fruitful period and the young people who took this on were from all walks of life: some who had graduated from university, some who chose to work in the Islamic field, men and women, and they took on their responsibilities with courage and self-confidence.[34]

By 1984 the organization had grown but was still run by the 'new youth', who were closer to the 'field leadership' led by Jebali than to the first generation of imprisoned leaders, according to Rouis. Later that year, after Ghannouchi was released from jail and re-elected head of the MTI, the youthful Rouis was elected to the movement's Consultative Council and went on to head the Sousse list for the 1989 elections. The organizational structure of the movement at this stage was small and young. In January 1983, Jebali announced a new Executive Bureau of just four men: himself as secretary-general; Abbas Chourou, a university professor aged 35 in charge of political relations; Salah Nouir, a schoolteacher aged 35 from Chorbane, near Sousse, in charge of media; and Mohamed Berriche, an engineer aged 25 in charge of finances.[35]

The repression targeted not just the movement's leaders, but its carefully nurtured centres of preaching. In mid-1981, at the moment of the crackdown, the movement was estimated to be operating in 300–350 mosques nationwide.[36] Soon, however, the regime installed its own loyal imams. Shortly before his arrest in mid-1981, the Lycée Technique teacher Nejib Khediri was prevented from taking to the pulpit in the Turabi mosque. In the crowd was Abdelfattah, an 18-year-old from Akouda, who was already giving religious classes in his own local mosque, and who regularly attended Khediri's classes:

> We were in the Turabi mosque, in Sousse, and I remember when they got in the mosque they didn't let Neijb Khediri go up to the pulpit and another imam began to speak instead. People began to pray out loud and to recite from the Qur'an to disturb him. The police entered the mosque, stopped the sermon, and the older people were taken to the police van. There was another with me who was supervisor of our Group of students, he was older than me, and he went into the toilets of the mosque and cut off the electricity and caused a blackout, so that when someone spoke you couldn't hear him on the loudspeaker. And as we left on a motorbike the police stopped us, they surrounded the mosque and interrogated us. That was how the first investigations began.[37]

The loss of the mosques pushed the movement underground, and that in turn required a reweighting of its organizational strategy to continue mobilization beyond the previous spaces of permitted activism.

The politicization of the movement came at a moment of acute political and economic crisis for the regime, and particularly for the increasingly infirm Bourguiba. Yet the effect of the MTI's public emergence in 1981 was to remove the top tier of leadership and preachers and to elevate less experienced student activists. In confronting the movement, the regime identified the MTI as a political, cultural, and intellectual threat, and excluded the Islamists from an already circumscribed political process. The movement's project would now be offstage, in social sites where limited activism was still possible, of which the first, and most dynamic, was the university campus.

Universities: A 'Zone Apart'

The university faculties in Tunis had long incubated political activism, especially among the left in the first decades since independence. By the early 1980s, population growth and economic development meant Tunisia's student population was rising significantly (it reached 34,000 nationwide in the 1982–83 academic year) and new faculties were established in the provinces.[38] In Sousse the Faculty of Medicine opened in 1974; the Higher Institute of Agronomy in Chott Meriem, to the north of the city, in 1975; the École Normale Supérieure, which provided humanities and arts-focused teacher training in 1982; the Faculty of Law, in Hai Riadh, in 1985; and the Faculty of Arts and Humanities, also in Hai Riadh, in 1990. For the Islamists, the new Faculty of Law, like the Faculty of Medicine in earlier years, quickly became an important pocket of activism: many al-Nahda leaders from Sousse and beyond studied law together here in the late 1980s.[39] Not only was the student population extending to sites beyond the capital, but the physical space of the university campus offered relative freedom at a time when formal politics remained tightly restricted. Although university security and the police were called in to curb confrontations between rival student groups, many former students gave detailed accounts of their freedom to hold meetings, to debate in public, and to publish their own newspapers. This was a fresh political opportunity, a newly expanding arena for action. The campus was also a dynamic environment, which transmitted ideas and organizational mobilization back into wider society. Ajmi Lourimi, a senior movement leader from Sousse who studied philosophy at university in Tunis from 1980, said:

When the students got enriched with Islamic views from the founders they started making the movement inside the university and then they got inside society. This is the transition: founders to university to society. After university they went back to their cities and started talking to people and made them conscious of the movement.[40]

Many who were students at this time believed they had brought a political awareness into the movement. The jailing of the leadership in 1981 only accelerated this process.

The student movement of the MTI took more extreme positions than the leadership. The decision in 1981 to seek formal authorization as a political party had only been made after intense internal debates: 70 per cent of the movement nationwide had been in favour, but only 53 per cent of their university students.[41] Many students argued that legalization would give recognition to the Bourguiba regime they so bitterly opposed. Within the universities, Islamist students gradually turned away from the main student union, UGET (General Union of Students of Tunisia), founded in 1952 and which, since a congress in Korba in 1971, had fallen increasingly under the influence of Bourguibist elements. In March 1985 the Islamist students established the rival Tunisian General Union of Students (UGTE), which soon claimed 20,000 members.[42] The union pressed for a formal break with the Bourguiba regime, what one former student described as a strategy of 'popular revolution' along Iranian lines, and which put it at odds with the MTI's more cautious formal political ambition.[43] The MTI held a serious internal debate, the Project of Priorities (*mashru ' al-awlawiyyat*) led by Ali Laarayedh, in 1982–86 to resolve this strategic difference and eventually concluded that the movement should focus on being a peaceful, civil political movement, an approach favoured by the jailed or exiled leadership at the time.[44] However, the more radical student element retained considerable influence.

The encounter with the left at university was physical. On campuses in the early 1980s there were clashes between Islamist and leftist students, especially the Marxist–Leninist group the Movement of Democratic Patriots (Harakat al-Wataniyyun al-Dimuqratiyyun, MOUPAD or WATAD). On 30 March 1982 at the Faculty of Humanities at La Manouba, near Tunis, around forty students were injured.[45] Even for those not present, this incident became a story of violence that galvanized others into action. Feelings of outrage spurred them to action; this was the emotional work of a 'moral shock' that sparked indignation and then mobilization.[46] For example, Jamel was at the time a secondary school pupil in Sousse who attended a meeting at the mosque at the Faculty of Medicine. One Islamist student who had been hurt in the La Manouba violence described to them what had happened.

He gave some details of the incident and all those who were present were soon crying out loud. He was so influential that if he'd said: 'Let's go to that place right now', everyone would have gone. And from that moment the MTI was prevailing everywhere.[47]

Most Sousse activists downplayed the violence, or put the blame on the leftist students, even though both sides were equally responsible. Some were more ready to admit to what had happened. Sahbi, a Nahdawi law professor from Akouda, had been a student at the Faculty of Law in Tunis in the early 1980s:

We used violence but only to defend ourselves. We were obliged to fight to defend ourselves. At the Faculty of Law, they said to us, 'We will kill you. We will slit your throats', because they knew we were Islamists.[48]

The Islamist students were not only fighting the leftists, but also pro-regime students, the Destourians. As Sahbi remembered:

We said that the universities weren't part of Tunisia but that they were a zone apart. And if we caught what we called a *flic* (cop), a student loyal to the regime, we would shave his head. We cut all his hair and sometimes we wrote on his head an F for *flic*.

The dynamic within the relative freedom of the campus was quite different from the inclusive, legalistic approach of the movement leaders outside.

The confrontation with the left was not just physical. It had a striking intellectual influence. Often Islamist students have been identified as tending to study scientific subjects and to shun critical thinking in favour of a more technical mindset. Hermassi, for example, describes Tunisian Islamists in the early 1980s as being most present in science faculties rather than teaching or humanities faculties.[49] One major quantitative study shows engineers are highly overrepresented within violent Islamist groups, and that non-violent Islamist movements too are generally made up of graduates with scientific degrees ranging from engineering, to medicine, pharmacology, and sciences, which require high scores in final-year school exams.[50] This was explained by relative deprivation, in which above-average students face frustrated ambitions because of a lack of job opportunities; psychological 'mindsets', including a desire to 'keep their social environment pure'; a preference for order, structure, and certainties; and strong group identity, which is prevalent among engineers and which might also attract them to Islamism.[51] However, the Islamists from Sousse diverge from this pattern. Many Sousse activists were doctors or engineers, in common with Islamist movements elsewhere, but many others studied non-scientific subjects including philosophy, sociology, economics, and, especially, law. After all, they were members of a movement founded not by scientists but by a philosopher (Ghannouchi), a lawyer (Mourou), and a theologian (Ennaifer). Among those Nahdawis I interviewed, the single most common degree course was law, ahead of medicine and engineering.[52] In the Tunisian context of the 1970s and 1980s, a law degree was more highly regarded than elsewhere in the region and for intelligent, aspiring students was as much of an elite degree as medicine or engineering.[53] The legal profession was also a redoubt for political activism across all parties. In later years the Order of Lawyers (Ordre National des Avocats) survived as one of the few places where it was still possible to act politically under the Ben Ali regime.[54] The presence of so many law students in the MTI may also reflect a particular pocket of Islamist activism that developed around individuals in the Sousse law faculty in the mid-1980s, which repeated the pattern established earlier in the medicine faculty.

In the accounts of the student experiences in the 1980s, many appear inquisitive and highly ambitious. Their career ambitions were not thwarted by relative deprivation, but by exclusion on the grounds of their political and religious beliefs. Youssef, a student from Hammam Sousse who studied at the elite engineering and sciences teacher-training college École Normale Supérieure de l'Enseignement Technique de Tunis, said:

We were products of the national state, meaning we had studied in schools after independence. We were the first product of the independent state. Ultimately, the country and our parents and our families and society were expecting that we would play a role in this country as high officials.[55]

All described a constant political debate on campus, focused around weekly student newspapers which were posted up on the walls, including Islamist papers called *The Political News* (*al-Hadath al-Siyasi*) and later *The Intellectual News* (*al-Hadath al-Fikri*).[56] Another activist, Abdelfattah, a sociology student from Akouda, studied at the Faculty of Humanities in Tunis (known colloquially as 9 avril, because of its location on Boulevard 9 avril 1938).[57] He stood for election to the student council in 1985–86, when the Islamists won two out of four student seats available, and he took part in preparing the student newspaper, which carried articles about the political positions of the MTI, as well as intellectual debates and discussions of student life.[58]

We had a newspaper we put on the wall, *al-Hadath*, and the leftists had their own newspaper called *al-Haqiqa* (*The Truth*), we called it *Pravda*, even they called it *Pravda*! We put the paper up every Monday. We prepared it and wrote it and we took content that came to us. We had one person whose handwriting was excellent and we wrote it on a Sunday and at 6am after morning prayers we had a place where we posted it up, a place reserved for the Islamic movement. It was a competition to see who would put theirs up first. We always got up early to pray and we went straight to put it up and stayed until many students were there so that no one could tear it down.[59]

They organized demonstrations and public meetings, campaigned to extend student rights, and to establish prayer rooms within the university buildings. They read and circulated writings by Sayyid Qutb, Hassan al-Banna, the Iranian scholar Ali Shariati, the Iraqi theologian Muhammad Baqir al-Sadr, and later the Algerian scholar Malek Bennabi, whose writings about the cultural and moral dispossession of colonialism and the significance of democracy for Islam were to prove particularly influential for the Tunisian Islamists.[60] The students read leftist thinkers too, under the influence of their political opponents. As one Sousse activist, who studied mathematics at university in Monastir in the early 1980s, said:

The polarization meant we didn't spare any effort to cultivate ourselves. Sometimes you'd find yourself in a discussion circle and you'd feel your weakness, so the next day you'd buy a book on that issue and that's why we were so cultivated. We read everything. Not only the books of the Muslim Brothers, but Marxist thought too. We read it all; we devoured everything.[61]

Though confrontational and often violent, the encounter with leftist students was also formative, not just shaping debating skills but broadening their intellectual resources.

Beyond the competition with the left, student life offered new ideas for young Islamists. Their studies provided a way to understand the increasingly fraught confrontation with the regime and a new vocabulary

in which to articulate their claims. Take, for example, the experience of
Hedi, a young Islamist student in Tunis in the mid-1980s. Hedi was born
into a family of farmers in Kalaa Kebira, then a semi-rural village outside
Sousse, and had begun to be active with local Islamists during his final
secondary school years. He did well in his baccalaureate, an achievement
celebrated by his family and local community, and he began at university
in late 1986, months before the final confrontation between the MTI
and the increasingly repressive Bourguiba regime. He read sociology at
9 avril and felt that despite his educational achievements he was still
excluded from playing a role in society, an exclusion that he felt physically as much as intellectually.

I want to be present, but you don't accept my presence. If you want to deny me
I will insist completely that I exist. But you deny me absolutely. You will not let
me exist as a student, or get my degree, or express a political position. So what do
you want students to do? Automatically I will find myself in a state of absolute
refusal whatever the authorities do.[62]

That exclusion became the source of frustration, first, and then a motivation for action. Here was the intellectual work that presaged the shift
towards confrontation.

Why did some have the right to give their position and opinion and their answers
and to participate and you were prevented from your own concept, or opinion, or
participation? There was no going back. It was time to take a political stance.
I was a student of sociology, not mathematics or physics, not just one plus one
equals two ... It was the first time you could choose that you were going to be in
opposition to the authorities, whatever the cost.

This realization came at a time of heightened tension with the Bourguiba
regime, which in 1987 began another major crackdown against the MTI,
arresting much of the leadership, including Ghannouchi. Hedi took part
in a series of MTI marches and demonstrations in Tunis protesting the
arrests, and narrowly avoided being detained himself. His sense of intellectual exclusion soon became constitutive: it pushed him to organize
avenues of resistance.

Effectively you passed through this political stage from only staying put and
discussing, to taking a position and then to applying this position. Applying the
position meant to galvanize the people, to stay with them, to lead political
meetings, to speak to the students, to sacrifice with the students, when you
knew at any moment the police could enter the room. One of your
responsibilities as a student was to live real freedom, not a fake freedom.

Hedi was arrested in January 1991 and jailed for four years. When he was
released he was not allowed to complete his final year of studies but

eventually found work in a tourism company. After the 2011 uprising he lead the al-Nahda bureau in Kalaa Kebira.

Beyond the formal political sphere, the university campus in the 1980s offered a site of relative freedom for Islamist activism that mobilized a new generation. Here physical and intellectual competition with leftist rivals was formative, shaping skills and pushing the students to explore rival intellectual traditions. The experience was also constitutive, providing a vocabulary of meanings through which to decipher the conflict with the regime and a motivation to organize a physical challenge to resist exclusion.

Building a Dissident Subculture

Beyond the elite-level political negotiations of the 1980s in the capital Tunis, the work of the movement in the Sousse region was divided between the rapidly growing student organization and what was called *al- 'amal al-turābī*, the more secretive grassroots work in society. In part this involved discussions about the political challenges both the movement and the country were facing, but this chapter argues it was most intensely focused on building a discrete community that soon began to function as a subculture based around pillars of identity, morality, and faith. Although most research on the movement has focused on the evolution of its political strategy, it was in fact these community practices that defined the MTI at the local level outside the university and which forged resilience that helped individuals survive the decades of repression under Ben Ali.

Despite the arrests of movement leaders from July 1981, the grassroots work was remarkably successful, not least because it involved small cells of the most loyal supporters. In a careful process of assimilation, they graduated from being sympathizers (*al-muta 'āṭifīn*) and members of what were called open families (*al-usar al-maftūha*), to becoming committed adherents (*al-multazimīn*) and members of the more secretive closed families (*al-usar al-mughlaqa*). Those who passed the training, which required meeting moral criteria for entry and securing the endorsement of two movement members, then swore an oath of loyalty (*bay 'a*) to the movement's leader or one of his representatives. The effect was to build a structure that reached from the central leadership, down to a regional leadership in the governorates, and from there down to small cells in the districts. Rachid, the mathematics student who had studied at Monastir university, was encouraged in 1983 to set up cells in El-Jem, a rural area south of Sousse, where he now worked as a teacher.

I was in charge of that region, with the sympathizers and the engaged in El-Jem and we had weekly meetings. I moved by motorbike all the time to have meetings, training, education, planning our work. It was all clandestine: we never announced a meeting.[63]

The movement developed a distinct sense of its position in Tunisian society, a subjective understanding of shared common attributes. In part, it was a product of a class dynamic. The MTI was by now largely a lower middle-class movement situating itself against the political and business elite. This was reflected in its 1981 political programme, which aligned the movement with the 'oppressed' and demanded a 'fair distribution of wealth'. It recurred in al-Nahda's 1989 programme, which talked of work as a 'right and obligation' and of an economic system based on the principle of 'from each man according to his abilities, to each man according to his needs'.[64] These young people represented what Abdelkader Zghal identified later as a 'new social periphery', resisting social marginalization and seeking to establish their place in society.[65] In the 1980s after graduation, the young Islamists became doctors, lawyers, engineers, academics, bureaucrats, and, often, schoolteachers.

At the core of their work was a continuation of the religious education and da'wa that had shaped the movement in its first decade. Small educational cells of five or six people met in private homes where they memorized verses of the Qur'an and hadith, and discussed commentaries on the texts, as well as addressing questions of belief and comportment. In their privacy they escaped the attention of the police and security forces. Saleh, a graduate of the Faculty of Shari'a and Theology in Tunis and a schoolteacher, led such cells in Akouda in the 1980s:

It was about purifying yourself, educating people on morals and virtues, and changing bad behaviour. These secret educational cells, they resisted and struggled even when many people were jailed in 1981. Most of the individuals in these educational cells received training in belief and education and that enabled their steadfastness ... They had a vision of the future.[66]

Faith, in other words, continued to play a central role in how the movement was organized and how individuals embodied their membership in the movement. Such experiences stand in sharp contrast to those analyses that see the movement through a largely political lens. One account, for example, considers the MTI in 1981 a political party whose 'religious goals were sufficiently vague to appeal to popular desires for cultural authenticity and increased religiosity'.[67] Another account argues that by the end of the decade the movement was no longer religious 'in any strict sense of the term'.[68] But the evidence from these Sousse activists suggests that even as the MTI was becoming a political and social force, it maintained a constant religious core to its activism that survived through the 1980s and beyond.

The educational cells read texts sent from the central leadership of the movement, the most important of which was *The Intellectual Vision and the Fundamental Approach* (*al-Ru'ya al-Fikriyya wa-l-Manhaj al-Usuli*), produced in 1986 as one of the results of the Project of Priorities. The pamphlet includes long discussions on the nature of belief as central to the Islamist project, elaborated through reference to Qur'anic verses. It then sets guidelines for the relationship between revelation and reason, and allows for a contemporary, contextual interpretation of the holy texts through independent effort, *ijtihād*. Though little cited in scholarly studies of the movement, this pamphlet was still frequently referred to by activists after 2011 as a guiding document, which again suggests that the idea that belief should be embodied in daily life remained a central organizing mechanism.

Not all activists came from religious families, or from families that were sympathetic to the new wave of Islamism. Instead, there are repeated accounts of how individual Islamists rebelled against their parents in pursuit of their new identity. One woman, Sayida, who became heavily involved in the *da'wa* side of the movement in the early 1980s as a schoolgirl in Sousse and then a student in Tunis, admitted her views had been hard for her family to accept.

I was convinced since the beginning from my readings that Islam was actually valid in everything, in politics and socially: I found it in all things. I was convinced that Islam had in it a universality. But frankly speaking we made many mistakes. In the 1980s we were very tough with our families. We were not lenient in our thought and in the way we imposed our ideas.[69]

Another woman, Farida, described how her new sense of morality put her in conflict with her parents about how they should conduct their lives:

We were trying to rectify morals. I started with my family. My late father, he was drinking alcohol and I told him not to. I even poured a bottle of wine down the toilet! There was no way to accept his behaviour. There is the licit and the illicit (*halāl wa harām*). But we were young, not like now, and in your twenties when you read something you want to apply it immediately.[70]

The forging of a new community often involved questioning and breaking their own family ties. New notions of correct behaviour were central to this.

As they broke with their families, the individuals of the movement worked hard to create a discrete subculture, a belonging to a distinctive bounded group built on a new ethical code. This was a community of common interests and shared values, shaped by daily practices ranging from religious study, shared social activities, mutual practical, financial, and emotional support, and new rituals of social cohesion. Farida, who was a teenager during the 1980s in Sousse, attended discussion circles at the Great Mosque in the Old City and became part of a small community of Islamist women who created for themselves a new way of life, separate from their previous life at home.

We were very thirsty for religion. We loved it and we found great goodness in it. We made a comparison between the first life we lived with our parents and then the one you lived with your girlfriends. We were meeting together in the week, and we went to weddings together, we went out together, for lunch and dinner and for sport. We joked with each other. We lacked many things but all that we did was *halāl*. Instead of going to a nightclub, for example, I went with my girlfriends and we enjoyed ourselves in a clean atmosphere (*jaww nazīf*), an Islamic atmosphere (*jaww islāmī*). Some considered that the people of al-Nahda were only praying and practising religion. No, no, no. We had everything, we went on camps, we went swimming, I played football, I went on trips.[71]

It is not just that these young men and women created for themselves their own, rich social life. It is that there was a sense of cleanliness or of self-purification as a prelude to changing society as a whole, a motif that recurs frequently in accounts of this period. This ethical community was reinforced through daily community activities. Pupils and students were encouraged to play football together as much as to study the Qur'an. One activist, Hafedh, an engineer from Kalaa Seghira, then a semi-rural village outside Sousse, described several layers of support that followed after he joined the movement. A group of activists helped him build his house, a neat single-storey building set back from the road behind a garden of fruit trees. A dozen-strong crowd, including some skilled stone masons, would come every Sunday and give their work for free. In turn, he would help others in their farms. Some of the connections he made surprised him: one fellow Islamist invited Hafedh to join him on an expenses-paid trip to Afghanistan to fight jihad against the Soviet army, an offer he quickly declined. Other connections were more social: activists gave each other emotional support, particularly on dealing with differences within the family.

When we met we advised each other, we spoke together and we prayed together; and especially in praying we showed great support to each other. If someone had a problem with his family, we would talk about it and advise each other. If you are in conflict with your father, they would say be correct with him because a father is someone sacred. Even if he doesn't pray you should deal with him correctly.[72]

Other work included marking the commemoration of the Eid holidays, collecting used schoolbooks and second-hand clothes for poorer families, gathering donations in money, olive oil, or wheat from local activists and sharing it with the poor, and arranging marriages within the Islamist community. This intermarriage between Islamist families was another way of binding solidarities. Individuals searched for like-minded spouses. In 1981 Habib, one of the early Sousse preachers, married a young woman from Sousse who had worn the veil for two years. 'You looked for a woman who wore the veil, even though there were few at the time', Habib said. Likewise, Saleh, the preacher from Akouda, married the daughter of Mansour Bennour, the Lycée Technique teacher and imam at the main Akouda mosque. Marriages linked prominent Islamist families in Sousse, including the Chemli and Makhlouf families, and the Gsouma and Nouir families. 'We married each other. We were a small society of our own,' said Khairi.

In search of social cohesion, this new community reinvented local traditions. Perhaps the clearest example of this was the reimagining of wedding ceremonies: costs were reduced, friends in the community made contributions, alcohol and gender-mixing were avoided, and new musical groups sang religiously inspired songs, avoiding the loud pipes and drums normally associated with Tunisian weddings. Hafedh, the engineer from Kalaa Seghira, was married in one of these new ceremonies, which he called an 'Islamic wedding' (*zawāj islāmī*).

Q: What was the difference between an ordinary wedding and an 'Islamic wedding'?
We did Islamic weddings, meaning there wasn't any dancing,
or drums, or mixing of genders and we spent only the minimum
amount of money, we didn't waste money. And the sisters were really
understanding: there was no need for gold. In the weddings the
women were together and the men were together with no mixing.
We have a tradition here that the groom goes to the cafe, which is the
emblem of manhood. But we didn't go to the cafe, we went to the
mosque and prayed in the mosque, and we did the contract of
marriage in the mosque, not at the local administration.

Q: Why was that important?
We did it in the mosque because there is humility (*khushū'*) before
God and there wasn't any disturbance. Everyone listened to each
other, there wasn't any mixing, and there was a kind of mercy in that.
And perhaps this represented a good sign for the future ... And these
marriages were a great event. It wasn't the norm. How was it possible
for someone to marry without drums and pipes? But we considered

these to be an innovation (*bida'*) because it was not part of Islamic tradition ... People married in order have children, a new generation, a correct generation, to serve their religion and nation.[73]

This new symbolic practice evolved over several years. It marked a new collective action, a way to separate themselves by their behaviour, and an effort to challenge established norms in the public sphere. This was an expansion of a growing repertoire of contention. Accompanying the new wedding was a new style of music, with religiously inspired songs (*nashīd*, pl. *nashā'id*). One Sousse activist, who started singing in the city aged 18 in 1984, described his songs as offering 'a cultural alternative' (*badīl thaqāfī*).[74] His group sang at weddings and at private family celebrations, and occasionally sang songs critical of the authorities. They drew on songs from an earlier generation of religious singers in Tunisia but also borrowed a repertoire from cassettes of singers in Egypt, Syria, and Iraq. They used instruments like the *bandīr*, a handheld frame drum with a snare, rather than the violins and pipes found at ordinary weddings of the time. Others who sang in such groups described *nashā'id* that referred not just to Islam but also to the Palestinian cause, or the religious meaning of jihad, and theatrical sketches to accompany the songs.[75] The invented traditions served both to inculcate a set of values through ritualization of the wedding ceremony or the *nashā'id*, but also to create an alternative way of being in the world. The new traditions established a continuity with an imagined past conceived of as more Islamic and moral than modern-day Tunisia. In the case of the MTI, these reinvented traditions helped to establish social cohesion and to reinforce a particular value system within the new community.

The forging of this dissident subculture was what Nira Yuval-Davis identifies elsewhere as a 'politics of belonging', with a selective narrative of the movement's self-identification reproduced from generation to generation, a strong component of emotional attachment, and an important ethical element, on which members of the movement drew to find their place in the world and to define their political struggle.[76] Collective identity could not be understood outside a whole set of social practices, from studying, to sports, to music, to social occasions like weddings. These actions produced close bonds within the Islamist community, dense networks that were inward looking and effective in mobilizing a social solidarity. It was less an attempt to create a utopia on earth, than to forge a particular community with a set of behaviours which corrected a perceived spiritual vacuum in society. The morality-focused community represented mobilization within the limits of a circumscribed political sphere and offered an implicit critique of the morality of the rest of society. It contested existing social norms. However, this construction of an inward-looking identity was exclusive and drew the movement away from political allies. The resulting isolation was a failing that al-Nahda itself later admitted: when the movement was confronted by a repressive regime, it had no allies to which it could turn.

The grassroots work began with small cells of committed followers, then used social practices of religious studies and reimagined traditions to forge a discrete dissident subculture. At its heart lay a sense of identity, a new moral code, and particularly the draw of faith that bound together a cohesive community. These often unnoticed and largely offstage activities were what most characterized mobilization within the MTI in the 1980s in Sousse. Activists built dense networks of social solidarity, which proved resilient in the years of repression that were to follow.

Confrontation

There were two major moments of rupture for the movement in the 1980s, when its political activism was no longer confined to formal political negotiations in the capital, in which it adopted a restrained language of political inclusion, or to offstage sites of mobilization in universities or the subculture community. In the first instance, a wave of repression in 1987 drove the movement to react in outrage and anger. In the second, a misperception of new political opportunities in 1989 pushed mass mobilization into the public space, with a confrontational vocabulary and street protests.

The demonstrations of 1987 were a sharp reaction to a new wave of repression by the Bourguiba regime. It was a time of worsening economic crisis. Income from oil exports halved between 1984 and 1986, a severe drought brought a disastrous harvest in 1986, and tourist income fell.[77] Bourguiba's government responded by turning to an International Monetary Fund structural reform programme, devaluing the dinar and beginning what would become a long-lasting reliance on conditional foreign loans. But the weakness of the regime coincided with a renewed sense of confidence for the MTI. Ghannouchi had been freed from jail in mid-1984, and then made a series of public announcements formally endorsing democracy and dropping previous criticism of the Personal Status Code, Tunisia's progressive family law legislation, in the hope of allaying fears about Islamist ambitions.[78] However, as the MTI's confidence grew, the regime turned against the Islamists once again. In early 1987 another round of student protests on campuses in Tunis was blamed on the Islamists, who were identified by the state and the official media as 'propagandists revealing their extremist theories and their obscurantist doctrines'.[79] On 9 March Ghannouchi was arrested and other MTI leaders were picked up in the days that followed. In response, the movement held a series of demonstrations in Tunis, often violently repressed by police, culminating in a 16 July 'resistance march' in the capital, under the slogan 'The movement exists for victory'.[80] Up to eighty MTI demonstrations like this were held across the country in 1987.[81]

An important demonstration was organized in several cities, including Sousse, on 17 May, a rare entry onto the public stage for a movement which until now had largely operated in the informal margins of life in the provinces. Walid, who was a medical student in Sousse at the time and who later joined the movement's Consultative Council, recalled:

After the arrest of the shaykh [Ghannouchi], the picture became clearer and we saw that Bourguiba was moving to eliminate and delete the movement. We decided not to remain spectators but to react, meaning to pressure Bourguiba in the street. We wanted to let the people know who we were so that the day they targeted us they couldn't say that we were unknown to the people. And we wanted to reveal that his policy was not just to isolate the movement, but to eliminate it.[82]

The movement delivered pamphlets to homes across the city. Activists wrote graffiti on the walls, with provocative slogans, such as: 'There is no God but God and Bourguiba is the enemy of God', according to one young activist involved at the time.[83] The challenge was not just to confront the authorities, but also to demonstrate that the movement was larger than the regime would admit. The MTI staged the march in downtown Sousse, one of the most public locations they could find, in a large square between the entrance to the Old City and the port, where buses gathered to take passengers out to the suburbs. It was not far from the regional police station and there was excitement at such audacity. Walid said: 'We challenged them. We came to their house in the middle of town and we did it!'. The march began at 1pm, when the crowds were largest, with pupils leaving school and workers leaving their offices for lunch. The activists dispersed around the square and then came together on cue. Jamel, another medical student who was present, remembered:

We were scattered here and there in a perimeter of 200–300 square metres and suddenly someone emerged and said: '*Allāhu Akbar!*' and that was the sign announcing the start, and everyone who heard the call gathered, and we shouted slogans and we walked for a few hundred metres before we were met by the police.[84]

The confrontation was violent: police opened fire on the demonstrators, injuring two before the march was broken up. Dozens were arrested and jailed, not to be freed until well after Ben Ali's November coup that year.

For those in Sousse, this march marked one of the first times they had organized in public in the city centre, well beyond the university campuses or the secretive grassroots work.

If the demonstrations were energizing, their result had the opposite effect. The regime demonized the movement as the agent of a foreign power. Reports in the official media detailed a 'Khomeinist network' which plotted to use violence to establish an 'obscurantist state'.[85] Diplomatic relations with Tehran were broken on 26 March, though there was never evidence of Iranian support for the movement. Around 3,000 MTI activists were arrested nationwide between March and August 1987, including for the first time many from the lower ranks.[86] In turn, Islamist activism grew increasingly radical. In August 1987 some on the outer fringes of the movement took part in bomb attacks against four hotels in Sousse and Monastir, injuring thirteen tourists, an act publicly repudiated by the movement leadership.[87] As it became clear Bourguiba wanted the death penalty for the MTI leaders, the language of the movement grew more strident. Jebali, now spokesman in exile, warned:

We will not stand with our arms crossed before this plan of extermination ... If the authorities go beyond the point of no return, our movement, in a position of legitimate national defence, will react against tyranny.[88]

More hardline elements were preparing an ambitious but unrealized overthrow of the Bourguiba regime, apparently with the knowledge of the movement's leadership.[89]

The movement was near defeated. The dozens of Sousse activists arrested in mid-1987 described months of detention and brutality at the hands of the police and their jailers. Walid, the medical student who had been present at the Sousse demonstration that year, was tortured in the Bouchoucha prison in Tunis.

Those centres of interrogation were very tough, without any control ... My family didn't know where I was and even my friends didn't know. Your family would go from police station to police station to ask for you, but they would not tell them if you were there. They were hard days: heavy torture, many incitements. I went through it all.[90]

Then came respite. Late at night on Friday 6 November 1987, Ben Ali, the former national security chief who had been promoted to prime minister only a month earlier, moved against the frail and increasingly erratic president. He summoned seven doctors to the interior ministry to pronounce Bourguiba's 'absolute incapacity' for office. In a dawn broadcast on Radio Tunis on the Saturday morning, Ben Ali announced that under article 57 of the constitution he was taking over the presidency.[91] To shore up his legitimacy, he promised political pluralism and aligned himself with Tunisia's 'Arab-Islamic identity', later freeing hundreds of MTI prisoners. Many other Islamists, including Jebali, returned from exile. The MTI leadership embraced the promise of change, declaring the coup 'a divine act meant to save the country from civil war'.[92]

If the 1987 march was a rare demonstration of the MTI's street power, the elections two years later offered a moment of semi-legitimacy in which to prove the reach of its organizational structure. The regime presented what seemed a promising political opening, and in turn the MTI signalled a willingness to participate on Ben Ali's terms. The opening began with a new political parties law in April 1988 and then, in November, a National Pact (al-mīthāq al-waṭanī) promising pluralist, democratic politics in return for an endorsement of Ben Ali's coup.[93] Most opposition parties signed the pact, as did one MTI activist, the lawyer Noureddine Bhiri. The MTI renamed itself the al-Nahda movement in December 1988, to comply with the new parties law, and wrote a new party programme in which it now advocated a civil democratic state, rather than an Islamic state, as well as calling for an end to economic exploitation and monopoly, Arabization in education and the administration, and prioritization of the Palestinian cause in foreign policy.[94] The movement applied for legal authorization on 7 February 1989, just too late to require a response before the coming 2 April elections but early enough to signal its desire to take part.[95] When the regime proposed that the opposition parties which had signed the National Pact should run as a united front, al-Nahda and others agreed. It was only the opposition of Ahmed Mestiri of the MDS, who believed his party could win alone, that prevented the formation of a common list.[96] Eventually, al-Nahda was allowed to run candidates in the election, but only as independents, under lists identified by the colour purple. This was the latest product of the Islamists' compromise in pursuit of inclusion. However, the al-Nahda leadership, like most others at the time, misread the situation. Though Ben Ali's rhetoric sounded new, in fact he would go on to change little of substance and stopped well short of significant democratic reforms. Unlike similar political openings in Algeria, Jordan, and then Morocco, the Tunisian regime never authorized the formation of an Islamist political party. On 6 June 1989, two months after the elections, al-Nahda's application for legalization was rejected.

In Sousse, as elsewhere, it was not the movement's regional leaders who were chosen as election candidates. This was partly because those convicted in 1987 were not eligible to stand, but it was also a strategy to put forward those on the periphery of the movement who might attract broader electoral support. In some constituencies the movement presented clerics with links to Zaytuna, in others lawyers and businessmen with a more 'liberal' Islamic discourse, and in others activists with a more 'radical' political vision.[97] Of the seven Sousse candidates, only the head of the list, Jaleleddine Rouis, was a true insider: by then the doctor from M'saken was a Consultative Council member and had only narrowly avoided arrest in 1987 by going into hiding for several months. His fellow candidates were respectable local figures who were movement sympathizers, not full members: Mustapha Ben Moussa, a pharmacist also from M'saken; Tarak Mokni, a university English teacher and whose relative Habib Mokni had been among the founders of the MTI; Hedhili Ben Ameur, a teacher from Kalaa Kebira; Mustapha Bouhelal, a teacher from M'saken; Saleh Hachem, a human rights activist who had been one of the early preachers in Sousse but had since distanced himself from the movement; and Zine el Abidine Attia, a legal clerk from a family of local officials in Enfidha.

The election campaign was vigorous and confident. Al-Nahda held dozens of well-attended public meetings, and distributed pamphlets outlining its political vision, which concentrated on reviving Tunisia's Arab-Islamic identity.[98] Abdelfattah, a young activist who helped organize the campaign in Akouda, described frequent tussles with officials from the ruling party, the now renamed Democratic Constitutional Rally (RCD), during which the Islamists acted with an excited defiance. The day before the Sunday vote was supposed to be a day without campaigning, but RCD officials drove through the suburb in taxis rallying support. Hamid Karoui, the Sousse-born justice minister and head of the RCD list in the city, visited the local market.

He was passing through the market and we surrounded them all and started whooping like Apache Indians and we threw purple-coloured pieces of paper at them and shouted: 'Down with the Destour! Down with the torturer of the people!'.[99]

Although al-Nahda perceived itself as acting in the interest of the nation, not merely the party, in pressing for democratic freedoms, in fact the movement was isolated on the political field. Activists from other opposition parties in Sousse saw the dominance of al-Nahda, particularly in the universities, but also felt their arrogance and reluctance to ally in broader alliances with leftist movements. The unauthorized Tunisian Workers' Communist Party (PCOT) had refused to sign the National Pact and considered al-Nahda to be as much of a threat as the regime. As one PCOT activist remembered: 'We had a slogan at the time: "Political

Freedom! No Destourians! No Khouanjiyya!" (*Ḥurriyya Siyāsiyya! Lā Dsātira! Lā Khouanjiyya!*). They were theocratic and ideological and they remained our enemies.'[100]

Although there was strong evidence of falsification of the results, the official count still attributed remarkable strength in depth to the al-Nahda movement. In Sousse, the list won around 27 per cent of the vote – more than four times as much as the combined results of the two other opposition parties in the constituency, Mestiri's MDS and the pan-Arab PUP.[101] Al-Nahda contested nearly every constituency in the country and did best in rural, socially conservative governorates in the south like Gabes and Kebili, but also did surprisingly well in wealthier, coastal, urban governorates like Tunis, Ben Arous, and Bizerte, where it won around a quarter of the official vote. Observers at the time put this coastal success down to large social and cultural fractures in society, the 'shock of modernity' brought by mass tourism to coastal areas, and a lower propensity for pro-RCD clientalist voting.[102] In Sousse, the RCD won around 70 per cent, and Karoui was rewarded with promotion to the post of prime minister in September 1989. Regardless of al-Nahda's strong performance as by far the largest opposition party with a formal tally nationwide of 14.5 per cent, the final results gave all 141 seats in the parliament to the RCD.[103] In a presidential election held on the same day, Ben Ali claimed 99.27 per cent of the vote.[104]

At first, what Burgat calls the 'electroshock' of the election results generated a tense standoff.[105] Within months of the elections, Ben Ali painted the Islamists as a critical threat to Tunisia, just as Bourguiba had done before him. It was only the state that should act as the 'defender' of religion, Ben Ali said. 'That is why we say to those who mix religion and politics that there is no place for a religious party'.[106] But he also allowed the movement to begin printing a newspaper again, for the first time since *Al-Ma'rifa* was shut down in 1979. The first edition of the new weekly, *Al-Fajr* (The Dawn), was published after several weeks' delay on 21 April 1990. Ghannouchi, who had left Tunisia in May 1989 for Algeria, issued a front-page challenge, committing al-Nahda to a struggle for freedom, justice, and respect for cultural identity against single-party rule and despotism. Al-Nahda, he said, was not a party-political project, but a liberation 'project of renaissance' built around Arab-Islamic identity.[107] A frequent target of criticism was Mohamed Charfi, a leftist academic appointed education minister days after the 1989 elections, who Nahdawis feared was intent on uprooting the Islamist social and cultural base in a project known as 'draining the springs' (*tajfīf al-manābi'*).[108] The movement's support among students continued to remain strong.

Results of internal student council elections in the 1989–90 academic year showed the Islamist UGTE won 111 seats nationwide, against just twenty-one for its leftist rival the UGET. In Sousse, the results were one seat apiece in the law faculty, and outright victories for the UGTE in the medicine faculty, the arts faculty, and the École Normale Supérieure teacher-training college.[109] However, the brief opportunity for expression afforded to the movement was quickly curtailed. *Al-Fajr* was shut down for three months after Ghannouchi wrote a critical article entitled 'The people of the state or the state of the people' in June 1990. The paper was finally closed at the end of the year, after it published an article by the lawyer Mohamed al-Nouri in October, entitled 'Military courts are exceptional courts, so when will they be annulled?'. Both al-Nouri and the paper's editor, Hamadi Jebali, were later convicted and jailed by a military court. The final editions of *Al-Fajr* were filled with lists of the latest arrests and convictions of Nahdawis across the country. The movement's frustration eventually pushed it into another rupture, this time more ominous than the 1987 protests. In November, Ali Laarayedh, the al-Nahda spokesman, warned of a new popular struggle:

We must continue the struggle because there is no longer any way to reach agreement with the authorities. Through demonstrations in the street, we will struggle for our rights and our country's rights.[110]

Once the regime began arresting al-Nahda's leadership from December, the movement's response intensified, with protests calling for the 'imposition of freedoms' (*farḍ al-ḥurriyyāt*) and coinciding with large-scale demonstrations protesting the US-led Gulf War against Iraq. And so, just as in 1987, the regime's sweeping programme of arrests to repress the movement shaped the street demonstrations, which marked a final phase of resistance.

There were, however, divisions within al-Nahda, not least over the appropriate stance to take on the Iraq conflict. Ghannouchi took a staunch line in favour of Saddam Hussein and explicitly critical of the Saudis, a position which mirrored that of the Islamic Salvation Front (FIS) in Algeria, while Jebali was much more critical of Iraq's invasion of Kuwait, which he said would open the region up to American control.[111] There were also disputes about how confrontational the movement's response should be to the disappointment of the elections. As Sahbi, the activist and law student from Akouda who had been imprisoned for student activities in 1983, said:

Some said it was a trial (*ibtilā'*) and that we should be patient and that there was a price to pay, and that sacrifices were needed, and even if we were killed we would be considered martyrs. We should put our lives in God's hands. The second view was for confrontation: we were going to be hit by the regime, so let us die standing up. We are not cowards. We should attack so that they will understand the movement has its own existence, its own base, and many people who will defend it.[112]

The movement, which was struggling to maintain a coherent leadership structure, rushed into confrontation even though many were opposed.[113] This meant increased numbers of protests, particularly on university campuses and at police stations after the arrest of fellow al-Nahda activists. There was also a rare act of violence at an RCD office in Bab Souika, in Tunis, in February 1991, in which a night guard was killed. Shortly after this, Mourou, one of the co-founders, publicly quit the movement in protest at the use of violence. The decision to issue strident public statements and to press for intense confrontation, succumbing to what Hermassi called 'the malady of impatience and haste', would be much debated and regretted within the movement in the years ahead.[114]

Charles Kurzman has argued that structural opportunities do not always align with perceived opportunities, that there is, in other words, a difference between objective and subjective definitions of political opportunity.[115] In his example of the 1979 Iranian revolution, he finds that the state was not particularly vulnerable but that Iranians decided to participate in protests on the basis of their assessment that the opposition movement had strengthened. In Tunisia in 1989 the state was also not particularly vulnerable to a popular uprising for democracy, but Islamists subjectively perceived their chances for dramatic change to be good. In this case it was a significant miscalculation. Al-Nahda misread its own strength and the real latitude for political change.

In Sousse there were several demonstrations. In April 1990, crowds gathered in the Old City to protest the takeover of a mosque by RCD officials, who had turned the building into a local party office.[116] A major rally was held between the Old City and the port in January 1991, in protest against both the Ben Ali regime and the US-led Gulf War. There were also confrontations between Islamist students and the police, particularly on the main road in Hai Riadh leading to the football stadium, which would also become a site of confrontation during the 2011 uprising. By mid-1991, hundreds of al-Nahda activists from across Sousse had been arrested. At least one died: Abdelwahed Abdelli, a fourth-year student at the École Normale Supérieure teacher-training college in Sousse, was shot in the leg, arrested, and tortured in jail. He died on 30 June.[117]

In both the 1987 demonstration and the aftermath of the 1989 elections, activists within the MTI and later al-Nahda emerged from their discrete sites of activity in university campuses and in morality-focused community-building projects and they broke explosively into the public sphere. In both cases, the ultimate trigger for action was anger at their exclusion, either through arrests or through ignored election results, and the penalty for their highly visible transgression in the public sphere was punitive: sweeping arrests and prison sentences. By the early 1990s, the movement had been entirely dismantled, its leaders forced into exile, and thousands of its members jailed. These moments of irruption generated extraordinary acts of public defiance and heightened self-confidence, pushing the movement into decisions it would later come to regret and eventually into a conflict it could not win.

★

Privileging the experiences of local level Islamist activists in the 1980s offers a new understanding of the MTI's politicization. Although most attention has focused on the formal political negotiations between the movement's leaders and the regime, and the clear efforts by Ghannouchi and his colleagues to find acceptance within the political process, other activism was taking place offstage. Here on university campuses young Islamists were shaping their ideas in competition with the left and coming to new understandings of their dispute with the regime. They were less keen than their leaders on seeking formal political inclusion. Beyond the university, grassroots work built a subculture forged around reinvented traditions and centred on identity, morality, and the continued practice of faith. It is only by excavating the informal offstage behaviours that we understand how the movement's activists understood their own identity as Islamists. When the cordon was breached between the careful public discourse of negotiation and the hidden mobilizing activities of the movement's base, the result was a series of sharp confrontations which led eventually to overreach on the part of al-Nahda and severe repression.

This is a portrait of a movement balanced between the state-level political ambitions of its leaders, students engaged in daily confrontations, and a grassroots subculture more focused on practices of identity, morality, and faith. This complexity, which is only ever hinted at in accounts of formal relations between the movement leaders and the regime, remained central to the movement's self-understanding just as its plasticity offered a repertoire of mobilizations. The bonds forged in the subculture provided the resilience needed to survive the next two decades of repression and to rebuild after 2011. However, the tension between the different understandings of what it meant to be Islamist, either competing for power in a pluralist political system or Islamizing from below through a moral community, remained unresolved. This ambiguity would be much debated during the years of prison in the 1990s and returned as a fundamental question after 2011.

4   Confronting Prison

> We considered prison to be a miniature version of the regime. We saw the power there. We saw how they were. It was the same logic as if the prison was the whole of Tunisia, the way they managed our lives in terms of our rights. The governor, the officers, they were all part of the system ... It was a whole implacable logic.
>
> *Hamadi Jebali, senior al-Nahda leader from Sousse, imprisoned from 1989 to 2006, including ten years in solitary confinement.*[1]

To look at the prison system in the Ben Ali era is to see where power took effect; where it acted not just to repress but also to generate resistance. If the preceding decades had been a time for Nahdawis to construct an imagined solidarity through a living subculture, here was the moment when that network faced its greatest strain. Viewed through the structural lens of political opportunities, the period of the 1990s and the 2000s would seem to be one characterized only by repression, a sharp downturn in contention in which the movement should have been exhausted and dissolved, no longer functioning as a force of mobilization. This is how the movement's history has often been explained. Most scholars considered the movement to have disappeared inside Tunisia, to survive only in exile, or that 'for all practical purposes, Nahda had become an offshore operation sustained by supporters in Europe and North America'.[2] Within Tunisia 'what remained of the Islamist movement was decapitated and fragmented'.[3] Several years later in the wake of the 2011 uprising, much attention would be paid to the movement's 'political theatre' of victimhood drawn from the repression its members suffered in the 1990s.[4] Yet between the movement's onshore disappearance and its post-2011 narrative of victimhood lies the long, unexamined prison experience. This chapter uncovers Nahdawi experiences of the prison years of the 1990s, not only to demonstrate the effect of coercion but also to reveal the self-critical debate and acts of protest that were generated in response to the punitive regime. Accounts from the prisoners themselves reveal a repertoire of resilience and the eventual reclaiming of the prison cell as a site of struggle. This was individual and collective work that was empowered by the strong pre-existing relationships between Nahdawis, who clung to that unity despite the fragmentation imposed on them. This sense of belonging was reinforced by familial support from outside the prison gates. But prison was also a new site of meaning-making, where Nahdawi prisoners not only identified themselves with a particular vocabulary, but where they also strove to recover dignity in the face of abuse and humiliation.

The Tunisian regime imprisoned the Islamists at a moment when other governments were reluctant to jail political prisoners because of the reputational cost. Prison had become, in the words of one human rights activist, an 'anachronistic mode of repression' of political dissidents.[5] Authoritarian regimes now deployed other forms of discipline, from the brutal death squads of Latin America to more subtle internal controls on employment, education, and travel. Even in authoritarian Syria, thousands of political prisoners were released in the 1990s because jail had become too politically costly.[6] In Tunisia, the political logic of repression was closely tied to the economic logic of *infitāḥ*: the priority of maintaining the stability needed to attract investment and a free trade deal with Europe were, as Gregory White argues, incompatible with political liberalization.[7] The instabilities generated by this economic path were answered by repression. In Tunisia, with its history of jailing leftist political dissidents in the 1960s–70s and Islamists in the 1980s, the subjection of dissent continued into the 1990s and beyond as a constant pillar in the reproduction of a system of coercion and surveillance. This should be seen as part of the making of centralized state power identified across the region, which relied not just on repression but on producing uniform subjects and constructing hierarchies of power.[8] Thus, although Ben Ali had begun his career in the military, it was through the internal security forces that he built a power base. He was made director-general of National Security, the highest position in internal security, in 1977 and again in 1984. Once president, he unleashed the 'security beast', expanding the repressive apparatus of state.[9] The number of police in the 1990s reached between 80,000 and 150,000, between two and four times its size in the mid-1980s, while the interior ministry budget grew to be half as large again as the defence ministry budget by 2010.[10] By 2005 Tunisia had the highest prison population rate in the Middle East, with 252 prisoners per 100,000 citizens.[11]

The al-Nahda prisoners referred to their years in jail as the tribulation (*al-miḥna*), reviving the name used by the Egyptian Muslim Brotherhood to describe its repression under Gamal Abdel Nasser.[12] Yet the coercive intent of the Tunisian authorities was to deny the prisoners the chance to regroup as their Egyptian predecessors had done in the 1950s–60s, or as had, more recently, Palestinians in Israeli jails or Republican prisoners in the H-Blocks of Northern Ireland. The Tunisian regime initially appeared successful, presenting itself in public as liberal and progressive, while acting in private with violence and domination. In public, Ben Ali's government spoke of a constant journey of political reform, the revival of a tradition of 'tolerant' Tunisian Islam, the defence of women's rights, and model economic growth. In private, in prison cells nationwide, it disciplined, deprived, humiliated, isolated, tortured, and sometimes killed prisoners in order to force al-Nahda into submission. The regime also engaged in a powerful propagandist attack on the weakened movement, insidiously eroding the Islamist narrative frames and depicting them as alien to 'authentic' Tunisian traditions. This state-sponsored denigration of the Islamists was to reverberate long after the fall of the Ben Ali regime in 2011.

Though the system was undeniably repressive, the regime cloaked its workings in pseudo-legitimacy. Within weeks of his coup, Ben Ali abolished the much-criticized State Security Court and reduced to a maximum of ten days the time a suspect could be detained before seeing a judge.[13] In June 1991, well before the key military trials against al-Nahda leaders began, Ben Ali appointed a special presidential adviser on human rights and set up a commission of inquiry to examine claims of human rights violations by his security forces, which admitted 'some abuses' but insisted these were 'individual and isolated acts' and contrary to government policy.[14] Ben Ali's own framing of the confrontation with al-Nahda is revealing. In an interview with *al-Hayat* in 1993, he described the Islamists as not just 'terrorists and criminals' but said:

They excluded themselves. They were rejected by all components of society, a society attached to its authenticity and values of tolerance and openness, from the moment that they proved to be no more than apostles of sedition and terrorism. As for us, we had no other choice but to confront them, by applying the law and yet without resorting to exceptional laws. For them, democracy is a heresy. Consequently, they are enemies of democracy and dialogue.[15]

Here he contested the essential Islamist assertion of 'authenticity' by claiming for himself the power to define and determine the boundaries of societal norms: the accepted meanings of 'authentic', 'tolerant', 'open', and 'democratic'. In defining and categorizing his population, Ben Ali framed his opponents as not merely law breakers but as located outside societal norms. What they could not be, in his framing, was political or social contestants. In this way he denied them their public voice and diminished the very serious political challenge they represented.

This chapter demonstrates what happened to the movement in the wake of the crackdown, and how members of the movement experienced repression. My focus here is not on those who went into exile, but on those Nahdawis who remained in Tunisia during the 1990s and 2000s, because theirs is an untold story. Life in exile was challenging in different ways, but the comparative freedom abroad allowed Nahdawis to build more sophisticated support networks than were possible at home. This included helping newly arrived Tunisians find housing and schools and providing cultural orientation.[16] Only a small number of Sousse activists went into exile (among them Zied Ladhari, a young lawyer who would become an elected deputy from 2011, and Afifa Makhlouf, the women's activist – both spent several years in France); most of those involved in the movement stayed inside Tunisia. This chapter shows that the prison regime made a determined effort to destroy the movement from within, using a range of coercive practices that were both physical and psychological. Yet, after the harsher early years of the prison experience, Nahdawis found the space to discuss with each other their struggle and what had led them to such a costly confrontation. There was a critique of strategic decisions by the leadership that emerged in parallel to policy revisions by the movement-in-exile. It was a long internal debate that was not easily resolved: the question of historic evaluations returned in the late 2000s and again after the 2011 uprising. Alongside this intellectual revival of spirit, the prison cell gradually became a site of struggle and, through hunger strikes and private study, a place from which to reclaim dignity. The repression of al-Nahda was also experienced by families, and especially women, who were forced to submit to another particular regime of control during their regular visits but who took advantage of those visits to re-establish a community of belonging.

Practices of Coercion

The repression of al-Nahda began with waves of arrests from autumn 1990 and culminated in two simultaneous show trials of 279 suspects at military courts in Tunis in July and August 1992. It was the third regime strike against the movement, following the trials of 1981 and 1987 under Bourguiba. Many thousands of Nahdawis were caught but, despite their earlier experiences, they had no preparation for the prison experience, in contrast, for example, to the Palestinians, who produced written pamphlets advising activists how to cope with jail.[17] Amnesty International estimated 8,000 men and women were arrested between September 1990 and March 1992 alone, while others within the movement claimed 30,000 were finally held in total, of whom around 10,000 spent a significant time in prison.[18] A small number escaped by going into hiding, while a few hundred left the country early enough to head into exile, most notably, and to the still-whispered chagrin of some, their leader Ghannouchi.[19] Judges at the heavily guarded Bouchoucha and Bab Saadoun military courts handed down life sentences to 46 al-Nahda leaders and jail sentences of up to 24 years to 219 others, in what international human rights groups said were 'unfair' hearings that followed 'pervasive' torture during interrogation.[20] The central charges were attempting to overthrow the government to install an Islamic state and conspiring to assassinate Ben Ali by acquiring a Stinger surface-to-air missile from Afghanistan in order to shoot down the presidential plane. Since the trials were held in military courts there was no appeal, merely a confirmation of all the verdicts by the Court of Cassation in September 1992.

The Bouchoucha and Bab Saadoun trials targeted the leadership of the movement, and only seven from Sousse were among the defendants, including: Hamadi Jebali, who was sentenced to seventeen years and six months; Ajmi Lourimi, then a political bureau member, who was jailed for life; and Bouraoui Makhlouf, from a prominent religious family in the Old City and the brother of Afifa, who was also jailed for life. Yet several hundred other Nahdawis from Sousse were jailed at smaller hearings which ran until the mid-1990s. For example, on 22 April 1993 the Criminal Circuit Court of Appeal of Sousse heard a case against nineteen suspected al-Nahda members.[21] The 23-page judgement offers a rare insight into the trial process at the local level. Eighteen defendants were convicted of burning a government building, and conspiracy to cause violence against a government official. Two were also convicted of distributing pamphlets that disturbed public order, belonging to a corrupt association, and writing graffiti.[22] One was convicted of sheltering a wanted suspect. The prosecution's case was that at dawn on 7 May 1991 the group had attacked a police station inside the Faculty of Law in Sousse, throwing stones and Molotov cocktails. One police officer was injured and the police opened fire on the attackers, hitting one in the leg. The defendants all denied involvement and several complained they had been tortured. They were fined and sentenced to jail terms ranging from six months to five years. Among them were three men who after 2011 went on to hold important positions in the regional bureau of the movement in Sousse and a fourth, Samir Dilou, who became a minister in the al-Nahda government after 2011. What the court document fails to convey is the very nature of the proceeding itself, and particularly the judge's tight control over what was included in the official transcript. In one rare account, an international observer who attended three similar trials during the 1990s of Tunisian human rights activists and political dissidents described how defendants' testimonies of torture were omitted from court summaries, how the word 'torture' itself was rarely used, and how defence lawyers used the courtroom as 'the site of extended challenge against the court'.[23] Although these cases were against communists rather than Islamists, it is highly likely the hearings were performed in a similar way. The unofficial narrative of the trial experience is striking:

> Physically, the courtroom was noisy and uncomfortable for defendants, lawyers, and observers alike ... The judge frequently slapped his hand on the table and used his microphone to shout down defendants and lawyers, cutting them off after a few minutes and thereby preventing them from developing their defence as they saw fit. When some of the defendants sought to name their alleged torturers, the judge cut them off and then refused to enter those names into the summary of the proceedings. Frequent interventions by the judge, the defence attorneys' often frantic attempts to intervene on behalf of their clients during their examination, the lack of amplification of the defendants' voices, and the generally hostile and dismissive attitude of the presiding judge conspired to make the proceedings chaotic at times.[24]

The practices of coercion extended even to the defence lawyers trying to insist on a fair hearing for their clients in the courtroom.

The authorities did not admit holding political prisoners, insisting that a Nahdawi prisoner was a criminal like any other inmate. Yet, in the first few months of the mass arrests in 1991 al-Nahda prisoners were held in large groups together and, despite routine torture during the initial interrogations, they at least were able to organize their lives in a way familiar to Palestinian or Irish Republican prisoners. Around 300 Nahdawis were held in the overcrowded Room Two of Sousse prison, with its single toilet and three small windows. They described praying together, studying the Qur'an, and singing, early in the morning before the guards came for an initial count and after the final count at night. 'When we were together, we didn't feel like we were in prison,' said Hamza, who was 27 years old when he was arrested at his home in Kalaa Kebira in 1991.[25] They organized study sessions: one lectured about the ongoing Palestinian peace negotiations. With the Nahdawis in Sousse was Mohamed Chemli, the regional bureau leader who was from a wealthy family. His relatives brought food and other supplies, including notebooks, for the prisoners. Others held elsewhere had similar experiences: study classes focusing on *fiqh* (Islamic jurisprudence), on Qur'anic commentaries, even discussions about married life, as well as games of chess, training in judo, and singing religious songs.[26] However, in October 1991, perhaps in reaction to the emerging political success in Algeria of the Islamic Salvation Front (FIS), the system within the Tunisian prisons changed.[27] Nahdawis were separated from each other and forced to share cells with ordinary criminals, usually four to a room, and were soon moved on to other prisons nationwide. So began the long and isolating prison experience.

Al-Nahda prisoners were immediately treated differently. They soon found they had the words 'special category' (*ṣibgha khāṣṣa*) stamped on their prison documents which separated them from the 'common law' (*ḥaqq al-'āmm*) prisoners. The Nahdawis referred to themselves collectively as the *intima* ', meaning 'belonging', reclaiming for their own use the vocabulary under which many of them had been repeatedly prosecuted since the first trial in 1981, namely the accusation of belonging to an unauthorized association. Special category status did not denote superior conditions but the reverse: a denial of many of the rights offered to ordinary prisoners. One Nahdawi, who smuggled out a detailed account of prison life, listed an array of deprivations suffered by Islamist prisoners: denial of physical contact during family visits; restrictions on the number and type of visitors; restrictions on how much they could spend on food and goods in the prison shop; and a ban on receiving money from visiting relatives.[28] But it was soon apparent that the Islamists would not be the only targets of prison repression: many other political dissidents, especially members of the Tunisian Workers' Communist Party (PCOT), were arrested from the early 1990s onwards and harshly treated.

The primary challenge of prison for the Nahdawis was repeated brutality. The worst torture happened in the first days after arrest, before the detainees were brought in front of a judge. Brutal techniques possessed their own grotesque vocabulary: '*falaka*', the beating of the soles of the feet; '*poulet rôti*', tying a prisoner to a horizontal pole by his hands and feet, like a grilled chicken cooking in a restaurant; '*avion*', tying a prisoner's hands and feet behind his back and beating him; '*bano*', the bath, or suspending the prisoner by his ankles and plunging his head into a bucket of dirty water.[29] Other punishments included electric shocks, burning with cigarettes, and sexual abuse, including rape, of both male and female prisoners.[30] In interviews, Nahdawis gave detailed accounts of many aspects of their prison years but, not surprisingly, avoided speaking of the violence they suffered. 'We in Sousse were under the baton of torture, the horrors of torture. It is humiliating to tell the stories of that torture,' said Jamel, who was held in Sousse prison in autumn 1991.[31] Hassan, who was jailed from 1991 to 1993, said: 'There was torture. They tried to get from me the maximum information to know the *organigramme*: Who is responsible for you? Who do you have links with? Who is below you?'[32]

The purpose of torture was not merely to extract information, but to provoke the rest of the movement into a violent reaction the better to repress it. Some were surprised how quickly al-Nahda collapsed. One Tunisian scholar noted at the time: 'No one expected that the movement could be so easily liquefied.'[33] However, contrary to the views of some who saw al-Nahda as an inherently violent organization, there is little evidence that the movement had a real commitment to an armed struggle against the regime, still less the resources to carry that out on anything approaching an Algerian scale.[34] Rhetorically defiant statements from al-Nahda leaders alienated ordinary Tunisians, yet they revealed not the militarism of the movement but rather its fragility at its greatest moment of crisis.

Torture was a shared experience that became emblematic in memories of the al-Nahda experience. Many of those I spoke to admitted revealing names and organizational information under torture, but because the arrests were so sudden and comprehensive there was no blame attributed to those who confessed. Although the worst of the torture was limited to the initial interrogation, the denial of medical treatment became a great physical challenge and many prisoners died of their illnesses in prison or shortly after leaving. In the case of the Sousse activists, these included Ali Nouir, the preacher and founding member of the Islamic Tendency Movement (MTI), who died of ill health six years after his release from jail, and Ezzedine Ben Aisha, a prominent activist from Kalaa Kebira, who died in his cell in August 1994 aged 33. In total, the movement listed nineteen Sousse 'martyrs' who since 1981 were killed, executed, or died from illnesses contracted in prison.[35] The violence was a proximate but often ghostly presence. Another prisoner from Sousse was in the jail where Ben Aisha died:

He died next to us, in the cell next to us, but we didn't realize for a whole year until someone came from another prison and told us that Ezzedine Ben Aisha was dead. It was very strange. You hear nothing, you see nothing.[36]

A shared experience of torture forged a collective memory of the prison challenge and another layer of belonging.

Beyond the physical punishments were other strategies designed to break the will of the prisoners. There were repeated efforts to force prisoners to submit to the arbitrary rule of prison officers. In the late 1990s in a Tunis prison the guards forced prisoners to salute an officer's cap left on a chair and a guard dog tied up in the prison courtyard.[37] Others described how non-Islamist prisoners turned informers; the Islamists referred to such a prisoner as a songbird, a 'lark' (qubbar), because they reported back to the guards on private Nahdawi discussions. Many al-Nahda prisoners spent long periods in solitary confinement, usually alone in a cell though sometimes in small group isolation and often for many months or, for more senior leaders, many years. Hamadi Jebali, who had led the movement in the early 1980s, spent ten years in solitary. Ajmi Lourimi, another senior Sousse leader, spent most of his sixteen years in jail in solitary. Human Rights Watch estimated that more than 500 political prisoners had been jailed in solitary confinement out of a 'political will to punish and demoralize these individuals, and to crush the Islamist trend they represent'.[38] Solitary confinement in what prisoners called the '*siloun*' (a derivation of the French *cellule*), meant being locked in a small cell that was suffocating in summer and freezing in winter, with a small toilet or plastic bottles serving as a urinal and with blankets covered in lice, being forced to wear a blue prison uniform instead of the usual ordinary clothes, or even to go naked, being denied family visits or food packages, and being made to take the weekly shower alone when other prisoners had finished washing.[39] As one prisoner recounted:

I was in a *siloun*, a small room with a toilet and you are handcuffed to the wall, naked, and at the tap even the water was limited. The water ran only when they opened the tap from outside. It was very humid, and there was constant torture and harassment.[40]

Isolation was also achieved by moving the prisoners from one jail to the next every few months, often without informing their families. This prisoner, Jamel, a doctor from Gafsa who had studied and had begun working in Sousse when he was arrested, was moved frequently during his eight-year sentence.

I was moved in twenty-two convoys from one prison to another. You lived without any stability. Tomorrow you don't know what will happen to you or who will be your cellmate. You can't pray in groups, you can't eat with your colleagues, you can't buy anything.[41]

As well as this physical isolation and instability, the prison regime imposed an information blackout. Authorized newspapers, usually the official Tunisian press, were sometimes available but often prisoners found the most interesting articles, usually involving the conflict in Algeria, had been cut out leaving what they called 'windows' (*shabābīk*) in the page. Wrapping from the soap or food brought by relatives was removed before it reached the prisoners, so it could not be used as notepaper, and pens were forbidden in the early years.

Occasionally the isolation took a public turn. Several Nahdawis formally disowned the movement in the national press. These public notices were all similar. Each was a paragraph long and gave the full name and identity card number of the individual who had written to the paper, followed by their disavowal of the Islamist movement and pledge of allegiance to Ben Ali, the Democratic Constitutional Rally (RCD), and his 7 November 1987 coup. One such notice, headlined 'A Clarification' read:

... he announces that he never belonged to what is called the al-Nahda movement and that he strongly opposes its principles and does not sympathize with its followers and that he is proud to belong to the Democratic Constitutional Rally.[42]

Another was headlined 'A Declaration of Innocence and Commitment':

... he announces that he is completely innocent of belonging to or communicating with or in any way dealing with what is called the al-Nahda movement, and expresses his absolute commitment to the principles of 7 November.[43]

A third was again headlined 'A Declaration of Innocence':

... he announces that he does not belong to what is called the al-Nahda movement, and expresses his repudiation and criticism of terrorism and extremism, and his commitment to the guidelines of the new era in laying the foundations of civil society.[44]

These notices may have been a bureaucratic necessity to allow someone to sign an employment contract or to resolve a difficulty with the local police or municipal administration. This would be in line with other administrative papers that quickly assumed great importance, including the Bulletin No. 3, which attested to a police record and a jail sentence of more than two months and which ex-prisoners often needed in order to be cleared for work.[45] However, for the individuals involved it also had its own punitive function. It was felt as a formal, public disavowal of not just the al-Nahda project but of their religious faith. As one Nahdawi said:

It was more significant than just resigning from the movement. It was not just to resign but to take up another position and to completely disown the movement as if we were non-believers, as if we had left God.[46]

It was also another effort by the regime to position al-Nahda as outside accepted societal norms, norms which required an explicit, public commitment to Ben Ali's legitimacy as president. There was much resistance to such public repudiations from within the movement, despite intense pressure from the regime on both Nahdawis and their families.

This array of coercive and disciplinary practices was intended to dissolve from within a movement that had challenged the regime. Prison coercion, which often mirrored conditions imposed on leftist prisoners in the 1970s, was intended to produce submissive, obedient subjects.[47]

However, those sentenced to longer jail terms eventually began to seek out ways to skirt the imposed isolation and to reclaim a shared belonging.

Evaluation

The Nahdawis were not docile victims of the prison regime. The worst of the physical violence was generally limited to the early 1990s and, although the coercive techniques continued for many years, the prisoners did find ways to adapt. Despite the frequently imposed isolation, some prisoners held extended discussions about the events that had led to the crackdown and particularly about how much responsibility the movement bore for its fate. These were not large, organized meetings, but rather discussions between two or three cellmates at a time. When one prisoner was moved on to another jail, he or she would take with them the ideas discussed and continue the debate with others in the new surroundings. In this way an informal, unwritten, and often critical assessment of the movement's past circulated through the jails, described by those involved as an 'evaluation' (taqyīm) along the lines of the Project of Priorities in the 1980s.

Separately, a formal evaluation was carried out by the leaders of the movement-in-exile. The leadership abroad, at least in the early 1990s, was unable to make direct contact with the Tunisian prisoners, which meant the review was not comprehensive and explains why another project of evaluation was felt necessary in the late 2000s and again in the post-2011 transitional period. In June 1996 the movement issued from London a long summary of its internal discussions, entitled 'Lessons from the Past, Present Problems and Future Ambitions', signed by Ghannouchi himself.[48] The document reads as an effort by the leadership to defend decisions made during the confrontation with Ben Ali but also, reflecting the reality of exile and the need to placate host governments, it redirected the movement away from its long-held political ambition. It made some striking admissions.

First, it noted that in the late 1980s the movement's political work had overwhelmed its cultural and social activities and brought it into confrontation with the regime: 'The supremacy of the political field over the da'wa and cultural fields had a negative effect on the path of the movement and the development of the awakening'.[49] The movement announced it would now eschew its former political ambitions, in favour of other projects:

We confirm the priority of the cultural and the social over the political, meaning that the political takes on new intellectual meaning and content so that it primarily serves the educational and cultural mission.[50]

Second, it accepted al-Nahda had failed to build alliances with other opposition parties and with the elite during the 1980s, which left it isolated in a highly polarized society. Third, it admitted that acts of violence undermined the movement's position. Even though al-Nahda's formal stance was in favour of non-violence, it acknowledged there had been some 'excesses' (al-tajāwuzat), including the throwing of Molotov petrol bombs and the attack on the RCD office at Bab Souika in 1991, which it admitted marked a turning point in al-Nahda's fortunes.[51] However, it also deflected blame for the confrontation, saying that the Ben Ali regime had taken a security-first approach following the 1989 election and that it was only after the regime had hardened its position that the movement too hardened its stance. Al-Nahda tried to avoid civil war, it said, by abandoning its confrontational approach in 1992, but it was not helped by the international situation, in which Islamist movements were increasingly targets of suspicion. It insisted the movement was committed to non-violence and to its 'Islamic identity'. And it appealed for 'national dialogue' and 'comprehensive national reconciliation' to solve the political crisis in Tunisia and asked its members to be patient.

However, the idea of reconciling with the regime was anathema to most prisoners. In their view, the repression that followed the elections and the brutality they suffered under interrogation demonstrated that this was not a regime open to negotiation. As Jebali said:

Ben Ali pushed everyone to conclude that this was a man we just couldn't deal with. We saw it was a waste of time. We must resist. Ben Ali, with his wrongdoing in prison and abroad towards our families, even towards the opposition that had allied with him, gave us evidence that it made no difference. It changed nothing.[52]

It was a view that would eventually change, but not until most prisoners had been released by the mid-2000s. Among the ordinary membership in the early 1990s there was still considerable frustration with the strategy of confrontation. Even among those in exile, there were signs of discontent. In 1993 and 1994 two senior Nahdawis in exile in Paris resigned and criticized Ghannouchi for favouring confrontation, which they said led to the crackdown.[53] Salah Karkar, in particular, grew increasingly distant from the movement while in exile until he was formally excluded in 2002. He argued for a renunciation of the political project in favour of training and education to bring back society's Islamic character, and declared that in some circumstances, such as Algeria and Afghanistan, Islamists were right to use violence.[54] Al-Nahda exiles and Tunisian observers sensed the movement was on the brink of collapse, 'torn and weakened by its own contradictions'.[55] After all, Ghannouchi committed a series of 'profound tactical mistakes', by leaving the country as early as 1989, through his radical vocabulary, and in overestimating popular support for a confrontation with the regime.[56] At the first congress in exile, held in Switzerland in December 1995, Ghannouchi, who had been granted political asylum in London two years earlier, was only narrowly re-elected president of the movement, winning just 52 per cent of the vote.[57] New internal laws were introduced limiting his powers by requiring the large Consultative Council to approve his nominees to the cabinet, the Executive Bureau.

Discussions within the Tunisian prisons tended to be yet more critical of the leadership, though given that this was not an organized process and that findings were not formally written down it is difficult to make a direct comparison with the mood in exile. It does at least demonstrate that discussions about adapting ideology and strategy were not merely confined to exiled leaders as commonly thought.[58] The strategic choices of the late 1980s were the most important topic under debate within the prisons, as well as the manner of decision-making within the movement. Many were frustrated that the leadership had rushed into the elections at full strength and then confronted the regime afterwards. Some prisoners, particularly those from the lower ranks, argued that the movement should have kept to its original risk-averse plan to contest only a handful of constituencies in order not to unnerve the regime. One young Sousse activist, who was born in 1968, said:

It wasn't necessary to enter the elections on the scale that we did. We could have entered only partially, and given the regime space not to be afraid of us or to panic about us ... There were also some who said the Islamist movement shouldn't involve itself in such a radical confrontation with the regime. They could have established some dialogue and been patient in the face of attack and not rush to a reaction. You shouldn't use up all your force in confronting the authorities. The Islamist movement, with its modest capacity, couldn't confront the authorities with their military capabilities. The best thing was to be patient, to take the path of dialogue, to make concessions, and to be silent in the face of insults in order to achieve other goals.[59]

A cautious approach to political entry was to become characteristic of other Islamist movements in similar semi-authoritarian circumstances in Morocco, Egypt, and Turkey.[60] Through their prison discussions, many Tunisian prisoners concluded that a more modest approach would be wiser if there was ever another opportunity for political inclusion. However, they also learnt that political zeal could undermine the original Islamizing mission. It was to implant in them a long-lasting wariness about the cost of prioritizing a state-level political project.

Many were angry that the leadership had opted for full confrontation with the regime. Rachid, the mathematics teacher who had been a local-level organizer in El-Jem in the 1980s, was deeply troubled. He had played an organizational role in Sousse during the 1989 elections and was already a member of the movement's Consultative Council. He spent ten months in hiding between December 1990 and October 1991. He was eventually arrested, then convicted in the military trial at Bouchoucha, where he was sentenced to eleven years in jail, which he spent in ten different prisons across the country. He argued that the movement had been right to take part in the 1989 elections, but had been wrong to confront the regime with popular demonstrations afterwards.

Even though the regime pushed our back against the wall I thought that we could have found a way out. If we had continued to try to normalize our situation and not pushed too hard for legal authorization perhaps we could have got out of it. The biggest mistake was, in my view, the plan of confrontation with the authorities. It wasn't well put together. I said that I had confidence in the morals of the leadership but not in their competence and strategy. Al-Nahda pushed too hard without having a plan of retreat, or an alternative. We spent years in prison and for what? Our movement didn't manage to free anyone. How could we believe that the authorities would give us freedoms after it had removed them all?[61]

Rachid spent two years in discussion with Abdelhamid Jelassi, a senior movement leader who played a key role in this prison evaluation, while together in a cell in Monastir. Jelassi was much more cautious about such policy discussions, arguing that the time of confrontation with the regime was not the moment to review previous strategies. 'The worst timing and climate to ask questions is the time of battle', he later wrote.[62] Rachid then spent two years with Ajmi Lourimi and Sahbi Aatig, two other senior leaders, in a cell at 9 avril prison in Tunis. By his own account Rachid was the pessimist of the group, while Lourimi was more optimistic and defensive of the leadership's actions. These debates showed how much space the prisoners had found in which to undertake this strategic reassessment.

Some complained that the leadership had failed to protect those thousands of jailed Nahdawis. A few even suggested the movement could have shown more defiance. Walid, who had just graduated as a medical student in Sousse, was arrested in May 1991 for taking part in a stone-throwing demonstration against police in the university district. He was among those convicted during the Sousse court case in 1993 and imprisoned until 2006. In his debates in prison, he argued with his cellmates that it had been a mistake for the leadership to dissolve the movement in Tunisia by seeking exile abroad:

They emigrated from Tunisia, some went to Sudan, some to Algeria at that time, and some went to Europe. But they refused to engage the movement in a confrontation with Ben Ali, despite the repression of Ben Ali, and more than that, they dissolved the organization.

Q: That was a mistake in your view?
At that time, it was a mistake.

Q: But was there another choice?
Yes, they could have continued the organization, undertaken training of those already enrolled in the movement and at least those remaining could have brought others to the movement. At the same time, they could have taken care of people inside the prison and those who had left prison. But when they dissolved the organization they cut the links between the prison and those abroad, and many people scattered and were homeless with no one to communicate with and without even knowing how to act. In addition, because there was no reaction from the movement, Ben Ali, instead of saying 'That's enough', he hit them again and again, and increased his repression.[63]

Such overt criticism was relatively rare, but clearly some among the prisoners and those Nahdawis left behind in Tunisia felt abandoned. They discussed among themselves possible methods of regime change: armed revolt, military coup, popular revolution, and electoral democracy. Nearly all accepted that non-violence was the only appropriate strategy for the future. They discussed popular protests in South Korea, Latin America, and Algeria, but understood the risk of trying for a popular revolution without sufficient groundwork. The hope of change through electoral democracy had been suffocated by the regime's response to the 1989 elections, and the choreographed RCD victories in subsequent elections. This process of debate, however, did shape the approach of movement leaders inside Tunisia in the 2000s, when they began to push cautiously for inclusion in the political system.

Alongside the extended debates among Nahdawi prisoners, the jail cell offered rare opportunities to debate with leftists, who made up the majority of non-Islamist political prisoners. One Sousse prisoner, Salah Nouir, spent some time in the early 1990s sharing a cell in Sousse prison with Hamma Hammami, the leader of the PCOT. From their shared experience of repression, they crossed what outside prison had been an unbridgeable divide. Nouir remembered:

He was next to me, by chance. We were very harmonious together, like friends. We told each other stories about the failures of our society. I couldn't believe how kind he was. There was no ideological battle because we were in the same boat, facing the same difficulties. There were values that we shared.[64]

This shared experience of prison repression may have helped push some in the movement towards an important opposition alliance that emerged in

2005, but such cross-ideological sympathies were short lived. A bitter polarization returned to political debates immediately after the 2011 uprising, particularly between the left, including the PCOT, and al-Nahda.

The very act of debate among the prisoners was an effort to recover a collective identity. Even if prison debates were ultimately inconclusive, they allowed a long period of internal reflection, which was to shape the movement's later strategy. Debate reinforced the frayed social bonds between prisoners and defied the isolating ambitions of the regime's coercive practices. If it was possible to debate, soon too it became possible to resist.

A Site of Struggle

For the Islamists, the hunger strike was a new technique of contention, adopted from a repertoire of protest previously used by leftist Tunisian prisoners in the 1970s, and by political prisoners in jails elsewhere in the world. Over time, the hunger strike became an increasingly common, cross-ideological method of individual and collective action against the Ben Ali regime both inside and outside prison. In Hibou's reading this self-denial of food and water was an act of despair that illustrated how diffuse the regime's techniques of control had become: the only freedom left was to deprive oneself of the freedom to eat.[65] But the hunger strike can be more than this, becoming a way to transform a prisoner's body from an object of power into a political expression of resistance.[66] Banu Bargu proposes that the hunger strike, particularly the hunger strike to the death, is a radical and disruptive act against an increasingly interventionist state. In her reading the hunger strike becomes a 'weaponization of life', advancing political goals through self-destruction in which hunger strikers, in her case Turkish communist prisoners, 'upheld the primacy of their political over their biological existence and advocated the withdrawal of consent from the existing order by way of self-destruction'.[67]

The Tunisian case presents a variant on this theme. Here the hunger strike was an act of political expression but not one that sought the Turkish prisoners' 'weaponization of life' nor the 'insurrectionary violence' of Irish Republican hunger strikers whose bodies too became 'weapons' in Allen Feldman's reading.[68] For the Islamists, the hunger strike was rarely to the death. Rather than fatal self-destruction, it was instead an act of calibrated violence against the self that generated dignity in the face of the repeated humiliations of the prison regime. Islamist prisoners made demands focused on improvements in living conditions, gaining access to pens and paper or more time to walk outside their cells, or they tried to force prison authorities to obey formal prison regulations. Many prisoners worsened existing illnesses and in some cases died as a result of these protests. Hunger strikers were harshly punished, with beatings, isolation, and crude force-feeding, a response that suggests the prison authorities felt a significant challenge to their authority. Just because the prisoners' demands were articulated within the framework of the legal system, rather than as a radical effort to overthrow the system, does not make them inconsequential. The prison system was acting arbitrarily, fragmenting Islamist solidarity, and, especially, humiliating them as individuals. In response, these strikes marked a call for respect and attention.

The prison experience could be described in three stages, according to one Sousse law student who was aged 19 when he began an eight-year jail term in 1991.

The first stage was the destruction of the movement: a ban on visits, prayers, studies, writing. I spent a year alone in a small cell, a very hard experience. The second stage was discovering yourself, understanding how to adapt. But then came the third stage: refusal.[69]

The stage of refusal began in the mid-1990s, as an act born out of frustration. There had been brief hunger strikes during the high-profile military trials in 1992, to protest conditions of detention and restrictions on media coverage. However, more concerted hunger strikes followed once the prison sentences began. Jamel, a medical student who had studied in Sousse, said the hunger strikes originated with the younger members of the movement.

Enough was enough. Most of the young people didn't hesitate to act violently towards themselves by going on hunger strike. No one cared about the hunger because we felt we were about to explode. We didn't even think of what long-term damage it might cause. People's patience had come to its limit. Most of the young people couldn't accept that we should bear it any more. They were no longer tolerant, no longer accepting this humiliation. Even if they felt the strike might harm them, they counted on their dignity because it was the only thing they had with which to confront others.[70]

By acting violently against themselves, denying themselves food and water, the prisoners retook control of their bodies. This was not irrational, nor emotion as a causal mechanism, but rather an end in itself, a 'moral emotion' derived from a sense of indignation over injustice.[71] Here too was meaning-making at work. The performative strike was not simply an act of protest, but rather reconstituted the self-respect the prisoners' jailers had tried to strip from them.

In November and December 1996 Nahdawi prisoners in Tunis, Mahdia, Gafsa, Gabes, Harboub, and Sidi Bouzid staged an organized hunger strike in the weeks before International Human Rights Day to claim their legal rights as prisoners and to demand an end to arbitrary punishments.[72] The prisoners had organized this several months in advance by sending notes to each other as they were transported from one prison to the next. As well as refusing food or refusing both food and water (a *'sec'* or dry hunger strike), others made themselves sick by drinking shampoo or cleaning fluid (known by its brand name 'Omo') in order to fill the prison infirmaries. The senior al-Nahda leader Abdelhamid Jelassi said the strikers were also resisting efforts by the prison authorities to prevent Nahdawis gathering together, either to share food, or to hold discussions, or to pray together. 'Our dignity and our unity were the treasures that we had to preserve,' he wrote later in a memoir of prison.[73] 'When we gathered in a room together, it gave us a chance to get to know each other, to be in solidarity with each other, and punishment lost its meaning.'[74] In late 1996 there were negotiations with the prison authorities and the strike was ended when improved conditions were promised. However, there were also punishments. In Mahdia prison dozens of the hunger strikers were beaten, put into isolation, or moved to other prisons as punishment.[75] Other prisoners were called before a judge and given up to two years' additional prison time added to their sentence.[76]

The demands of the hunger strikers were for minor regulatory changes, rather than against the broad target of the regime. In accounts of the prison experience, whether in interviews or in published memoirs, there was little exaggeration of resistance but instead a recurring reference to self-limiting demands. Bouraoui Makhlouf, one of the Sousse prisoners sentenced to life, spent forty-seven days on hunger strike at Borj El Amri prison, near Tunis, from December 2003. He demanded an end to his solitary confinement, more time outside his cell beyond the fifteen-minute walk allowed each day, and the provision of a television set, which was the only demand to which the prison authorities eventually acceded.[77] Rachid, the mathematics teacher, described frequent brief hunger strikes for modest goals. In Sidi Bouzid prison in 1998, he went on hunger strike when the newly arrived governor curtailed his daily walks outside his cell. He was sent to a punishment cell for ten days for his trouble. Then in 1999 at Grombalia prison, in Nabeul, he again went on hunger strike to demand transfer to a prison in the Sahel to be close to his family in Sousse. Eventually, he was transferred to Monastir prison. Then at Monastir he began another strike to demand better lighting so that he could read, and a longer daily walk outside his cell. 'It was a chronic malady that I had. I kept making small problems for my demands.'[78] Just as his sentence was coming to an end in 2002, he staged another strike in Messadine prison to demand that the court remove repeated sentences from his conviction.

I said to the governor: 'I am not asking for an amnesty. I just want your injustice to be just. I was convicted to this sentence and I served my time, so why make me do it again for nothing?' I really didn't want an amnesty, I wanted my rights.[79]

Jelassi also wrote, for example, about how he challenged one prison official over the right to pray, which he insisted was protected by prison regulations. 'I don't follow measures that violate the rules,' Jelassi told him.[80] These were not merely material demands, but an effort to hold accountable a regime that was acting arbitrarily.

Testimony collected by human rights groups at the time reveals that prison conditions did gradually improve from the mid- to late-1990s.[81] Nahdawi prisoners were now allowed to eat together and to have copies of the Qur'an. In October 1997 Nahdawi prisoners at 9 avril prison in Tunis were allowed to pray together in the prison courtyard, which Samir Dilou, one of the inmates held there, described as a 'fundamental change'.[82] Ali Laarayedh, the prisoner who endured most solitary confinement, was allowed a pen in 1996, and the following year a notebook too, as well as access to more books and to pro-government newspapers. Although his one window was still almost entirely boarded up, lighting improved in his cell from 1998, and the duration of family visits was increased to twenty-five minutes. From May 2004 he was allowed a television in his cell.[83] These incremental material improvements were not negligible; the risks the prisoners took for them were grave. Though these were not strictly fasts to the death, several died as a result of their hunger strikes or from untreated illnesses that were worsened by their protests.

The hunger strike soon grew into a central element of political resistance to the Ben Ali regime, a common call for justice activated across the political spectrum, inside and outside prison. In April 2000 Taoufik Ben Brik, a freelance journalist and human rights activist, went on a high-profile hunger strike for forty-three days after he was accused of spreading false information and defaming public institutions.[84] In June 2002 the lawyer Radhia Nasraoui announced a hunger strike to protest the reimprisonment of her husband Hamma Hammami, the PCOT leader, who had emerged from four years in hiding.[85] A rare opposition coalition in 2005, uniting Islamists with communists and others, was launched with a high-profile hunger strike in Tunis. To some activists, the hunger strike became so common as to be banal and was less and less appreciated for its political significance.[86] But for the Nahdawi prisoners this was resistance too, against efforts to separate the Islamists and against a policy not just of coercion, but of humiliation. The hunger strike was an act of violence against the self that explicitly challenged the legitimacy of the Tunisian regime and exposed the state's illusory promise of tolerance.

If the hunger strike was an act for dignity, then for some few prisoners there was dignity too in committing themselves to a private regime of contemplation and study. The daily reading of the Qur'an, when prisoners were eventually allowed copies of the book from the mid-1990s, recurs as a common theme.

Even though these conditions were catastrophic, there was a great potential for patience. When you repeated over and over the parts of the Qur'an that you memorized it was the greatest refuge for us. The day passed as if it was just an hour.[87]

Jelassi, the senior movement leader, found a similar refuge in writing in his cell. In the early years of the prison experience this was highly constrained: prisoners were given only half a page and a few minutes to write a letter to their families before the censor went through them, erasing any mentions of hunger strikes or punishments. However, in later years the prisoners were allowed to write longer letters. Even under the eye of the censor, Jelassi found relief in the act of writing to his wife and of drawing cartoon-strip stories for his daughter.

For the prisoner of opinion, writing didn't just fulfil the function of communication, rather you gained a dimension of existence. By writing, the prisoner manufactured another world which made you forget the harsh and bitter real world ... It was as if I was shouting: 'I am present, I am alive.'[88]

Eventually Jelassi managed to obtain his own pen, which he hid in his cell for seven years because it offered him a sense of his 'humanity': 'I am thankful for that pen. It saved a part of me. It was a friend to me in difficult times.'[89]

Rachid, the frequent hunger striker, gave the most detailed account of this experience of routine study. He pointed to personal faith as a way of achieving contentment even in the prison environment.

We held strongly to spiritual issues and it was well founded, because that is how we faced that infernal machine. We experienced its torture, but despite that we were very content. People don't imagine this. Perhaps they think Islamists have pretensions or that we exaggerate. But it's true. Once in Sidi Bouzid prison I was in individual detention, alone in a cell. At the end of my bed was the toilet and close to my ear a place to pray and eat. A guard asked me: 'What do you do during the day?' I told him: 'I do my prayers, then breakfast, then I recite the Qur'an by heart, then I read my newspaper, then I read a book from the library but sometimes I don't have time to finish my work.' The guard was very hard, very bad, and he mocked me ... But when I was in Sidi Bouzid I felt bliss, the happiness of someone who is alone. Believe me after eight months there, when I was transferred to Grombalia, in my heart I cried that I'd lost that chance. It was splendid. It was something extraordinary ... Believe me those twelve years in prison were a digression that passed in just a few seconds. I was very much at ease, as if nothing had happened.[90]

These experiences were confined to those prisoners serving longer jail terms, who had lived through the brutality of the early years of the prison repression in the 1990s and who had reconciled themselves to a long period in jail, often alone. They also depended on the particular regulations of an individual prison and its governor. Rachid's experience of 'bliss' in his cell was confined to eight months he spent in Sidi Bouzid under a particular governor who operated a more relaxed regime, allowing him longer walks and the chance to buy additional food in the prison shop. Much may have had to do with the individual prisoner: Rachid was determined to study his way through his jail term. As well as reading the Qur'an, he spent eight years teaching himself French from newspapers and prison library books. Still, these descriptions of contentment behind bars are a striking disruption of assumed histories of persecution. They also echo experiences recorded elsewhere, even among less religious prisoners. For example, Gilbert Naccache, a Tunisian leftist who was jailed in the 1970s and who wrote a memoir-novel in his cell on cigarette packets, also described not only the brutality and isolation of prison, but also the 'intense jubilation' of writing without the guards noticing, and of other 'periods of joy, exaltation, bursts of laughter, songs'.[91] In another context, Richard English describes how Republican prisoners in Northern Ireland in the 1980s took seriously to reading and studying. He quotes one prisoner as saying: 'There is nobody who was on those wings who didn't enjoy themselves tremendously and say they are the best time I've ever had in jail.'[92]

Hunger strikes soon became a regular part of the prison experience, not just for Nahdawis but for other political prisoners too. In some cases, they brought small improvements in the quality of life of the prisoners, but they also transformed the prisoners' cells into sites of struggle and their bodies into subjects of resistance. Most Nahdawi prisoners were released one or two years before the formal end of their sentences, often in a series of presidential amnesties which began in the late 1990s. The gradual relaxation of repression was the result of opposition groups and international human rights groups publicizing these frequent hunger strikes and poor conditions, which embarrassed the regime abroad and distracted from its propaganda of tolerance and reform. It may also explain the slow improvement of prison conditions in the 2000s. In that sense, the hunger strikes achieved some of their aims, but these actions carried further implications. Beyond the well-documented evidence of brutality, the Nahdawis' own accounts of the prison years also speak counter-intuitively of feelings of 'dignity', 'contentment', and even 'bliss'. This is not to exaggerate a biography of resistance, for the al-Nahda movement was severely depleted from the early 1990s onwards and many individuals were physically and psychologically harmed. Rather, it is to suggest that in this prison experience we find the unexpected seeds of a future revival of the Nahdawi community. All acknowledge that this could not have happened without the sustenance offered by families outside the prison walls.

Support from the Outside

Given that the logic of the prison regime was that it should extinguish al-Nahda entirely, it was inevitable that this repressive power should reach beyond the prison walls. Mothers, fathers, wives, husbands, sisters, and brothers of imprisoned Nahdawis were disciplined, through harassment, interrogation, physical beating, and frequent impediments during prison visits. Women in particular were identified as a target for surveillance because through their enduring relationships with their husbands, brothers, and sons they became a vital pillar of support. Such repression was, of course, strikingly inconsistent with the regime's constant positioning of itself as a champion of women's progress. The much-lauded rights of Tunisian women were merely secondary to the priority of repression.

Many women were targeted because of their involvement in the movement. Monia Ibrahim was one of the senior female figures in the movement in Sousse, and the wife of Abdelhamid Jelassi. She was aged 24 and pregnant when her husband was arrested on 6 April 1991: he went on to spend nearly seventeen years in jail. Ibrahim herself was arrested in April 1994 in Sousse by a Department of State Security intelligence unit, the Information Brigade (*firqāt al-irshād*), and was sentenced to eighteen months in jail but then was released in June 1994, when an appeal court ruled she had no case to answer. Despite the ruling, she spent five years under strict surveillance. She had to report three times a day at two security offices in Sousse. She was banned from leaving the city without authorization and was subject to frequent interrogation. Although qualified as a psychologist, she could only find menial employment. Ibrahim described her life in an open letter in May 2004, published by an opposition website:

I didn't stop asking 'Why?' And I always got the same answer, which was roughly: 'We know you, it's not about you, it's about your husband!' What law or custom punishes twice, first the person and second their family?[93]

At the time her husband was in Borj El Amri prison, near Tunis, in solitary confinement. He had spent fifty days on hunger strike to demand access to reading books, notebooks, letters, newspapers, and a television. The impact of his sentence was felt well beyond the prison cell. Ibrahim wrote:

Sentencing by the court is not just the deprivation of freedom; it also deprives you of your mental and physical health and leads to a state that is synonymous with death, but a slow death. What my husband is enduring in prison and what we are suffering outside has pushed my 13-year-old daughter to ask herself whether she too will be deprived of her freedom and chained up as the daughter of parents considered undesirable by the security services. Her questions sum up how she has lived since birth, an existence filled with policemen, prison guards, gloomy visits, and a metal grill separating her from a father she no longer knows because she was born five months after his arrest and because she has been allowed only one direct visit since.[94]

Estimates of the number of female detainees in the Ben Ali era range from 300 to 1,500, but female political prisoners were often jailed without trial, released, and jailed again in arbitrary fashion, according to one striking collection of female testimonies.[95] The coercion of imprisonment also touched wives and children outside jail; children could be excluded from state schools and from obtaining university scholarships.[96] Even the unvoiced threat of future imprisonment had an immediate repressive effect. It was not just the women of al-Nahda who suffered like this, for women with other political affiliations were also imprisoned or targeted for repression. A wave of arrests in 1992 targeted female members of the communist PCOT. What was at first a crackdown targeting only the Islamists soon widened to envelope all political dissidents.

The women of al-Nahda were subject to an array of coercive practices, especially if they were members of the movement themselves or if their husbands were in jail or had fled into exile. Many were held for the unauthorized collection of money or donations, which meant that any financial support given by sympathetic friends or relatives could be turned against the women as evidence of criminality. Amendments to the penal code introduced in 1993 made Tunisians liable to prosecution for activities conducted outside the country if they were considered an offence under Tunisian law. Thus a meeting with other Nahdawis abroad, in France for example, was grounds for arrest and conviction on return to Tunisia.[97] Once under arrest or in prison, the women of al-Nahda were often subject to violent abuse: torture, beatings, sexual assaults, and, on some occasions, rape. As early as 1993 Amnesty International documented accounts of forced undressing, abuse, threats of rape, and sexual assault suffered by female al-Nahda members and other female political dissidents after arrest.[98] There were also informal acts of control. Many women were told to stop wearing the hijab and some even to divorce their husbands if they wanted to continue their jobs. The wife of one Sousse activist came under considerable accumulated pressure to divorce her husband, who had been a local-level activist in the movement. As a schoolteacher she was the sole breadwinner for her two daughters while her husband spent eight years in jail. Her husband's brother, not himself a Nahdawi, was jailed and forced to shut his restaurant. She agreed to the divorce in order to keep her job, though shortly after her husband was released from jail the couple remarried and had a third child.[99] Other prisoners tried as much as they could to shield their children from what was happening. One Sousse activist, Abdelfattah, was arrested in 1992, five months after his first son was born, and was released from jail the following year. He chose not to tell his son that he had even been to prison: 'That was my choice. There are others whose children knew everything. I chose not to tell him because I know psychology: I didn't want to put up a barrier between us.'[100] Several years later, when his son was a teenager and had won a place in the highly regarded Lycée Pilote in Sousse, the boy found out about his father's past in the playground.

He was insulted by one of his friends who said that his father was in jail. He came home and said: 'Someone said you were in jail!' I talked with him and told him it was my choice not to tell him so he would grow up as a normal child. One day he should know his father was in jail, but not because he was a criminal but because he was struggling for a new idea and way of thinking, and in the end my son accepted that.[101]

His account reveals the calculations made by individual families. It also showed that even a brief prison sentence had remained public knowledge in his local community, such that it might leak out more than a decade later in a children's playground.

Yet within these practices of coercion lay unexpected opportunities to engage, however briefly, as a like-minded community once again. Prison authorities made the weekly family visits as difficult as possible, restricting access to the closest family members and then forcing them to wait in line for several hours before the brief audience with the prisoner was permitted. The result was that on the day of prison visits large groups of mothers, wives, and sisters met at the prison and spent several hours talking, spreading news, offering reassurance, and reinforcing community bonds. One al-Nahda activist, Kawther, a schoolteacher in Sousse, visited her husband in prison during his 19-month jail term and, with her sister, spent eleven years visiting her brother Rachid, the mathematics teacher, in prisons scattered across the country. The regular visits were a source of solidarity:

Outside the prison we talked together. Everyone talked about the conditions they were facing ... When we met, us women, we tried to give each other resolve. We weren't sad, we didn't cry, no, no. You found love, humour, we told each other jokes, that was normal. We gave each other resolve. We were happy and we believed the day would come when we would triumph. We were not afraid.[102]

A visit, which for Kawther was usually once a month, meant leaving home in Sousse at dawn in order to join the queue at the prison gate by around 9am or later, depending how distant was the prison. Each visitor carried a package of food for their relative, known as the '*couffin*', or basket, which the prisoners depended on to augment the poor-quality prison food when they were not on hunger strike. The *couffin* was subject to its own arbitrary controls. Pens and paper were forbidden, as were certain types of food, including *mulūkhiyya* stew and '*uṣbān*, a Tunisian style haggis.[103] Some prison guards insisted that fruit should be delivered already peeled so it would not last.[104] On other occasions the deposit of the *couffin* was restricted to the day after the visit, in order to force visiting relatives to stay overnight in the nearby town or abandon the visit altogether. The wait to deposit the *couffin* could be several hours, and in this time there was again the chance to pass on news of other members of the movement and to offer support to those struggling to manage their lives. Most of these women, with their husbands in jail, were now responsible for financially supporting the family through poorly paid menial work, as well as paying for the food and travel involved in a prison visit. The mutual support during the visits was a rare moment of encouragement but also reshaped individual views about the rights of single mothers and the role of women in the workplace. The experience of being financially responsible for their families later encouraged Nahdawi women in the post-2011 transition to take a 'practical stance' on women's rights, notably endorsing the Personal Status Code, defending women's rights in the workplace, and taking on leadership roles in commissions within the constituent assembly, a stance some have likened to that of women in Europe after the Second World War.[105] After the long discussions in the queue came the actual moment of the visit, which was brief and anticlimactic. As Kawther described it:

You were already really exhausted and then there was the visit but you just had a short moment to ask: 'How are you?' And then that was all. And it was done through a metal grill at first, and then through a telephone handset, and we spoke just a couple of words, a minute or two, no more. Just to check he was still there and alive. And there was a guard on either side listening to what we said ... Once in the prison in Messadine, my husband was there, and I said: 'There is news from Algeria about Bouteflika.' Suddenly the guard stopped me. It was forbidden. You spent the whole day in a queue just to say: 'How are you?'[106]

After a long day of travelling and queuing, these few minutes were frustrating and insubstantial. For the prisoners themselves, they left mixed feelings. Jelassi, in his prison memoir, described how his wife, Monia Ibrahim, would leave her Sousse home at dawn to visit him in Kasserine prison, travelling and waiting for hours just for a ten-minute encounter and a late-night return to her home. Jelassi, on the other hand, would wake at the usual hour and take only five minutes to walk to the visitors' room for their brief meeting: 'I came out of the visitors' room feeling the blame. I was sleepless over the suffering of the visit. For them it was a hardship, and for me it was a pleasure.'[107] The prison regime was effective at circumscribing the encounter between visitors and prisoners, but it failed to see the opportunities for collective dissent that remained hidden within its systems of control.

The visits brought solace to the prisoners, but they offered as much to the visitors themselves. The challenge of travelling often long distances to prisons across the country, sometimes only to find a relative had been transferred unannounced to another prison elsewhere, was oppressive. Yet, the encounter at the prison gates brought the visiting women a chance to bond together week after week.

*

This chapter has recovered accounts of the prison experiences of al-Nahda to demonstrate the nature of carceral repression and the resilience it generated. The accounts of individual Nahdawis, men and women, reveal the complex regime of coercion, with punishments ranging from physical beatings to humiliation, isolation, and exclusion. Yet they also show how within a few years of the crackdown against al-Nahda, individuals began to resist in different forms. There were long private debates, which rebound individuals together in a collective project even at their most vulnerable moment. Ironically, it was to prove easier to hold such discussions within the prison walls than it would be in later years when prisoners returned to their homes only to face the more difficult challenge of social exclusion. Along with the debates came acts of physical resistance, ranging from hunger strikes to moments of intense study which forged a sense of dignity and self-respect. Regular visits from families, mostly mothers, wives, and sisters, offered some succour to the prisoners but also another layer of reassociation for the broader al-Nahda community.

The prison experience revealed how awkward the relationship within the movement had become between political ambition on the one hand and cultural, social, and religious objectives on the other. There were significant disagreements among the prisoners about the strategy adopted by the movement during and after the 1989 elections, and about the nature of the confrontation with the regime. In exile, there was an explicit acknowledgement that political ambitions had overwhelmed other elements of the Islamist project. This period of strategic review exposed the challenge of pursuing the 'comprehensive' conception of Islam, first proposed at the 1981 press conference. Though the ambiguities of the project became evident as a result of this prison evaluation, they were by no means resolved. While the review in exile directed the movement away from its political goals for strategic reasons, in Tunisia the reality of repression within and without the prison walls meant formal political work was all but impossible in the 1990s. The direct experience of repression meant many grew wary as individuals of the cost of political ambition. When Nahdawis returned home from prison, they encountered a social exclusion that was often even more repressive than incarceration and so they continued to reconsider for themselves what shape the Islamist project should take.

5   Beyond Social Exclusion

> When we left prison, we were in a bigger prison. Meaning what? You were not free with your time. You were restricted. It's true that you'd left the worst of prison, but personally in the morning at 8 am I had to go to the police station in Kalaa Kebira and sign, and in the evening too. Also twice a week I had to sign at the National Guard station and at the regional police station in Sousse. You weren't in charge of your time ... Even people that I knew, neighbours, people who sympathized with you, they wouldn't dare speak to you. They passed in front of you but couldn't speak to you. Why? Because they thought they would be arrested and taken to the police station and interrogated. That was the most severe punishment.
>
> *Hamza, an al-Nahda member from Kalaa Kebira, imprisoned in 1991–93.*
> *Unable to return to his job in a private topography firm, he worked as*
> *a waiter for many years before finding a job in a tourism company.*[1]

The architecture of repression imposed on the al-Nahda movement endured well beyond the prison experience. Some Nahdawis, like this Kalaa Kebira activist, left prison in the 1990s; others returned home in later years when their sentences were completed or thanks to a series of amnesties beginning in 1999.[2] Though ostensibly free, they were deprived of their independence, isolated from the community, and humiliated by arbitrary police raids, interrogations, arrests, and enforced daily reporting at police stations. They were ostracized from political, economic, and social life. This chapter draws on the experiences of Nahdawis to explore this long post-prison episode, which ran through the 2000s until the uprising in 2011. Rather than endorsing the received scholarly understanding of the movement as a defeated recipient of all-pervasive state repression, these accounts instead reveal a complex web of survival, individual and collective resilience, ideological reorientation, and strategic debate.

For the small group of activists in Sousse who were bold enough to be concerned with political parties or human rights groups at the turn of the millennium, it seemed al-Nahda had almost entirely disappeared. One former head of the Sousse branch of the Tunisian Human Rights League (LTDH), a focal point for the activist community, described the gradual reappearance of a pro-democracy movement in the city in the early 2000s, but said Nahdawis were nowhere to be seen: 'Al-Nahda moved against Ben Ali and then exported its activities abroad and the movement played no role in life here or in the regions.'[3] Another Sousse activist, a member of the Tunisian Workers' Communist Party (PCOT), said the local al-Nahda leadership remained absent until the uprising: 'In fact we only knew the al-Nahda leadership here after 14 January 2011. We met the democrats at the UGTT [Tunisian General Labour Union] for strikes or in the LTDH, but the Islamists weren't ever there.'[4] Al-Nahda was dismissed as a movement only in exile, whose former loyalists in Sousse were repressed, inactive, and silent. This became a view reflected more widely. Salwa Ismail, writing in 2006, talked of the story of Islamism in Tunisia appearing 'complete': 'The movement is thought to be at an end ... The expansion and multiplication of mechanisms of control and incorporation has served to neutralize Islamist opposition and to suppress other forms of independent activism.'[5] In the view of Hibou, the regime deployed a complex web of control, which extinguished the Islamists not just as a political force but even as individuals:

Having come into close contact with physical death, they experience, outside prison, what they themselves call a 'social death' that is often even less bearable: the extreme difficulty, or even the near-impossibility, of having a social or even a private life.[6]

As an expression of an individual and collective project, al-Nahda appeared spent.

This chapter, however, looks beyond the narrative of 'social death' to ask what happened to individual Islamists who returned home from jail in these years and what it meant to be Islamist when it was no longer possible to be so. From their own accounts it is clear, first, that some Nahdawis in Sousse were resilient and that this resilience affected their understanding of the Islamist political project. The effort required to survive, both materially and psychologically, plunged these men and women into unfamiliar surroundings, new workplaces, and a new, inferior social status. Some struggled, others prospered, all were forced to rethink what their Islamist belonging meant to them as individuals. Second, unlike Islamist movements elsewhere in the region, there was relatively little participation in this period in social and charitable work. The work that did take place often involved those on the movement's periphery, who were on the fringes both in terms of their position in the hierarchy and their ideas. They pulled the movement in new directions. Third, though the movement was more resilient than it seemed, this resilience exposed the fault lines within al-Nahda. Under pressure in the 2000s, the movement disaggregated into its diverse components. Here we find al-Nahda sympathizers, with a wider freedom of movement and more inclusive political vision than senior leadership figures; young men and women, who were becoming drawn to Islamism in a personal spiritual quest; and the rump leadership, who focused almost entirely on a political survival strategy. In this decade of repression, with the many debates and challenges it provoked within al-Nahda, the fault lines between the different projects of the 'comprehensive' vision stand out.

Navigating the 'Bigger Prison'

By the early 2000s the regime had dampened all significant political competition. Not only did Ben Ali amend the constitution in 2002 to lift term limits on the presidency once again, but the ruling party, trade unions, and loyal opposition were on hand to endorse his candidacy as president in 2004. While al-Nahda and the PCOT remained unauthorized, other opposition parties were allotted a quota of nineteen seats in the 1994 parliament and 34 in 1999 (out of a total 182), despite their tiny share of the vote. Ben Ali's constant invocation of 'reform' operated as an effective method of control and coercion.[7] Economic growth reinforced his position: gross domestic product more than trebled between 1986 and 1999.[8] It was into this landscape in the early 2000s that Nahdawis began to walk free from jail.

Though the prison experience was hard, the period after jail was commonly considered harder still, with its twin pressures of isolating individuals from their community and diminishing their social status. Once a prisoner returned home he or she was subject to a period of administrative control (murāqaba idāriyya), theoretically included as part of the initial prison sentence, although sometimes arbitrarily imposed or extended. Police and security officers were not commanded by clear orders from above, but rather were given latitude to be 'more or less pernickety, aggressive, systematic or intrusive' in their exercise of power over the Nahdawis.[9] Administrative control could run for up to ten years, according to the penal code.[10] The state had the right to decide where ex-prisoners would live, and to ban them from certain professions, including as a lawyer, public official, doctor, vet, midwife, and employee at a school or university.[11] Nahdawis had to report regularly to local and regional police stations as well as National Guard offices, where at the appointed hour they had to sign their names in a notebook, which they themselves had to buy. This was accompanied by routine humiliation as well as repeated interrogation about sources of income, new employers, and daily life, often beginning in pseudo-familiarity: 'What's new?' (shnuwa *jdīd?*). Police officers raided houses day and night, searching homes for incriminating books, newspapers, or political pamphlets.

Nahdawis found themselves socially ostracized. In the 1980s weddings had been an opportunity for the movement to strengthen social bonds and to articulate new religious and cultural expressions. Now several men described how they struggled to find a bride, which left them outside the social norms of their communities and intensified their despair. Rachid, the frequent hunger striker, was freed in 2002, but was unable to return to his job as a school mathematics teacher. His sister and son-in-law collected him from the prison gates and brought him back to their house in Hai Riadh, where for the first time since his arrest in 1991 he saw his elder brother, a secular senior government bureaucrat who had not visited him in prison. They drove together to the family house in the village of Chorbane, south of the city, and grilled a lamb to celebrate. However, few neighbours attended the party; even some of his nephews did not dare appear. Some months later Rachid began working as a private tutor, visiting pupils in their homes, but he remained single. 'I looked for someone to marry but I was refused frequently. I came from a known family but there were lots of refusals. They said: "We're not refusing you, but your cause".'[12] Eventually in 2004, at the age of 44, he was engaged to a woman he had met as a student in the 1980s. Her father, a farmer, was a graduate of Zaytuna, which signalled a sign of shared religious commitment. 'He was looking for the right sort,' Rachid said. The celebration, however, was modest.

When I did get married there was just a small attendance in the countryside at the wedding. Usually they have hundreds of guests but we just had the closest of relatives. People were afraid. Even my nephew, who is very close to me, didn't come. That was hard.

Most Nahdawis stayed away from their local mosque, fearful of police interrogations, and either prayed at home or stayed conspicuously at work on a Friday lunchtime. Not surprisingly, some despaired of the movement's future. One local member from Kalaa Seghira said: 'We told ourselves that it was done with al-Nahda, adieu to al-Nahda, there is no more movement.'[13] The effect of this programme of restrictions was to isolate them not just from society but to make them question their own convictions too, to 'alienate us from ourselves', as one said.[14]

Beyond this arbitrary punishment, there was pressure on social status. Administrative control made it hard to find work. Former teachers and civil servants could not return to their jobs, and the regular signing requirements deterred employers from taking them on. Doctors set up private clinics, but others found themselves resorting to menial jobs, working among the traders in the Sunday market, on the poorer southern side of the city. It was an uncomfortable reversal: those who had once held high social status within the Islamist community and who had been the first in their families to attend university were now reduced to penury. Salah Nouir, a Consultative Council member who had studied at the Sorbonne, had been banned from his job as a French-language teacher since 1981. When he left jail in 1995, aged 45, he could only find work selling sweets from the back of a bicycle in the market. He signed twice-daily at the local police station and once a week at the National Guard headquarters. At first, he tried to disguise his identity:

> At first, people didn't know me. But here in our country people want to know all about you: Where do you come from? What did you do before this work? I lied and said I was a truck driver but they didn't believe me, and they began to understand the story. And then they started to avoid me. They were afraid when they spoke to me. We were completely isolated. Even from our parents, even my brothers, my uncles, my cousins. Everyone was afraid, because if someone knocked on my door he would be summoned by the police.[15]

He was not the only Nahdawi in the Sunday market. Alongside him was his cousin Ali Nouir, the prominent preacher. He had a stall selling clothes in the market before his death in 2000. Some suggested they fared better in the market than other stallholders because they were more honest with their customers, but few prospered during this period and all regarded it as a long indignity.

There were, however, occasional opportunities to defy the isolating impact of the administrative control system. Many Nahdawis attended the wedding in November 2006 of a daughter of Hamadi Jebali, the senior Sousse leader who had been freed from jail earlier that year and who was now leading the movement inside Tunisia. It was a rare and brief opportunity for them to revive what one called their kinship (*luhma*). The police tried to prevent the wedding from taking place at all. Murad, the son of a local bank clerk, was a friend of the groom but not yet a member of the movement. He arrived at the marriage hall dressed in a smart suit.

> But in the hall I found nothing. It wasn't like a party, and there were no cars, there was nothing. What was happening? I was in a taxi. I got out and I saw the police in civilian clothes. The marriage hall was upstairs with a cafe downstairs and the hall was lit up and I saw the lights. So I entered into the cafe and I said: 'Isn't there a marriage upstairs?' and they said: 'No there's nothing.' The police were watching me.[16]

Murad called his friend the groom, who told him they had had to move the celebrations to his family house to avoid the police restrictions. The police not only closed the marriage hall, but also took the names of those trying to attend and recorded their car licence plates, and then closed the streets leading to the family house, preventing the musicians and caterer from reaching the party.[17] Nonetheless Murad found his way there, and suddenly emerged into the bosom of the reclusive al-Nahda community:

I knew almost no one and I knew that the people there would be mistrustful and had the right to be mistrustful. 'Who would welcome me?' I wondered. And then as I came in someone came to me and greeted me and he was smiling, and he brought me in and it was Mr Hamadi. I've never forgotten. I entered into al-Nahda by way of the big leaders, not just anyone ... It was a party with lots of people and yet look how he welcomed me. He saw me hesitate and he came to greet me as if we'd known each other for years; not at all distrustful even though he should have been ...

Someone said to me: 'Are you al-Nahda?' I said: 'No', but then they told me stories about their experiences. The groom said to me: 'I have friends who I thought were my friends but they didn't come. But you came, even in this climate!' I saw it as a normal thing to do but really the embargo Ben Ali put on them, even on their families, it was horrible to live through. Everyone was avoiding them.

He later married Jebali's second daughter and became an al-Nahda member himself.

A secondary effect of repression was to shift Nahdawis from public sector jobs into the private sector. Many former teachers or civil servants now ran modest market stalls, bookshops, or groceries. They were forced into entrepreneurial work in a country that valued more highly the social status and stability of government employment, which was known, in a Tunisian saying, as being as solid as 'a nail in the wall' (mismār fī al-ḥāʾiṭ).[18] However, there were several ways of navigating these obstacles. Foreign-owned companies, for example, were more open to recruiting former prisoners and accommodating their regular police station visits. With its large port, Sousse had become an important centre for exports and several foreign companies had taken advantage of the tax discounts offered in 1972 to set up factories in industrial zones in southern Sousse and further south. Thirty years later, the city's Islamists became unexpected beneficiaries of this policy. In prison, Hafedh, an engineer and activist from Kalaa Seghira, had befriended a Frenchman who later found him work repairing machinery in a French factory in Sousse:

It was as if it came from heaven ... I told my employer I had problems of having to sign but he saw me working and that I was capable, and he had confidence in me. He said: 'There are twenty-four hours in the day: come when you want and leave when you want, just give me eight hours of work' ... I discovered the regime didn't have control over foreign companies, they couldn't tell them not to employ this or that person.[19]

Another company, Leoni, a cable-manufacturer headquartered in Nuremberg, Germany, played a particularly important role. The firm had a factory in an industrial zone in Messadine, south of Sousse, operated by Leoni Tunisie, a firm headed during this period by Mohamed Larbi Rouis, an al-Nahda sympathizer from a prominent religious family in nearby M'saken. Rouis's father had been a Zaytuna-educated cleric and his brother, Jaleleddine, sat in al-Nahda's Consultative Council and had headed the movement's electoral list in Sousse for the 1989 elections. Leoni became a protected source of employment for Islamists. The head of the local al-Nahda bureau in Kalaa Seghira after the 2011 uprising, a former schoolteacher, had worked at Leoni in Messadine for six and a half years after leaving prison. Another al-Nahda activist from Sousse, who was prominent in training young Islamists in secret, worked at Leoni from 2007 as an accountant. Another employee working in human resources since 2004 was one of Jebali's daughters.[20]

I do not mean to exaggerate or romanticize resilience against the punishing weight of administrative control; for while some Nahdawis in Sousse navigated around the restrictions, many were suffocated by the weight of repression. Several admitted giving up hope that their movement would ever return and were reconciled to a life of poverty and social exclusion. For others, the commitment to an ordinary life, whether through marriage and a family or the constant search for secure employment, was their own challenge, their own mundane but self-affirming act of what James Scott called 'prosaic but constant struggle'.[21] Moreover, behind the individual acts they also held tenaciously to their religious belief and their idea of the Islamist project.

'Living Islam in Our Daily Lives'

The post-prison experience was not merely about enduring regime controls. It also forced Nahdawis to reassess what it meant for them to be Islamists when it was no longer possible to mobilize for their project. Stripped of the political, the meaning ascribed to being Islamist became closer to what it had been in the 1970s: an emphasis on morality and correct comportment in line with religious commitments like prayer and fasting, but this time as individuals in the privacy of their home or workplace. Where in the 1970s and 1980s there had been overt community-building among the like-minded, now it became a brotherhood that was more imaginary than realizable. What they clung to was a diluted, individualized remnant of the imagined solidarity forged in earlier years. Hamza, the Kalaa Kebira activist, said:

We were brothers before God. Even when we didn't talk together they stayed present in our hearts. I was sympathizing with the conditions of the others and I really wanted to be with other political prisoners, but I assessed our conditions and I stayed far away.[22]

Another Nahdawi, a preacher and Consultative Council member who worked in cheap restaurants during the 1990s and 2000s, described a similar withdrawal into the individual:

This is the value of being an Islamist in very suffocating conditions: to be Islamist in these conditions the minimum is to preserve Islamic ethics, to preserve trust in God, to preserve the Islamic project which will be victorious and it's enough for you to do your prayers, to do your fasting, to have successful relations with people. It's enough that you have unwavering convictions to trust in. This is how it is to be an Islamist. You don't have any other choice.[23]

This was more than retrospective rationalization. These were religiously committed men and women who had been punished for their political beliefs and who were now trying to find shelter in their Islamic reference during a long period of hardship.

The sense of a moral code emerges also in their approach to business. Several emphasized the moral rationale behind private-sector commerce, which they believed distinguished them from other shopkeepers and businessmen. Youssef, formerly a teacher from Hammam Sousse, began working in construction after his prison term and eventually obtained his own licence to run a small firm of builders. He identified a religiously inspired value system as the backbone of his success: honesty towards his employees and clients; arriving at work on time; completing projects when promised; and paying his staff promptly and equitably. It was what he called 'living Islam in our daily lives'.

For me, religion was a personal issue. I retained my religious convictions and commitments. For those who belong to the al-Nahda movement, religion was the embodiment of religious values, living religion in your values, the Islamic values, that is what was important. So we lived Islam in our daily lives. The most important thing for us was reflecting religion in your daily behaviour, in your daily transactions, in your work, that was the important thing, a long way from the folklore side, like beards and so on. That's not important.[24]

Youssef's assessment of that period was not one of hardship. Instead, he said of his construction work: 'Really, it was a positive experience for me. It was excellent.' This sense of an ethical advantage recurred frequently in accounts of this period. Another Nahdawi, for example, spoke of those selling cheap goods at market stalls as drawing on their 'stock' (*raṣīd*) of religious morals in governing how they dealt with customers.[25] Separately, the al-Nahda leadership was gradually embracing a market economy which became explicit after 2011, a path well-trodden by other Islamist movements, who, paradoxically, tended to be more committed to implementing the free market Washington Consensus than the regimes with which the Western financial institutions preferred to work.[26] However, these accounts do not quite align with the religiously affirmed 'theology of prosperity' identified by Patrick Haenni as indicative of an evolving Islamism.[27] Instead, the emphasis here was on morality as an advantage, rather than an explicit religious endorsement of capitalist prosperity. Besides, among Nahdawis in Sousse, the shift from public to private sector employment did not last. After 2011 many took advantage of a general amnesty for former political prisoners and returned to work as teachers or in the administration. Youssef, for example, gave up his construction business to return to work as a schoolteacher. Many found returning to work in the public sector more attractive in terms of status and job security than continuing with their small businesses.

The bigger puzzle, however, is why Nahdawis did not take more advantage of the societal return to personal religiosity that marked the 2000s. This religious revival was a familiar region-wide pattern. It was a reaction against US-led wars in Afghanistan and Iraq, and was fuelled by the increasing availability from the late 1990s of satellite television channels. Nahdawis in Sousse watched al-Jazeera (launched in 1996 with Qatari funding), Iqraa TV (a channel of religious and social programming set up in 1998 by a Saudi businessman), and later al-Resalah (Saudi-funded and broadcast from Cairo since 2006) and al-Hiwar (established in London in 2006 by Azzam Tamimi, who had close contact with Ghannouchi in exile). One element of this wave of religiosity was the emergence of Qur'anic study groups, which responded to growing demands for knowledge about religious tradition and discomfort at growing consumerism and corruption.[28] These associations received surprising official protection thanks to the launch in 2007 of Radio Zitouna, a religious channel owned by Ben Ali's son-in-law Sakher al-Materi, which aired Qur'anic discussion programmes.[29] Although nominally secular, the Ben Ali regime in fact deployed an array of techniques, from security controls to information dominance and symbolic production, to expand control over the religious sphere. Similarly, other regimes including Egypt, for example, also extended their presence in the religious sphere. Yet, such efforts have been shown not always to bring a regime social control, but instead to generate challenges from other actors and to increase an appetite for religious resources.[30]

One al-Nahda activist and former prisoner, Chokri, set up a small Qur'anic association in his home in the old city of Hammam Sousse in

2005. The work began discreetly, with small groups of boys and girls meeting on Fridays and Saturdays for classes led by Chokri and his sister. The initial emphasis was on correct behaviour and family life.

The goal was to educate children in the old city at first: how to bring up children so they don't use vulgar words. Women came to give classes to the mothers about how to raise children and we brought an expert to speak on marital relations.[31]

Chokri also invited some of the preachers within al-Nahda in Sousse to give talks in private. His small association offered a different style of learning to the staid and poorly attended state-run Qur'anic centre in Sousse. Chokri's goal was a return to the non-political ethic of the movement in the 1970s and 1980s, which focused on creating a cultural alternative, an Islamic subculture:

For many people, learning the Qur'an was about having a shaykh with a stick who would beat you if you made a mistake. But we didn't do it like that. We did it gently and we tried to offer a community. We went to the beach together, we did sports, we organized outings, and we did cultural events. We tried to create a certain ambiance and there was no extremist dimension. People still think religion is just going to the mosque and praying, but it's more than that. It's our whole life.[32]

His association survived until the uprising of 2011 and then expanded rapidly. During the repression of the 2000s, these studies offered a rare breathing space for members of the movement. Sayida, a middle-aged Nahdawi from Akouda who worked during the week in Tunis, attended a Qur'anic class in the capital. She worked in a law office and began wearing a hijab again but was careful not to discuss her religious beliefs at work, even though she felt the environment around her relaxing. In her view Radio Zitouna offered a chance for Nahdawis to renew friendships.

There was a margin of freedom and this is why we profited from this freedom to meet, to rebuild ourselves anew. The idea spread again, especially among those who had gone for years without any meeting, the older ones.[33]

However, among Sousse activists these examples were more the exception than the rule. Remarkably few Nahdawis spoke of participating in such study groups, even though they appeared to offer the sort of new political opportunity of which social movements tend to take advantage. The repressive effect of prison and administrative control deterred them from any risky endeavours. If this was an opportunity for mobilization, it was not perceived as one. For most, their religious conviction remained private.

More than this, older al-Nahda members showed some disdain towards this religious revival, particularly the return of hijab. The new style of dress became suddenly popular in large cities and was explained at the time as a search for identity and as a response to the Afghan and Iraq wars, or as popular among a new upper-middle class looking to express themselves in a consumer society.[34] The regime tried to curb the popularity of the veil. In 2006 it launched a new campaign against the headscarf, which the Minister for Religious Affairs, Boubaker al-Akhzouri, described as 'un-Islamic', 'unpatriotic', and an 'imported' concept, though this failed to stifle what was fast becoming a widespread phenomenon.[35] Yet rather than celebrate the new presence of the hijab, many al-Nahda women instead saw it as symptomatic of a superficial religious understanding. In the 1980s, in the view of many women in the movement, the hijab had two significations: as a political affiliation and as an ethical commitment. As Sayida, the Nahdawi from Akouda, said:

In the 1970s and 1980s there was a hijab that meant political belonging, of belief and of a message, the idea of the Islamic Tendency Movement. Ninety per cent of those wearing the hijab belonged to that project—the idea that Islam could solve the problems of the contemporary world *and* that reviving Islam was like a method of life, a model of life in all fields. Perhaps if you met a woman in the street wearing a hijab and you didn't know her, you would say: '*al-salām 'alaykum.*'[36]

However, she said, the hijab that re-emerged in the early 2000s was worn by most women in a different manner, 'without conditions or any political engagement or awareness'. The new attention to the hijab, in her view, lacked the particular set of practices and beliefs of the al-Nahda project.

They were wearing hijab and they didn't even pray ... The new generation they were not like we were. Sometimes they had ideas totally against ours: they wore the hijab but their minds were interested in other things, and they even went to the nightclubs. You never imagined finding a girl in the nightclub dancing and wearing hijab!

Another female al-Nahda activist, Kawther, who was a schoolteacher in Hai Riadh, said the widespread appearance of the hijab on the streets in the late 2000s gave her sufficient protection to wear it herself at work. However, she lamented the lack of religious understanding that accompanied it:

It's only a worn as decoration. It doesn't have any value to these women. It's not worn as a duty, no ... Now the veil (*khimar*) in Tunisia is just an article of clothing that's very ordinary. It's decoration.[37]

For these women, the hijab they saw proliferating in society was merely an identity claim and had lost its purpose as both a political signifier and a means of achieving an ethical life.

In her research in mid-1990s Egypt, Saba Mahmood suggests that acts like fasting or wearing the hijab function not merely to mark political allegiance or identity but to cultivate modesty.[38] It is an argument which mirrors the disciplined formation of the Christian self in the monasteries of the early Middle Ages or the Tablighi approach to *da'wa* work as a mechanism of reform.[39] Yet the interpretations drawn by these Nahdawi women complicate Mahmood's binary distinction between Islamist activists, for whom the veil signalled an Islamic revival, and members of piety circles, who instead saw the veil as a way to achieve modesty from the outside in, through the 'training and realization of a pious self'.[40] In the Tunisian case the evidence suggests that Nahdawi women saw both political and ethical conceptions as intertwined in their project. When in the 2000s formal Islamist activism was largely impossible, so Nahdawis sought refuge in an ethical conception of their Islamism. What they felt dismissive towards were those women who wore the veil merely as an identity marker, without either a political or ethical dimension.

Understandings of what it meant to be Islamist in these straitened circumstances focused on the private and the moral, rediscovering ethical comportment and renouncing the more ambitious political project. Nahdawis went back to the meanings present at the movement's origins, which prioritized the moral condition. These understandings were reflected in the moral work ethic for those fortunate enough to find jobs. Yet, the understandings also retained a particular interpretation and history, which left them out of tune with the satellite preacher-led religious revival of the 2000s.

Recruiting the Next Generation

Perhaps the most unexpected activities of the al-Nahda movement in this period emerged among the younger generation who began to discover and study Islamist ideas for themselves. In Sousse this was a small but significant group: some were the sons and daughters of Nahdawis (the 'children of the movement', *abnā 'al-ḥaraka*), but surprisingly some were new to al-Nahda. They were influenced by events abroad, notably the 11 September 2001 attacks and the March 2003 invasion of Iraq, as well as growing religiosity at home, and were encouraged by what they could read on the internet or the religious programming they watched on satellite television. Their focus was not on al-Nahda or its political project but instead the search for a new religious authority, which might offer an antidote to the self-serving official Islam relayed through the state media and the mosques.

Two different paths into the movement illustrate the absorption of the new generation. The first is perhaps the more anticipated. Nejib was the son of a daily labourer and grew up in a small village on the road west from Sousse to Kairouan. He was sixteen at the time of the 11 September attacks. Neijb learnt about Islam and the Qur'an from an uncle, who had been in the Tablighi Jamaat and who gave him books to read on *fiqh*, the hadith, and various Qur'anic commentaries. He joined a local Qur'anic study group, the Association for the Preservation of the Holy Qur'an in M'saken, which was indirectly connected to the al-Nahda movement: it was led by Shaykh Mohamed Tahar Rouis, a local imam who was the father of Jaleleddine Rouis, head of the al-Nahda list in the 1989 elections, and Mohamed Larbi Rouis, the sympathetic director of the Leoni manufacturing company. Nejib took part in competitions of commentary, memorization, and rhetoric, though this was always under the gaze of the political police. 'I remember I was in Tunis for a Qur'anic competition at the Ministry for Religious Affairs. There were more security officials than competitors!' he said.[41] Despite the Rouis family connection, Nejib described his belonging (*intimā*') to the Islamist movement as an individual, personal search led by his Qur'anic studies and reading. He became known in his village as someone to call on for Qur'anic recitation during social occasions like engagements or funerals, though he was forbidden from preaching in the village mosque. He described his strong personal reaction against the 'official Islam' of the regime that appeared on television, in newspapers, and in the Friday sermons at the mosque.

The official Islam was the Islam that expressed the options of the regime, a contradictory Islam, and you felt it was an affected model just to silence people. It justified the choices of the regime but at the same time it was at war against the Islamic awakening (*ṣaḥwa*), and even freedom of religion and of belief, and it fought against the simplest form of religiosity, whether the beard or the hijab. And that was what put you off official institutions ... I began to differentiate myself from many of my friends and peers.[42]

After the uprising he moved quickly to join al-Nahda at university in Sousse and then rose up the regional leadership structure.

The second path, which also brought a young teenager into the al-Nahda fold, began independently of the movement. Faouzi, from Kalaa Seghira, was inspired by watching the Egyptian preacher Amr Khalid on satellite television and fell in with a group of Salafists while studying at the Higher Institute of Management of Sousse.[43] They tried to spread their *da'wa* and implicit in this was a direct challenge to the legitimacy of the Ben Ali regime: 'Of course when we talked about Arab-Islamic identity we must talk about who is blocking and preventing these freedoms'.[44] They were arrested in a nationwide crackdown on extremism that began with the December 2003 anti-terrorism law, with its broad definitions of terrorist offences.[45] Faouzi was jailed in 2004 for five months and was then excluded from the university. Eventually in the late 2000s, he made contact in his neighbourhood with a Nahdawi and the movement carefully drew him in, encouraging him to reconsider his earlier Salafism. By 2014 he was head of the al-Nahda youth section for Sousse and a member of the movement's regional bureau and had married the daughter of a senior al-Nahda leader.

The chains of transmission of ideas involved in recruiting Faouzi are striking. He was initially told about the movement's experience of repression and was eventually brought to a secret meeting with Moncef Ben Salem, a mathematics professor and senior leader in the movement from Sfax.[46] It was an important moment:

I thought it was impossible to meet someone like this and then there he was in front of me. He gave me great moral encouragement. Even though he was an old man he was still talking about working for freedom.[47]

From that point, Faouzi was drawn into small study groups of young al-Nahda sympathizers, who were meeting sometimes in private homes, sometimes in the main public library in central Sousse, and sometimes in rented summer houses by the beach. One key guide for them was Nouri, another activist from Sousse who was an older mathematics student in Tunis and better acquainted with Islamist readings. He was the son of an al-Nahda prisoner who had died in 1998 shortly after being released from jail. From 2006 Nouri ran the youth committee in the al-Jahiz forum organized by Slaheddine Jourchi, a journalist and former Progressive Islamist, in Tunis.[48] It was a rare and influential intellectual discussion group which met regularly on Saturday mornings to discuss subjects that were virtually taboo for public debate: notions of consultation (*shūrā*), criticisms of dictatorship, and ideas about democracy. Nouri then tried to recreate a similar intellectual discussion among young Sousse activists, though with a focus that was more explicitly Islamist than the Tunis forum. It was a struggle given the sterile absence of debate among the younger generation, a climate he and others frequently described as 'desertification' (*taṣaḥḥur*).[49] In these Sousse meetings the groups would read books and focus on subjects like the history of Islam, studies of the Qur'an, the life of the Prophet, how to pray, the importance of fasting, and moral questions like the perils of drugs, smoking, and drinking.

These young friends were also aware of the growing Salafist phenomenon, which was strong in Sousse. Although Sousse was portrayed in the media as a secular tourist city and a stronghold of the ruling party, it was also a source of Salafism from the early 2000s. One of the two Tunisian assassins of the Afghan opposition warlord Ahmad Shah Massoud was a textile worker from Sousse who had been living in Belgium.[50] Many of the hundreds of young men arrested in the crackdown following the 2003 anti-terrorism law were from Sousse and around a third of those involved in the Suleiman incident of December 2006–January 2007 were also from the city, particularly from the poorer, industrial southern quarter of Taffala, near the *louage* station. The Suleiman incident was an audacious but 'shambolic' attempt to stage an armed Salafi uprising against the regime.[51]

Some Salafists Nouri met advocated political change through violence and a few went to fight in Iraq in the mid-2000s, fuelled by ideas from writings like Ayman al-Zawahiri's tirade against democracy, *The Bitter Harvest*.[52] In contrast, Nouri's group read advocates of non-violent political Islam including Fahmi Huwaidi, an Egyptian newspaper columnist; Tariq al-Bishri, an Egyptian judge; Mohammad Salim al-Awa, an Egyptian scholar; Burhan Ghalioun, a Syrian opposition figure; and Yusuf al-Qaradawi, including his *Islamic Awakening: Between Rejection and Extremism*, which Nouri understood as a criticism of blind obedience and intolerance. Nouri described this intellectual process as installing 'intellectual immunity' (*al-taḥṣīn al-fikrī*), immunizing their minds against the rigidity of Salafism. He saw this dispute over different Islamist visions as having replaced the intellectual contest of the 1970s and 1980s, which was predominantly between the Islamists and the left. The problem was that Salafists opposed political participation.

In the university in the 2000s there was no longer a challenge like before from the leftists, no, the challenge was *inside* the religious school, the issue was the idea of *kufr* (unbelief). They believed entering parliament with democracy was *kufr*, and that the basis of change was armed struggle, that the basis of change was to build an Islamic emirate, and then *takfir* (an accusation of apostasy) for all those who took part in democracy.[53]

This intellectual immunity meant finding a response to Salafism from within Islam and refusing to accept the Salafi characterization that al-Nahda merely represented an 'Islam light' trend. It also meant accepting ideas from other political movements, for example, adopting the notion of Tunisians as 'citizens' (*muwāṭinūn*) not 'subjects' (*raʿāyā*), an idea Nouri said he learnt from the Democratic Forum for Labour and Liberties (Ettakatol), a centre-left opposition party.[54]

There is a difference between patriotism, meaning we die and we are loyal to the homeland, and citizenship. OK, I give myself to the homeland but the homeland must give me something, let me feel like a citizen, and among even the simplest rights are the issues of participating in the drafting of public policy, participating in building a future Tunisia.[55]

This distinction between citizen and subject was widely felt among political dissidents, as if Tunisians were unable to exercise their full citizenship because the regime forced them to withdraw from public life through censorship, surveillance, manipulation, and co-option.[56] The concept of political participation was just one of many points of difference with the Salafists.

The question of this physical proximity and intellectual rivalry with the Salafists in the 2000s recurs with remarkable frequency. Another al-Nahda activist, Nabil, who was the son of a Zaytuna-educated imam and who went on to head a local bureau in Sousse, at one stage considered leading a group of Salafists in the city. Though he had not been a member of al-Nahda before the crackdown of the 1990s, he became involved with a group who tried to restart al-Nahda in Sousse as a political force in the mid-2000s. However, the more senior leaders, who were only just emerging from prison at the time, were cautious and told them to rein in their ambitions. At that stage friends in his small group joined the Salafist movement in the city, some of whom were travelling to Iraq to fight in the anti-American insurgency: 'There were networks of connections at first between our ideas and theirs. But they considered themselves as waiting for jihad and us as cowards, and so there was an intellectual conflict.'[57] However, he remained close to them and watched them return from fighting in Iraq where they had felt betrayed because they were undervalued. Nabil was asked to join and lead the Sousse group, but eventually refused.

They were very angry, and they weren't convinced of my point of view. There was a difference of ideas and the influence from outside Tunisia was stronger than from inside. They felt that al-Nahda couldn't change or resist Ben Ali, but that they, with their new ideas, could do a lot.

Soon after came the crackdown that followed the 2006–07 Suleiman incident; many in Sousse were arrested including Nabil, who was eventually jailed for six months for attending an unauthorized meeting.

On university campuses there was an effort among a small number of students to test the limits of activism. However, there was much less evidence of this in Sousse than in other cities, like Tunis and Sfax, where groups of students calling themselves the Independents (*al-mustaqillūn*), who were openly Islamist supporters, managed to be politically active.[58] In the Faculty of Law in Sousse there was a small group of students in the mid-2000s, who later became members of al-Nahda, but who were at the time active within the main student union, UGET, and who were reading in private what texts they could download from the internet by Hassan al-Banna and Sayyid Qutb.

Some in this student group were also among those meeting under Nouri's guidance in Sousse. Instead of identifying themselves as Islamists at the university, they rallied behind issues like opposing the ban on the veil in the university and defending Arab-Islamic identity. They challenged the regime's cultural values and its imposition of a French-style and Francophone education system in the university. In the later 2000s the student group would meet privately to discuss moral issues: prayer, fasting and resisting alcohol, drugs, and smoking.

In the final months before the 2011 uprising these young people grew more confident. Several described a summer training camp in mid-2010, when they rented a house for a week in Chott Meriem, a tourist beach-front area in northern Sousse. There a group of fifteen to twenty like-minded young men and women from Sousse, Monastir, and Sfax spent the week studying and playing. They swam in the sea, cooked couscous together, and then studied books, read the Qur'an, and stayed up late in discussion. One night Abdelhamid Jelassi, the senior al-Nahda leader, came to give a talk about the movement, its history, and their training for the future.

A new generation came to the movement in the years before the uprising and focused their debates on questions of identity, ethics, and behaviour. For them the ideological challenge with the left, as fought by the older generation, had been replaced by a more urgent challenge from the Salafists. The emphasis was on correctly interpreting the holy texts, understanding the appropriate source of religious authority, and thinking about moral or behavioural issues. Ideas of political participation for this generation, at least in Sousse, were still very limited.

Activism Outside Al-Nahda

The 2000s saw a return to political activism across Tunisia. The weight of repression lessened, in part because of pressure from international human rights groups but also because the regime now focused more on the security threat from nascent Salafist groups than on the apparently exhausted political opposition. Gradually, it became possible for dissidents of all political backgrounds to become active. They found their voice in a revival of associations, especially human rights groups which resisted regime co-option and began to challenge the political calm.[59] However, the reawakening of the self-described 'democratic left' raised awkward questions. They rallied around the call for the release of the several thousand political prisoners still in jail, most of whom were Nahdawis, for few among the rights activists would endorse the brutal torture, long jail terms, and arbitrary judicial system. Yet many leftists were reluctant to cooperate with the Islamists and saw al-Nahda still as an illiberal threat.[60] It would take much work to dissolve this mistrust.

For al-Nahda in Sousse the most public activism was found not among the leaders, but on the periphery of the movement; those who had been members but not in the leadership hierarchy, and who had avoided long prison sentences. They were also on the intellectual periphery and tended to have strong personal friendships extending across political boundaries. These individuals were less interested in al-Nahda's own political advancement and instead favoured broader goals like democratic reforms and human rights causes, while all the time retaining a deep personal religious commitment. They were so much on the periphery of the movement that after 2011 many in this group chose not to rejoin the newly legalized al-Nahda.

In Sousse in the early 2000s, there were only a few formal settings for oppositional civil society activities. The local branch of Amnesty International brought together academics, lawyers, and human rights activists, including Moncef Marzouki, a doctor who in 2001 founded the opposition party Congress for the Republic (CPR), before going into exile in France the following year.[61] At least two al-Nahda members joined the Amnesty branch, including Yahya, one of the first preachers from the 1970s who had become a civil society activist. The group would meet at an office on the second floor of a block on Rue Anatole France, in the city centre, to organize petitions and letter-writing campaigns. They worked on rights abuses abroad but rarely on Tunisian issues, for such were the limits on their activities set by the regime. Nevertheless, it offered a new chance for Sousse's few dozen activists to meet. For the Islamists it was particularly poignant given their experiences of repression. One of the Nahdawis involved was a lawyer, Zied, who had been arrested in May 1991, aged 17. After a year in prison he was prevented from returning to his state school and was forced to finish his studies in a lower-quality private school. Despite being under administrative control, he then completed a law degree at the Faculty of Law in Sousse. After 2000 Zied joined the Tunisian Association of Young Lawyers, even though it was dominated by supporters of the ruling party, and then began working with the Amnesty branch in Sousse. Despite limits preventing their work on Tunisian issues, he described one lecture when a lawyer from Gafsa came to talk about the history and development of the death penalty in Tunisia. Always there were policemen outside and sometimes inside the office, monitoring their work. For Zied, his Amnesty membership became a proud 'personal challenge', an effort, however modest, to stand up to the abuses of the regime.[62] 'What encouraged me was that you found respectable people from other trends in human rights work. In Amnesty it wasn't just normal people, but real people who struggled.' He also became increasingly self-confident with the policemen waiting outside the office. 'I became indifferent towards them. I wasn't committing a crime, I was defending rights and freedoms.'

By the mid-2000s there was increasing pressure in Sousse on the local branches of Amnesty and the LTDH as the regime clamped down on their new activism. Some Nahdawis began to work with an unauthorized human rights group, the International Association for the Support of Political Prisoners (AISPP) founded in 2001. They gave material and psychological support to former prisoners and their families, trying to find employment for those without work and medical care for the sick. They turned discreetly to the private clinics of doctors who had been with the movement in the 1970s and 1980s but who had avoided jail and repression. For others, the focus shifted to the opposition Progressive Democratic Party (PDP), which in 2001 had openly welcomed former al-Nahda members into its ranks, offering a form of political cover. A Sousse branch of the PDP was established in 2004 on Rue Soeur Joséphine, in the central Trocadero district, and several al-Nahda civil society activists including Yahya joined. It became the 'only refuge' in the city, he said.

From early 2003 the PDP began a remarkable rapprochement among all the major opposition parties. Led initially by exiles abroad, including senior al-Nahda leaders, it began with a joint statement, the 'Appel de Tunis', calling for the release of all political prisoners and a new constitution for a political system based on popular sovereignty, the peaceful rotation of power, and the freedom of belief.[63] At the time Ameur Laarayedh, a senior Nahdawi in exile and brother of Ali Laarayedh, argued for a common front to push for a democratic transition, beginning with the release of political prisoners, a general amnesty, and free elections.[64] Building on this foundation, the leaders of the PDP in Tunis formed a political front in October 2005 with other opposition parties ranging from the communist PCOT to al-Nahda. Though the regime dismissed this 18 October Collective as 'an unnatural alliance', it grew in ambition, beginning with a high-profile hunger strike and eventually producing a shared vision on women's rights, the lifting of the ban on the veil, freedom of conscience, and on the relationship between religion and a civil democratic state.[65] Nationally, it marked a moment of opposition compromise and unity, as well as the first overt return by al-Nahda to some form of political activism in Tunisia.

In Sousse five men gathered in the PDP offices to support the 18 October Collective with a three-day hunger strike, an event that launched several years of cross-party discussions in the city. Al-Nahda's regional leaders were conspicuous by their absence. However, one of the five hunger strikers was Tahar, a gently spoken lawyer who had been twice forcibly conscripted into the army in the late 1980s as punishment for his Islamist activities at university in Sousse. Once freed from the army, he opened a shoe shop and raised enough money to complete his law degree at a private university and then from the late 1990s began attending Amnesty, LTDH, and PDP meetings in Sousse.

The impetus began with one of the PDP members, Moncef, a civil society activist and former Progressive Islamist, who had been present at the Tunis hunger strike. He pushed for the Sousse branch to hold its own strike in solidarity. Historic tensions between the left and the Islamists threatened to overwhelm it from the start. Moncef said:

I insisted but the others said they were afraid or there was a political calculation. Here on the left we didn't have enough leftists and there was a fear of the Islamists. The PCOT was afraid that the Islamists would surround and swallow up this strike.[66]

The night before the strike, Moncef met with the local head of the PDP at his home, prepared a mattress, and drove into the party's office in the city centre and slept there until morning. At 8am they formally declared the hunger strike was on. Dozens of police soon gathered on the street outside but by the end of the day four others had joined him: the former Nahdawi, Tahar; a member of the local PCOT branch, Nasser Ben Romdhane; another PDP member; and an independent activist. 'It was an extraordinary day,' Moncef said. A photograph of the strikers dated 30 October 2005 shows the five crouched against a plain wall, each making the sign of a victory salute. Above them a banner read: 'The Movement of 18 October. Hunger but not submission' (*Harakat 18 Uktubir. al-juw' wa lā al-khudū*').[67] Personal relations were important in securing this rare cross-party unity. Moncef was distrustful of al-Nahda, who he felt still nurtured the goal of an Islamic state, but he said of his Islamist friend and fellow hunger striker Tahar:

I didn't see the other Islamists in Sousse from 1991 until about the last five days before 14 January [2011]. But he is a real activist, a democrat and I trusted him … I'd known him for a long time because we were in the same political family. He is very gentle and brave and I respect him. Especially, it was the fact that he was the only face of the Islamic family in regional political life. We were obliged to work with them.[68]

Ben Romdhane, the PCOT representative, was also distrustful of the Islamists. The communists felt they had continued the struggle against the regime throughout the 1990s and early 2000s while the Islamists equivocated and still held to the possibility of striking a compromise with

Ben Ali. In his view, though they might be prepared for a temporary alliance, they could not imagine a shared political programme with the Islamists.[69]

Tahar, the al-Nahda hunger striker, also faced pressure from his fellow Islamists before taking part in this joint venture. 'My Islamist friends said: "What do you expect from these people? Don't take part!" I said: "No! We must be present."'[70] Until the hunger strike, Tahar had been attending Amnesty and PDP meetings but not speaking up. '2005 was the first time I spoke,' he said. 'The government said the Tunis strikes represented no one so we did our own strike here.' Except this was an individual challenge: there was only one Nahdawi in Sousse involved in this ground-breaking opposition alliance. The movement's regional leaders did not take part in the action or in the discussions that followed, even Hamadi Jebali, who was released from prison in 2006. In fact, there remained a lasting groundswell of mutual suspicion between the left and al-Nahda.

The Sousse hunger strike was brief, but from this one action emerged a committee of around fifteen people, made up of the five strikers plus representatives from other opposition parties and human rights groups like the LTDH. They met in the local PDP office over the following years and debated the draft texts that were sent from Tunis, which discussed the shared political vision the major parties were trying to compose. Eventually, the collaboration dissolved ahead of the 2009 presidential election in a disagreement about whether the coalition would put forward a single candidate for the vote. Ironically, after the 2011 uprising al-Nahda leaders in Sousse held out the 18 October Collective agreements as a sign of their consensual ambitions. At the time, however, shared action with other opposition parties was limited to a handful on the periphery of the movement. They had a broader interpretation of the Islamist project and were more open to engaging with their leftist rivals on cross-party human rights issues. It is striking how many of these Sousse activists, including Yahya, Zied, Tahar, and others, chose not to re-join al-Nahda once it was formally legalized in 2011. Nor were they the only element of the movement searching for new opportunities for mobilization during these straitened times.

A New Political Strategy

These activities on the periphery of the movement took place largely beyond the oversight of the senior leaders, most of whom were still in jail or were heavily restricted by administrative control. Formal political activities within al-Nahda were thought to have been confined to the movement-in-exile, which held three congresses in Europe over two decades, and which met with other Tunisian opposition activists.[71] Ghannouchi himself lived in London for most of the 1990s and 2000s, giving speeches and leading the movement-in-exile. However, there was eventually a revival of formal political activities within Tunisia as senior leaders began to come home from jail, though this work has often been overlooked. For the activists of Sousse, it quickly became apparent how hard this would be. Rachid, the mathematics teacher who had struggled to find a wife after leaving jail in late 2002, hoped to revive his political activities as quickly as possible. He refused to accept the administrative control order under which he had to sign in with the police in his home village some twenty miles from the city rather than in Sousse itself, even though senior Nahdawis warned him not to be confrontational. Then in 2004, ahead of the legislative elections of 24 October, he attended a meeting of the leftist party the Movement of Renewal (Ettajdid) in Hai Riadh.[72] He spoke briefly to the gathering of a few dozen activists to warn them against participating in another rigged election.

I said: 'We, the Islamists, we tried it with Ben Ali and we lost everything so what will you do with these elections? You're giving legitimacy to these elections!' They tried to convince me that it was better to do something, even a minimum.[73]

The next day Rachid was summoned to the Hai Riadh police station and was told a report had been written about his attendance and that he had no right to attend further political meetings. His signing for administrative control was to be increased from once a week to every day. 'I was terrified,' he admitted. That was the end of his political activism until 2011.

Some movement leaders adopted a conciliatory attitude once they were out of jail. Their goal was a negotiated survival, not a return to the costly resistance against the regime that had shaped their approach before the crackdown. Perhaps the most important moment was the return in February 2006 of Jebali, after sixteen years in jail.[74] Jebali was the most senior Nahdawi from Sousse and from 2006 led the al-Nahda movement within Tunisia. His return brought new momentum:

When I left, even before me, we regained confidence. We knew Ben Ali could no longer attack us. There was a group inside the country that started to organize itself. Not only the social aspect of the family, but the organizational and political aspect also started.[75]

Jebali received visitors, Tunisian political figures as well as foreign diplomats, at a fifth-floor apartment in Sahloul, in Sousse, which became the base for the project to rebuild the movement.[76] After a two-hour meeting with Jebali in August 2006, a US diplomat reported to

Washington that nine al-Nahda leaders had written to the Ben Ali regime a month earlier saying the group was 'ready to turn the page' and wanted to restart 'political life'.[77] They received no response. Jebali told a journalist that 'reconciliation' with the regime was now an 'urgent necessity' to allow Tunisia to face the challenges of globalization. 'Unfortunately some insist on treating us as "terrorists", whereas we should all look to the future together,' he said.[78] Later in the year Jebali repeated his request for 'reconciliation' when he was asked by the opposition newspaper *al-Maoukif* what he thought of other Nahdawis who were pushing for a strong, united opposition under the more confrontational 18 October Collective banner.[79] Jebali was forced to deny any disagreement with the Collective, but emphasized again that Tunisia now needed 'comprehensive national reconciliation' (*al-muṣālaḥa al-waṭaniyya al-shāmila*).

For some years there had been rumours of behind-the-scenes discussions between al-Nahda representatives abroad and emissaries from the Ben Ali regime.[80] These may have been no more than 'pseudo-negotiations', as Vincent Geisser describes them.[81] Nonetheless, the Islamists were open to an accommodation with the regime as a 'strategy of political survival', in contrast to those like Marzouki's CPR who called for Ben Ali to go. It was also an attempt to secure the return of exiled Nahdawis.[82] Al-Nahda was seeking a compromise like that made by Morocco's Islamists, the Party of Justice and Development, which conceded the religious legitimacy of the monarchy in return for entry into a tightly controlled political process.[83] In 2002 Ghannouchi argued for a transition towards a 'symbolic presidency' with limited powers.[84] Then at al-Nahda's eighth congress, held in London in May 2007, the movement suggested it serve as a 'constructive opposition'.[85] Ghannouchi said he was open to dialogue with the regime, making explicit the contrast between the 'moderate' al-Nahda and the violence of the Salafists behind the Suleiman incident.

However, even among those Nahdawis in Sousse there were already differences over the identity of their movement. Ajmi Lourimi, who had joined as a teenager in the late 1970s, left jail in July 2007 and soon wrote an article in *Mouatinoun*, an opposition newspaper, arguing that al-Nahda needed a dramatic structural and ideological overhaul to adapt to the new realities.[86] Parties were too preoccupied trying simply to exist rather than trying to develop. As he put it, they were caught up fighting the 'battle of presence' (*ma'rakat al-wujūd*) rather than the 'battle of renewal' (*ma'rakat al-tajdīd*). Of al-Nahda, he said:

It is not possible for the movement to return to what it was in the 1990s ... We are living in a new international situation, but that new international situation meant many transformations and these transformations naturally produced an intellectual, ideological, and political realignment and it's not possible for the Islamic movement and al-Nahda in particular to be isolated from that realignment and those transformations ... It is inconceivable for the movement to be along the lines of what it was in the 1990s or the 1970s.[87]

Lourimi was arguing for greater openness and a shift in vision towards a reformist, human rights-based agenda. He explicitly aligned himself with the 18 October Collective, which he described as 'simply the most important political step in the country in recent years'. Others flinched at such public calls for radical rethinking. In an open letter dated three days after Lourimi's interview, Abdelhamid Jelassi, recently released from prison and now living with his wife in Sousse, wrote that it was important to maintain movement unity. He delivered a cautionary warning, which prioritized organizational integrity over intellectual debate, the battle of presence over the battle of renewal:

Our movement is now more visible and public. Many important questions come up for public debate in which everyone contributes, and it is for the general good of the country and the people that the goal is to investigate the truth. But though people are eager to clarify ideas and to argue positions we should not forget to take care to defer to the right of the brotherhood and to preserve friendly, harmonious relations because we have no greater reserves than that ... As for what shortcomings may be found in what is actually present in our performance, individually or collectively, we should draw from it whatever are the necessary lessons and results, and this should not imprison us in a circle of self-flagellation (jald al-dhāt). For if we fell short yesterday, so we will stand determined not to fall short today, and if our return didn't exceed twenty per cent of what was available yesterday, for example, then tomorrow it will be eighty or ninety per cent.[88]

Where Lourimi spoke of bold rethinking and political realignment, Jelassi spoke of the history of the movement, public discretion, and most of all 'the miracle of preserving al-Nahda's presence and unity'. Intellectual revision was being debated, but there was always pressure pulling in a more conservative direction.

In the coming years, even Lourimi began to sense that the gulf between the movement and the Ben Ali regime was narrowing. In a long assessment of the movement published in 2009, he argued that al-Nahda, after years of confrontation, now saw the need for 'stability and reconciliation' and favoured reconciling with the regime.[89] This was a movement in 'new clothes' undergoing a 'natural evolution' (al-taṭawwur al-ṭabīʿī). In another essay written a few months later, he described al-Nahda's stages of development, from a movement of Islamization (aslama) through daʿwa and education of the individual in the 1970s, to a political project in the 1980s that quickly overwhelmed the other aspects of the movement, became confrontational and strove to take power but failed. Now al-Nahda had reached the next stage:

The goal of the movement became not taking power but participation, and so began the slogan of joint work with the opposition and serious, comprehensive national reconciliation instead of the slogan of complete Islamization (*al-aslama al-kāmila*) and of taking power (*iftikāk al-sulṭa*), and it moved to the call for mutual recognition (*al-i'tirāf al-mutabādal*) and to considering the project as the task of society as a whole not the task of an individual party, and it became clear it was impossible to return to the first stage of Islamization and that it was impossible to continue the second stage of taking power.[90]

This was a newly emerging discourse of cooperation, inclusion, participation, and pragmatism, which saw the challenge ahead not as al-Nahda's project alone, but as a society-wide endeavour.

This debate demonstrates that for al-Nahda the rethinking of the project had its roots in internal debates conducted within Tunisia and not just among exiles abroad. More significantly, we see that intellectual revision came well before the strategic behavioural change of the post-2011 period. It was not simply the pressure of contingent political competition that produced ideological change. This complicates the inclusion-moderation hypothesis often deployed to explain Islamist transformations, which argues that these organizations 'moderate' their behaviour once they are allowed to participate in the political process.[91] Instead, Tunisian Islamists engaged in intellectual revision as a result of long-term political exclusion, rather than inclusion. Francesco Cavatorta and Fabio Merone argue this is explained by the twin pressures of repression and 'societal rejection' during the Ben Ali years.[92] The internal debates among Nahdawis in Sousse and elsewhere reveal the detailed mechanisms by which some sought to rethink their movement's intellectual project against the resistance of colleagues. They crafted a new vocabulary of contention, embracing liberal ideals of democracy, a civil state, equality, and freedom of conscience. They took advantage of new opportunities for cross-party cooperation and discussion. And they pressed the senior leadership to acknowledge the changing political climate and to address the mistakes of the past.

During the late 2000s a small group of around a dozen individuals from the movement in Sousse began holding discreet meetings in each other's homes to discuss reviving the organization. The priority was an evaluation (*taqyīm*) of al-Nahda's past actions, particularly during the late 1980s and early 1990s. It began as a series of informal discussions and then by 2009 a written document began to circulate to a limited audience of loyal Nahdawis in Sousse, and elsewhere in the country. The document, which remains secret, was a history of the movement's actions since its founding as the MTI in 1981 and included the same assessment made in the early 1990s, both in prison and simultaneously in exile abroad: that al-Nahda had overreached in its confrontation with Ben Ali. Those most involved in the process of evaluation in Sousse tended not to be the more religiously inclined preachers, who had dominated at the start of the movement in the 1970s, but those with more political leanings, who were often involved in student activities in the late 1980s and who went on to play important roles in the movement's regional leadership structure after the 2011 uprising.

One such meeting gathered around a dozen men and women from Akouda, a semi-rural district in northern Sousse, for a discussion led by Jelassi. They met in autumn 2010 at the home of the sister of one Nahdawi, on a sandy, undeveloped road near the sea in Chott Meriem. Each had received discreetly in advance a compact disc, which contained a document, which was a history and evaluation of the movement from the 1980s and the changing international environment since then. The purpose was, first, to study the movement's past. It was evident to nearly everyone that serious mistakes had been made in the early 1990s. Second, there was a more mundane effort to rouse the near-defeated individual activists and to tell them they were not forgotten. One activist described how Jelassi tried to encourage them that the movement would one day return:

We had sacrificed and struggled for an idea and a project and it would be a shame if all these things were in vain, he [Jelassi] said. We have a message and we must return to this goal and revive it ... 'We must try at least', he said. 'We should not surrender' ... We said: 'How are we going to serve the world? Let's not be negative and let's try to revive the organization' ... It made us regain hope that we could progress, and that this tyrannical police state couldn't eradicate the movement, that it was a Godly movement (ḥaraka rabbāniyya) and its project was not materialistic, not about individuals, but about an idea, a civilizational project, that we want the best for the Muslim community, to revive the glory of Islam, to revive the values that came through the rightly guided caliphs.[93]

Despite Jelassi's efforts in this meeting and others, most activists at the time were pessimistic about al-Nahda's chances of revival.

In the end the task of evaluation was interrupted and left incomplete by the uprising, which began within weeks of this meeting. Quickly, al-Nahda presented itself as a party of the revolution; the policy of reconciliation with the Ben Ali regime was quietly forgotten. The concerted effort of the late 2000s to revive al-Nahda as a political movement now bore fruit and explains why the movement was so quick to profit from the political vacuum created by the fall of the Ben Ali regime. A process of intellectual and strategic rethinking had begun well before the real possibility of political inclusion in a transition away from authoritarianism. Yet, the debates during these years of social exclusion also suggest that deep-seated tensions about the broader strategy and vision of a contemporary Islamist movement remained unresolved.

*

The post-prison experience was one of punishment, restriction, and thwarted ambition for the Nahdawis of Sousse but it did not always mean their 'social death'. Instead, these accounts reveal individual stories of resilience against an architecture of repression that was designed to ostracize these men and women for the crime of their Islamist project. They channelled their religious commitment into a moral project. Individual determination now stood in place of the community of activists. Those on the periphery felt more at ease collaborating with their leftist rivals, crossing the ideological bridge in the spirit of shared democratic enterprise. The younger generation, in turn, met in secret to discuss the intellectual challenge of the new religiosity of the satellite channel generation. Meanwhile, the small core leadership struggled to regroup and consider the once unthinkable compromise of reconciliation with a regime that had tried to eradicate them.

Here lay the groundwork that allowed the rapid return of the movement as a political force after the collapse of the Ben Ali regime. However, here too lay exposed the tensions at the heart of the movement, which became yet more pronounced in the political freedom of the new Tunisia. The bold political project of the late 1980s had not merely been abandoned but criticized too from within as a dangerously ambitious overreach for which thousands had paid a heavy penalty. At the level of political leadership there was an entire, and not always unopposed, volte-face, in which the necessary cost of survival was reckoned to require reconciliation with the regime. The battle of presence had won out against the battle of renewal. Meanwhile, lower down the movement hierarchy, individuals were reclaiming the Islamist project for themselves. For some it meant renouncing the ambitions of the party in favour of a broader, shared democratic agenda, for others it meant rediscovering the ethical and moral compulsions that had driven the movement in its initial stages in the 1970s. The tension between costly political ambition and personal, moral commitment was already emerging. After 2011 it would only deepen.

6   Rebuilding and Fragmenting

> Are we a political movement with an Islamic background? Are we fundamentally an Islamic movement that has a political dimension? Or are we a political movement with no religious dimension? It needs to be theorized, to be thought through in depth. I believe that we have a comprehensive project, with politics, economics, religion, art, everything in the Qur'an. But how can we implement this for people? It needs much more reflection.
>
> *Rachid, imprisoned 1991–2002, member of al-Nahda's regional bureau in Sousse and the national Consultative Council.*[1]

The uprising that brought down Ben Ali was not of al-Nahda's making. Like all other political parties and the regime itself, the movement was caught unaware, even if some of its members took part as individuals in the many demonstrations that shook the country from 17 December 2010 onwards. Protests began in the small town of Sidi Bouzid, in central Tunisia, where an unlicensed vegetable seller, Mohamed Bouazizi, burnt himself to death in despair at his financial precarity. Young people, lawyers, and local trade unionists rose up in demonstrations in other towns across the marginalized interior. They were confronted by police and security forces firing into the crowds. The protests reached Tunis, beginning in the poorer suburbs and then, in the second week of January, reaching the imposing Ministry of Interior on Avenue Habib Bourguiba, in the heart of the city. Initially slow to act, the Tunisian General Labour Union (UGTT) finally called a general strike for Friday 14 January 2011; Ben Ali fled the country that afternoon, finding shelter in Saudi Arabia. An official inquiry later put the death toll from a month of protest at 338.[2]

Once Ben Ali had fled, al-Nahda reacted rapidly to the new opportunities. Communities of Nahdawis moved quickly to meet, organize, and structure themselves anew. On 30 January, Ghannouchi flew back into Tunis for the first time since 1989. Within a week his office issued a new 'founding statement' and the movement finally secured legal authorization on 1 March.[3] Al-Nahda emerged victorious from Tunisia's first free elections on 23 October 2011, winning in all but one of thirty-three constituencies and dominating in urban Tunis almost as much as it did in rural Tataouine.

Accounts of al-Nahda's behaviour in the period after the uprising have focused on the leadership's strategic choices during a transition away from authoritarianism. These analyses often underscore the constraints on al-Nahda and the acts of compromise that followed, highlighting political competition and negotiation between Islamist and secular political elites.[4] However, another approach to understanding al-Nahda in this transitional period is to ask how its choices affected the internal dynamics within an organization that had for many years enveloped a diverse membership. Islamist movements have often been seen as divided between those who have ambitions to acquire state power and those who prioritize their relationships to the community.[5] Yet al-Nahda combined both a formal political party and a religious social movement in one organization, not just as a response to authoritarianism but even once the political process had opened up to pluralist competition. This ambiguity was evident in the name under which it ran for election in 2011: the Party of the Movement of al-Nahda (Hizb Harakat al-Nahda). Such blurring of the lines reflected the trajectory of an organization which from the early 1980s tried both to compete within the political process and to build a grassroots subculture. This careful interweaving began to unravel as the movement reckoned with the new political opportunities now available. An internal debate quickly developed about whether to continue both political and preaching projects simultaneously within a single organization, or whether to spin off a separate political party, like the Freedom and Justice Party in Egypt, the Party of Justice and Development in Morocco, or the Islamic Action Front in Jordan. As Tunisia's transition away from authoritarianism gathered pace, so the division deepened between those who favoured competing in the formal state-level political process and those who, disaffected by party politics, preferred projects of Islamization from below, whether through preaching, civil society groups, or charitable activities.

Islamist organizations are as heterogeneous as other social movements and their strategies and ideas adapt to the changing political context. It is not merely that they shape the new landscape, but that they in turn are shaped by it. The mistake, then, is to conceive of such movements as dogmatic and static when instead their ideologies are in constant interaction with their political and social environment.[6] There had already been moments of intellectual and strategic adaptation throughout al-Nahda's history: when it first reached out beyond an original *da'wa* project in the late 1970s; when it endorsed democracy, a civil state, and the Personal Status Code hoping to enter the political process in the

1980s; when it reprioritized cultural and social work over the political during the repression of the 1990s; and the subsequent push for 'reconciliation' with the Ben Ali regime in the late 2000s. Al-Nahda's shift towards a commitment to democracy was not unique, but instead a feature common to most political groups in Tunisia since the 1970s.[7] The era after 2011 should therefore be seen as another phase of adaptation in which the meanings Islamist leaders gave to their movement's actions were transposed once more. In this new era, al-Nahda began to describe itself no longer as Islamist but, in Ghannouchi's own words, as 'a civil party with an Islamic reference' (*ḥizb madanī dhū marji'iyya islāmiyya*) and later as 'Muslim democrats'.[8] Yet this semantic switch took the movement into uncertain territory and, at least initially, amounted to little more than a rhetorical display which guarded the Islamic tradition without providing a new theory of governance. In that respect, the movement shared characteristics with other Islamist groups in the region with similarly superficial ideological visions. This latest challenge of adapting to new democratic competition within a globalized economic world order produced a deep structural and intellectual crisis within the movement.

This chapter demonstrates how al-Nahda rebuilt itself in the months and years after the fall of the Ben Ali regime, and why it began to fragment. It considers the movement's campaign for the October 2014 legislative elections, and the profound implications of election defeat on ordinary members. Following defeat, the movement made a decisive, hard-to-reverse commitment to politicization, becoming a political party that would for the first time formally separate itself from religious, social, and cultural activism. However, in the eyes of many Nahdawis the pragmatic steps their leaders took to be accepted within the new political process undermined the movement's electoral legitimacy, diluted its ideological vision, and weakened its organizational structure. The experience of al-Nahda demonstrates that ideological evolution and political pragmatism can have a significant organizational cost.

Rebuilding

Sousse was not at the forefront of the uprising that toppled Ben Ali and, for the most part, the city remained calm until the day Ben Ali fled. Several Nahdawis and other political activists spoke of their disgust when on Sunday 9 January 2011 they saw thousands of their fellow Sousse residents out on the streets, not challenging the regime but celebrating the victory of the local football team, Étoile Sportive du Sahel, over their rivals Espérance Sportive de Tunis. Yet the uprising did touch Sousse, with protests by doctors in front of the Farhat Hached hospital, daily demonstrations by lawyers and human rights activists outside the UGTT headquarters downtown, and some violent confrontations between students and the police in the university district of Hai Riadh. Some Nahdawis attended these protests, while others watched cautiously from a distance. Once Ben Ali had fled, however, they moved quickly to remobilize.

It was men and women by then in their late forties and early fifties, who had been student activists in the 1980s and often prisoners in the 1990s, who led the rebuilding. This gave a particular hue to the new movement. It was no longer a defiant young generation newly empowered by their university experiences but an older more cautious middle class who led the process.[9] They brought an instinctive return to a style of organizing familiar to the secretive years of the 1980s.

In early February in Kalaa Kebira, around two dozen Nahdawis held an initial meeting in one of their homes. Among them was Mohamed Chemli, the activist from a wealthy business family who had led the movement in Sousse in the late 1980s and who was to be again leader of the regional bureau in 2011–17. The next meeting in Kalaa was larger and included Jaleleddine Rouis, the doctor from M'saken who had led the al-Nahda electoral list in 1989 and who went on to succeed Chemli as head of the regional bureau in May 2017. Hedi, an ex-prisoner and former student activist from Kalaa, was present:

It was like a dream, not reality ... You invited people you knew, people that you remembered, and the brothers started rapidly gathering and everyone took up an activity, whether political or street work, and we started reviving things on the basis of the old mentality. Not on the mentality that you're now a party, but on the old way, as if you were spending from your previous knowledge: not through scientific organization, but through coordination, meetings, mutual respect, and the solidarity between brothers.[10]

A founding meeting was held and everyone attending proposed a candidate to lead the al-Nahda office in Kalaa. Hedi was elected as the bureau leader, or local general secretary (al-kātib al-ʿāmm al-maḥallī), with around a dozen others elected to lesser positions. Similar informal meetings and votes were held in all sixteen of the administrative districts across the governorate in February and March 2011, creating a much wider network of local offices than had ever been possible in the 1980s, when the movement was unauthorized. These local offices formed the first structural layer of the movement, and the main organizing centre for all ordinary members. A larger meeting was then held in central Sousse to elect the movement's regional bureau. Every local office presented four candidates for election to the bureau, which Chemli was chosen to lead as regional general secretary (al-kātib al-ʿāmm al-jihawī). A dozen other Nahdawis, including two women, were chosen for various roles, including: structure and organization; political work and relations with parties; administration and finance; women and family; youth; education and training; culture; and media. This regional bureau then reported up to the movement's central structures: the administrative offices; the national Consultative Council (*majlis al-shūrā*), which was made up of 150 directly and indirectly elected members and which met every three months; and the smaller Executive Bureau (*al-maktab al-tanfīdhī*), which included Ghannouchi, whose title was simply 'president of the movement'.

In the early 1980s supporters of the movement graduated through various secretive ranks from sympathizer and member of an open family, to committed adherent and member of a closed family. But now the movement operated as an open political party, with a formal application procedure for entry to the one level of membership on offer. On the application form, candidates for membership had to give their name, date of birth, identity card number, level of education, profession, address, family status, and some indication of the role they hoped to play within the movement. Each had to be proposed by an existing member and to agree to abide by nine conditions, including: to 'respect and defend Arab-Islamic identity and the principles of human rights and the gains made in the country'; to respect the decisions made by al-Nahda; to participate in the movement's activities; to follow the pro-gramme of cultivation (*tathqīf*), education (*tarbiya*) and training (*takwīn*); to pay a regular financial contribution; and to act correctly, with good behaviour and good morals.[11] Even when the membership process was updated in May 2016, when the movement became a party, al-Nahda maintained as one of the conditions of membership 'good behaviour and morals' (*al-sulūk al-ḥasan wa-l-akhlāq al-fāḍila*).[12]

Movement organizers emphasized participation in activities, which ranged from football games to religious, political, and intellectual training through the revival of the small study group known as 'the family' (*al-usra*). The *usra* was to envelope the new member in a support-ive network of familial bonds; it was an explicit re-creation of the imagined solidarity of the 1970s and 1980s. These groups replicated the close-knit study cells of the past, which were directly comparable to similar study groups in other Islamist movements in the region.[13] The goal was not to attract new followers, but to educate, cultivate, and reform those already within the al-Nahda embrace. As Nabil, now the leader of a local bureau in Sousse, described it:

The new generation doesn't have the original belonging to the al-Nahda movement, they don't have a familial belonging. They need to study the history of al-Nahda in order to know about it, because they are not joining a new party

formed recently but an old organization ... The *usra* becomes a second family.
They give training in religion, morals, in how to deal with people, in behaviour ...
And we develop our vision of society from a religious view.[14]

The group of around ten members met weekly. They would gather at
their local al-Nahda office or in one of their homes to follow a predeter-
mined programme of mostly Qur'anic study, drawing from a monthly
booklet sent by the movement's central office in Tunis known as the
'educational notebooks' (*al-kurrāsāt al-tarbawiyya*). This would include
short passages from the Qur'an that were to be memorized, as well as
commentary on the Qur'an and hadith, and stories from the life of the
Prophet. The Qur'anic commentary was excerpted from Sayyid Qutb's
In the Shade of the Qur'an, which had been the most popular commentary
read by Islamists across the region, while the hadith were from *The Forty
Hadith* (*al-Arba 'in al-Nawawiyya*), drawn from the widely read work of
the jurist Sharaf al-Din al-Nawawi (1234–78). The religious discussions
were broadly linked to contemporary political challenges. One woman,
Fatima, an Arabic teacher who joined the movement in 2011, described
her regular *usra* meetings in a women's group at the al-Nahda regional
office in central Sousse.

The discussions are religious but even on religious subjects we connect them to
political problems. We always try to find a link, for example, between the life of
the Prophet, or verses of the Qur'an, and what is happening in political life ... We
always try to show the Qur'an is not isolated from life but is anchored in life. We
always try to take conclusions, to extract laws and rules, and to make a link
between the past and contemporary life.[15]

The ambition here, driven by the activists from the 1980s, was to return
to a carefully ordered, collective project that encompassed both the
religious and the political in one comprehensive understanding.

In the first months of 2011 there was a rush of young people eager to
join the newly revived al-Nahda. On university campuses across Sousse
those few students who had tried to organize discreetly on an Islamic
platform before the uprising were now suddenly able to gather openly
without fear. They formed the Islamic Youth in the university and in
April 2011 held a small rally in the Faculty of Law in Hai Riadh, with
posters and banners hung from the courtyard walls with such slogans as
'Arab-Islamic Identity', 'Civil State with an Islamic Reference', 'There is
No Glory for Us Except Through Islam', and 'Down with Circular 108',
referring to the ban on the hijab in government institutions dating back to
1981. At this stage the group was still under the strong influence of
experienced al-Nahda activists: a few weeks later Rafik Abdessalem, a
senior al-Nahda exile and son-in-law to Ghannouchi, was invited to the
Faculty of Law to give a talk about democracy.

However, soon the movement began to lose influence over the students as more young people joined, bringing with them different and often Salafist-influenced ambitions. One organizer, Nouri, who had been involved in youth discussions in Sousse before 2011, admitted they soon lost control:

> The idea was to preserve this Islamic phenomenon but there were some difficulties. In some places we couldn't control some of the statements that were attributed to the Islamic Youth in the university because they weren't actually the ideas of the al-Nahda movement. The group had the title 'Islamic' and we soon saw it included Salafists, or members of Hizb al-Tahrir, people who believed that democracy was blasphemy (*kufr*).[16]

The challenge was not in trying to find young people sympathetic to an Islamic cause, but in distinguishing the al-Nahda project from a range of positions extending from reformism to much more hardline interpretations of Islam's role in society. In October 2011, for example, a group of Salafist-influenced students staged a major demonstration at the Faculty of Arts and Humanities in Sousse because a female student had been turned away for wearing a *niqāb*, the full-face veil. It was not organized by al-Nahda and led to a major standoff with the university administration, as well as some minor violence. A similar but more prominent demonstration in favour of the *niqāb* followed in November at the Faculty of Arts and Humanities at La Manouba in Tunis.[17] Nouri and others renamed the student group Al-Nahda Youth in the university in the hope of excluding those with more extreme views.

Tremendous energy and ambition went in to the rebuilding of the movement in the first months of 2011, when it was still unclear what the transition might bring and when there was a real fear of a return of the Democratic Constitutional Rally (RCD) regime. Many of the former activists of the 1980s yearned to revive the al-Nahda they had once known: to rebuild the project of internal educational training and the tightly bonded community. However, the problems encountered early on by the student organizers on university campuses hinted at the substantial challenge that lay ahead.

Fragmenting

In Tunis, al-Nahda's central leaders found themselves drawn into a fast-moving and uncertain political process, where long-term strategic ambition gave way to reactive policymaking. In the first months after the fall of Ben Ali, the newly legalized movement portrayed itself as the primary victim of the former regime. It aligned itself with the populist spirit of the uprising against what it framed as an elite-led transition. Al-Nahda voiced popular demands: the prosecution of security officers responsible for killing demonstrators, the removal of corrupt judges, and a 'final break with the former regime and its choices, symbols and methods'.[18] In late June 2011 it walked out of the 155-member transitional authority, the High Commission for the Realization of the Objectives of the Revolution, the Political Reform, and the Democratic Transition, describing it as an effort by the leftist elite to curtail al-Nahda's political freedoms.[19] In its campaign for the October 2011 elections, the movement did not shy away from its religious character, but presented Islam as a 'supreme centrist reference' (al-Islām bi-i 'tibārhu marji iyya wasaṭiyya 'ulyā).[20]

However, despite winning the elections and taking 89 out of 217 seats in the assembly, al-Nahda soon found itself conceding ground to its critics. Short of an overall majority, the movement went into coalition with two secular, centre-left parties, Marzouki's Congress for the Republic (CPR), to which the Islamists were already close, and Mustapha Ben Jaafar's Ettakatol. The task of the National Constituent Assembly was to draft a new constitution to consolidate newly won political freedoms. Al-Nahda revealed its ambitions early on when it proposed in the spring of 2012 that the shari'a should be 'a fundamental source of legislation' (al-sharī 'a al-islāmiyya maṣdar asāsī min maṣādir al-tashrī ').[21] There was a sharp critical reaction from politicians, civil society leaders, and the media, as well as a long debate inside the movement's own Consultative Council. Ghannouchi was soon forced to announce that al-Nahda would no longer seek inclusion of the shari'a in the constitution because the concept remained 'unclear' for most Tunisians.[22]

Other compromises soon followed. The movement initially proposed that 'attacks on the sacred' should be criminalized, effectively an attempt to outlaw blasphemy. This was included in the closing statement of the movement's July 2012 congress and the following month al-Nahda submitted a draft bill to criminalize blasphemy, proposing a punishment of two years in jail and a large fine. However, during long negotiations in the assembly al-Nahda was forced to drop the idea of criminalization, and to settle instead for the vaguely worded Article 6 of the new constitution, which committed the state merely to 'protect the sacred', without specifying what was held sacred, who might decide this, or what such protection might entail.[23] The movement also acceded to demands from other parties for a semi-presidential system of government, rather than the parliamentary model it had first preferred, and it withdrew a proposal to state explicitly that Islam was the religion of state.

More significant still was the compromise towards the former regime. At its 2012 congress al-Nahda had committed to ban senior RCD figures from political life.[24] However, two years later, in April 2014, the leadership reversed its position. It just managed to convince enough al-Nahda deputies in the assembly to defeat by a single vote a draft article of the new Electoral Law that would have excluded former senior regime figures from contesting elections.[25] These self-limiting concessions were considerable and disproportionate given the size of al-Nahda's electoral victory and the balance of power in the assembly, but they demonstrate the lengths to which the movement had to go to reassure its rivals, a challenge shared by many Islamist movements in the region.[26] The effect of years of hostile media and regime propaganda against the Nahdawis could not be easily undone.

The coup against the Muslim Brotherhood in Egypt in July 2013 intensified pressure on al-Nahda to concede ground, especially after the killing of hundreds of Brothers in Cairo in mid-August. Most of al-Nahda's policy concessions had been made well before the coup, yet the fall of the Brotherhood came as a profound shock. At first al-Nahda strongly resisted efforts by opposition groups to imitate the populist demonstrations in Egypt; Ghannouchi warned against 'anarchist solutions' and 'blackmail'.[27] However, there had now been months of street protests condemning lapses in security following a Salafist attack on the US embassy in September 2012 and the assassination by Salafist cells of two opposition politicians in 2013, Chokri Belaïd, who was shot dead in Tunis on 6 February, and Mohamed Brahmi, who was shot dead on 25 July.[28] Political and media critics accused al-Nahda of being unwilling to confront Salafist violence, a fault that some Nahdawis admitted themselves.[29] The movement leadership was left with little choice but to accept a negotiated exit from office. After months of talks, al-Nahda left government in January 2014 but only after ensuring that the constitution had been formally adopted, fresh elections promised, and a commitment made to keep the Constituent Assembly in place, an assembly in which al-Nahda was still the largest party. The four civil society groups, led by the UGTT, which oversaw this long negotiation to unseat al-Nahda won the Nobel Peace Prize for their 'decisive contribution to the building of a pluralistic democracy'.[30]

The exigencies of holding office, drafting the constitution, and dealing with widespread security and economic anxieties had inevitable repercussions on the deeper structures of the movement. As hard as Nahdawis in the regions worked to rebuild their organization, to restart the *usra* training, and to recruit a new generation, it soon became clear that their primary struggle would be maintaining al-Nahda's structural integrity. This was not the first organizational crisis for the movement. There had been internal differences of opinion in the past, for example, in the late

1970s when the Progressive Islamists split away from the increasingly politicized Islamic Group, or in 1991 when Mourou and others resigned from al-Nahda in protest at its confrontational strategy. However, the struggle to reconcile competing viewpoints after 2011 became the most serious internal conflict in the movement's history.

The most pressing challenge lay with the new generation of supporters and their misunderstanding of or disillusionment with the movement's teachings. Al-Nahda activists in local offices across Sousse tried to organize educational and religious training for their new young members but soon faced conflicts. Hedi, the leader of the Kalaa Kebira bureau, found many new members who either hoped al-Nahda would be a direct replacement to the RCD clientalist party machine and that membership would bring them personal advancement and influence in the community, or, alternatively, hoped that al-Nahda was intent on Islamizing the Tunisian state to a much greater degree than it admitted in public. It was disconcerting to find both ambitions meeting in one organization, particularly those with more hardline religious beliefs.

Some religious young people came on the basis that the movement was Islamic and so they should support it . . . But they were looking for an extremist religious movement and they didn't find it. There was a shock (*rajja*) and many of them began to accuse the movement of not being Islamist at all but secular.[31]

Hedi considered this a failure on the part of al-Nahda, which, under pressure to defend itself in the face of successive national political crises, had not pursued its internal educational programme for new recruits as carefully as intended.

We should have paid specific attention to them because they were not brought up inside the movement. They felt they should be in the movement but they couldn't find how to do that, and the movement didn't give them enough time to adapt and make them understand they should go through stages until they found their real place.

Soon the demands of being in government began to overwhelm internal training. To movement outsiders al-Nahda had to emphasize its democratic credentials. To insiders it had to stress a continued connection with the Islamic reference while competing with the growing ideological appeal of the Islamic State in Iraq and Syria (ISIS), which in Ghannouchi's view had 'disfigured' political Islam.[32]

Not only did local offices run their programmes of education and 'cultivation', but al-Nahda also ran national workshops to explain to the new membership the history of the movement and the nature of its project, and to defend the growing number of concessions it was making at the political level. One of the students at the Faculty of Law who joined al-Nahda in 2011 and became an organizer within the movement in Sousse, spent six days at a training conference in Tataouine in 2012 with around 300 others. There were classes about the history of al-Nahda, and its intellectual vision, as well as debates about the role of the shariʿa, interspersed with group prayer sessions and religious discussions. He, like many others, had believed that the shariʿa should be a source of law, but he now argued that al-Nahda should wait until there was less resistance to the movement from within the government administration.

In any state when the executive authority takes a decision and has no structure to influence that project, it can't apply it. If we decided to apply the shariʿa we would be in confrontation with the whole apparatus of the state: judicial, executive, legislative. We'd find not one Islamist. As al-Nahda we have our project, but we don't have the apparatus to apply it.[33]

His objection was pragmatic, not intellectual: at present there were simply too many obstacles preventing proper application of the shariʿa. Other young members absorbed different elements of the official discourse from the workshops. One female student, aged 24, from Hammam Sousse, who ran the youth section of her local al-Nahda office, had attended several workshops at which there were long debates over policy.

Many young people demanded that this term 'shariʿa' should be in the constitution as a source of legislation. Some students had different ideas and argued that the shariʿa alone is not Islam, but that Islam is bigger and more important than the shariʿa. We say there are a minimum of principles that must be present in society first.[34]

Her argument was intellectual: only in a truly just society with neither poverty nor inequality could the shariʿa properly be applied. Such comments indicated the reach of the movement's internal diffusion of its new policy positions. Yet loyal youth activists like these were few in number. Both they and the older generation of Nahdawis frequently admitted the challenge they faced in retaining young supporters. Many new arrivals walked away rather than accept the al-Nahda project. The movement was ageing. Young Tunisians were less and less drawn to the movement as it shed its subcultural activism in favour of a new political formation.

Al-Nahda fragmented not just among its young members. Several activists who had played prominent roles within the movement since its earliest years chose not to rejoin when al-Nahda was formally legalized in March 2011. In their words, they remained believers in the Islamic project and supportive of al-Nahda but from a position outside the movement. This demobilization affected those who had been most involved in working in alliance with other political movements, or in civil society or human rights organizations and who were influenced by a human rights discourse and a more inclusive, cross-party societal project. The process fits patterns observed elsewhere, in which collective action operates in cycles of mobilization and demobilization, which can mean activists dispersing from a movement, being drawn into organized polit- ical institutions, or finding new avenues of activism framed by different agendas.[35]

Tahar, the lawyer and former Nahdawi who had taken part in the 18 October Collective of 2005, was one of those who chose not to rejoin al-Nahda. Instead he invested his energy in establishing a local cultural heritage organization, which was open to Tunisians of all political backgrounds.

I work more freely in an association than in the party. All the rules in the party limit your situation and you end up opposing or confronting other parties. That's political life but we're not used to it and we need to learn the way of accepting others. I respect al-Nahda and at heart I'm with them but I'm not a member. I prefer to be able to speak freely with others.[36]

Others who took a similar path after 2011 included Yahya, who had been one of the earliest preachers in the movement in the 1970s and who, after four years in prison, went on to work in Amnesty International and in the Progressive Democratic Party (PDP) in the 2000s. He ran, unsuccess- fully, on an independent list in Sousse in the October 2011 elections, and though he remained close to the Nahdawi community he did not rejoin the movement. One of his close friends, Abdedayem Noumi, who had been involved in religious training in the late 1970s in Sousse and who then also became involved in civil society work, had also decided not to return to the movement and was particularly aware of the incongruity between his new work and his former al-Nahda identity.

My work now is in civil society and I want to be seen to be independent. I want to be able to criticize anyone in a fair way and I couldn't do that if I was a member of al-Nahda. My work includes inspecting prison conditions and meeting prisoners, some of whom al-Nahda wouldn't approve of, like former members of the RCD [Democratic Constitutional Rally] or homosexuals or Femen activists.[37] I couldn't imagine al-Nahda accepting that. But I put human rights first and in that sense my ideas have evolved more than al-Nahda's. The Qur'an says that all sons of Adam are created equal: there is an Islamic idea of liberty. But most in al-Nahda don't understand this even though this is the real culture of Islam. Religion brings us to the real sense of being brothers with all, having equal respect for all, including non-Muslims.[38]

He had absorbed new priorities of rights and liberties that he felt his fellow Nahdawis had not yet embraced, though he was careful to continue to present his views within an Islamic framework. Such individuals demobil- ized from a network of Islamists into a very different network of civil society activists, drawing from a new global discourse of human rights and advocating certain values or cultural systems rather than specific political programmes. Their experience of cooperation in the 2000s with activists outside the al-Nahda community so deeply affected their sense of purpose that they repositioned themselves in networks traditionally dominated by the secular left in Tunisia. Yet, demobilization was not absolute. They maintained a familial relationship with al-Nahda as well as rearticulating the inspiration they drew from the Islamic tradition.

Al-Nahda suffered political defections. Most prominent among those who left was Hamadi Jebali, the Sousse leader who was prime minister between December 2011 and February 2013. After his public proposal for a technocratic national unity government was rejected by the al-Nahda leadership, he resigned as prime minister. He gradually distanced himself from the movement before leaving in December 2014, in frustration at its decision not to put up a candidate for the presidential election. In a remarkably frank statement, Jebali warned that the al-Nahda project was facing 'serious challenges' and was losing sight of the goals of the revolution, risking a return to a 'system of tyranny and corruption':

I promised myself that I would be among the victorious fighters for the gradual, peaceful approach of the revolution so as to avert a catastrophe for our people, our region, our nation, and indeed the whole world ... I find it very difficult to meet this goal today while remaining loyal to the framework of the organization of the al-Nahda movement.[39]

Another who left was Riadh Chaibi, a former Consultative Council member who resigned in mid-2013, saying that al-Nahda was more interested in power struggles than in achieving the call for social justice that was behind the uprising.[40] There were similar departures at the local level. Fattouma Attia, elected in 2011 as one of four al-Nahda deputies from Sousse, resigned from the movement in early 2013 and later joined a secular party, Afek Tounes. Others rebelled within the movement. Despite the many workshops to justify postponing implementation of the shari'a, 21 of al-Nahda's 89 originally elected deputies in the Constituent Assembly voted for a failed amendment in January 2014 that would have made the Qur'an and the Sunna principal sources of legislation in the new constitution.[41] The same day, 17 al-Nahda deputies voted for another amendment that if successful would have removed the state's protection of freedom of conscience.[42] In April 2014, as many as 39 al-Nahda deputies defied the leadership by voting with other opposition politicians to try to exclude former regime officials from political life.[43]

Of course, the new opportunities and challenges presented by the uprising brought difficulties to most political parties. Many suffered internal crises even more damaging than those facing al-Nahda. Some of the old political forces almost entirely petered out. The PDP, once the most significant opposition force in the Ben Ali years, won only 16 seats nationwide in the 2011 elections and just one in 2014, when it ran under a new name as the Republican Party (al-Jumhuri). The CPR and Etta-katol suffered many defections and a collapse in popular support. The CPR won 29 seats in 2011 but just four in 2014; Ettakatol won 20 seats in 2011 and none at all in 2014. New parties also struggled. Nidaa Tounes (the Call of Tunisia), the anti-Islamist party established in 2012 to challenge al-Nahda and which won both the legislative and presidential elections in 2014, suffered a deep structural split in 2015 trig-gered by an internal power struggle.

Beyond the political disagreements that had become typical of all major parties in the years after the uprising, al-Nahda struggled with its own internal fragmentation. This was not simply a disagreement over political strategy or the choice of individual candidates for office, but evidence of a profound structural and intellectual debate within a move-ment trying to adapt itself to the new demands of post-2011 Tunisia. Nowhere was this more apparent than in the October 2014 legislative election campaign.

On the Campaign Trail

Al-Nahda's election campaign in Sousse revealed the movement's efforts to reframe its narrative. It drew ambiguously from its Islamic heritage while also offering technocratic solutions to contemporary social and economic challenges. These directions issued by the central leadership were adapted and reshaped by local activists, who felt constrained by the consensus-seeking caution of their leaders.

Al-Nahda had performed well in the first elections in October 2011. Nationwide the movement won 37 per cent of the vote and eighty-nine Constituent Assembly seats, each allocated by proportional representa-tion through closed lists in multi-member districts. Al-Nahda achieved its strongest results in the rural, socially conservative southern governor-ates of Tataouine, Gabes, Medenine, and Tozeur. But it also won more than 40 per cent of the vote in some heavily urban areas: northern Tunis, northern Sfax, and in Ben Arous, near Tunis. In Sousse, the results broadly reflected the national trend: the movement won 34 per cent of the vote and took four of the ten seats on offer. It won in fifteen of the sixteen electoral districts in the governorate, doing well in a mix of settings including: M'saken, a small religious town to the south of Sousse; Hai Riadh, the lower middle-class suburb in the university district; Kondar, a thinly populated rural area; and Sidi Abdelhamid, an industrial zone on the city's southern edge. Only in Hammam Sousse, the wealthy home of Ben Ali, did al-Nahda come second, behind the National Destourian Initiative, a party led by Ben Ali's former defence minister Kamel Morjane. Four Nahdawis from Sousse were elected to the assembly: Hamadi Jebali, head of the Sousse list and the candidate chosen as prime minister; Monia Ibrahim, the long-time activist and wife of Abdelhamid Jelassi; Zied Ladhari, a young lawyer born in 1975 who had spent a decade in exile in France; and Fattouma Attia, the business-woman who later resigned in 2014. A fifth Nahdawi, Kamel Ben Romd-hane, a former political prisoner from Kalaa Kebira, replaced Jebali in the assembly after he was made prime minister in December 2011.

Three years later, ahead of the second general elections on 26 October 2014, al-Nahda was in a much less favourable position. Not only had it been forced out of government but it had faced frequent criticism in the media for the slow pace of economic recovery. It was now challenged by a more united opposition, in the shape of Nidaa Tounes, led by the veteran former interior minister Beji Caid Essebsi, who had grouped together former regime figures, leftists, and trade unionists in an anti-Islamist alliance. Even before the ballot, al-Nahda campaign organizers in Sousse feared a 'punishment vote' against them from poorer communities who still felt economically marginalized.[44] Al-Nahda's private polling identi-fied Nidaa Tounes as the main rival in Sousse, yet because there was so much infighting within Nidaa, including the resignation of the party's Sousse regional coordinator in December 2013, al-Nahda activists believed they faced a poorly organized opponent weakened by personality clashes and lacking grassroots depth.[45]

When al-Nahda chose candidates across Tunisia for the 2014 legisla-tive elections it tried to broaden its appeal, selecting businessmen and individuals who might attract 'modernist' voters.[46] In the Sfax 2 con-stituency, for example, the al-Nahda list was led by Mohamed Frikha, an entrepreneur who had launched an airline but had never been an al-Nahda activist. Its rival Nidaa Tounes adopted a similar approach. In Sousse, Nidaa chose candidates who were well-known public personal-ities including Ridha Charfeddine, president of the Étoile Sportive du Sahel football club, Zohra Idriss, a wealthy hotelier, and Faycel Khelifa, the head of the Étoile Sportive handball club.

However, al-Nahda's regional bureau in Sousse took a different approach. It ran a democratic but inward-looking selection process in which local members prioritized popular activists from within the move-ment, rather than those with public standing in the city. Zied Ladhari, the young lawyer elected in 2011 who had been the movement's national spokesman, was picked as head of the list. With him were two women who were prominent within the movement but not well known outside it: Monia Ibrahim, the activist elected in 2011, and Afifa Makhlouf, an activist from a Nahdawi family who had lived in exile in France and who now led the women's section of the movement in Sousse. Also selected was Ajmi Lourimi, the former political prisoner. Other candidates were a lecturer in engineering, a schoolteacher, and two young female students. The candidates were chosen for their 'technical aptitude', said Ladhari.[47]

Movement leaders were careful in the way they framed their narrative, diluting religious references and making a nationalist appeal to a broader range of voters with promises of economic recovery and restored security. The movement's 2014 election manifesto was titled 'Towards a Rising Economy and a Secure Country', addressing the two central issues on which al-Nahda had failed to make much progress while in government. A campaign leaflet handed out at rallies in Sousse, 'The al-Nahda Movement in the Service of Sousse', was even more prosaic in its technocratic ambition. It gave a list of seventeen pledges for local change which addressed a mixed population of city-dwellers, businessmen, and farmers, and included promises to: turn village councils into elected municipal bodies; rehabilitate the tourist sector; revitalize industrial zones; address public transport shortages and traffic jams (a pledge common to several different parties in Sousse); complete a local deepwater port project; turn the city's port into a tourist attraction and move commercial shipping elsewhere; modernize the fishing industry; improve services to farmers; review projects that harmed the environment, including run-off canals leading to the sea; and create a southern entrance to the city. The emphasis was on local, civic projects and there was a determined effort to avoid any issues that were ideologically inflected. This was not a unique approach: the Islamist Party of Justice and Development (PJD) in Morocco had pursued an identical strategy in the elections of November 2011, barely mentioning religion and instead focusing on technical problems of job creation, corruption, and minimum wage increases.[48] This reflected the broader concerns of the voting public. Opinion polling in 2013 by Arab Barometer, for example, showed that in Tunisia, as across the region, citizens' two leading concerns were overwhelmingly the economic situation (poverty, unemployment, price increases) and then financial and administrative corruption, well before concerns about enhancing democracy, achieving stability, or curbing foreign influence.[49]

Strikingly absent in al-Nahda's campaign was any program for a religious reshaping of society. Instead, the religious vocabulary deployed by both al-Nahda and its rival Nidaa Tounes was uncannily similar, suggesting the two were drawing on symbolic markers that were so widely shared they now conferred little in the way of distinct political identity. This was not the straightforward Islamist-secularist polarization it appeared to be. The al-Nahda election pamphlet began with the invocation 'In the name of God, Most Gracious, Most Merciful' and ended with a Qur'anic quotation. Precisely the same format was used in Nidaa Tounes' national manifesto, with the same invocation and another Qur'anic quote to end. Nidaa had taken a Qur'anic phrase as the title of its election manifesto: 'The Accountable Pact' (al-'Ahd al-Mas'ul), a phrase which, ironically, al-Nahda had previously used in its 2011 election manifesto.[50]

The primary difference between the two rivals was that al-Nahda had identified a series of local priorities on which to campaign, whereas Nidaa Tounes' Sousse candidates campaigned almost entirely on national issues: restoring 'respect for the state' (haybat al-dawla), fighting terrorism, and creating jobs. Nidaa preferred less frequent, larger, and more spectacular rallies. For example, in late October 2014 thousands of supporters from the Sousse, Monastir, and Mahdia governorates were bused in for an evening rally at the large Foire Internationale de Sousse, on the outskirts of the city. For several hours before Essebsi took to the stage, organizers played long video sequences showing scenes from Tunisia in the early years of independence, with women dressed in knee-length skirts and their hair uncovered and with long shots idolizing Bourguiba, the independence leader, who was shown being kissed in the street and addressing parliament. Essebsi's efforts to inherit Bourguiba's symbolic resonance were always explicit.[51] At one stage a video montage showed a reanimated bust of Bourguiba pronouncing his endorsement of Essebsi from beyond the grave as the crowd held up lighters as if at a music concert and chanted 'Beji! President!'.

Al-Nahda campaigning was rather different. One afternoon halfway through the election campaign, a group of male and female Nahdawi activists gathered in their office to prepare for a few hours of door-to-door campaigning before sunset prayers. Organizers practised talking points and the group prayed together before leaving the office. One student activist, Qais, aged 21, explained how he was taught to approach voters:

If they ask why there's no shari'a in the constitution you answer that this is the first step, that Tunisia is a Muslim country and that though of course whoever is Islamist wants shari'a, there's a lack of understanding about what it means. If it's a secular young person and he drinks, you say the party program is not to close bars but to convince people by dialogue not to drink.[52]

Out on the streets, in a middle-class district near the al-Ghazali mosque in central Sousse, Qais tried to win over a young voter, dressed in jeans and smoking. He said to him:

Just one simple question: are you with the parties of the former regime? Or are you with the parties of the revolution? Al-Nahda is of the revolution, so at least say you'll vote with the revolution!

Local activists often went well beyond the formal movement narrative, which underlined consensus, cooperation, and national unity, to present al-Nahda instead as defending a revolutionary cause that was now endangered by the return of the former regime to political life, a clear allusion to Nidaa Tounes. It reflected the very real fears of local al-Nahda activists, who were angry about the revival of the former political elite and long delays in the transitional justice process. Their concern was that leftists might ally with Nidaa Tounes and exclude the Islamists from the political process, repeating the history of the early 1990s. Meanwhile, the al-Nahda leadership in Tunis refused to rule out a future coalition government with Nidaa.

On another day a local al-Nahda branch organized a small rally on a patch of barren land in Hai 9 avril, a poor, working-class area of western Sousse. A crowd of a few hundred gathered on plastic chairs before a stage where four candidates sat. Sweets and al-Nahda flags were passed around, and the announcer led the crowd in chanting the movement's slogans, 'The People want al-Nahda Again' (al-sha b yurīd al-Nahda min jadīd) and 'Loving Tunisia is not just words' (maḥabba Tunis mish klām). A day earlier a handful of Nahdawi activists had come to the neighbourhood to hand out leaflets. Blankets hung from balconies airing in the sunshine and a cart passed through collecting some of the many piles of rubbish filling the streets. The Nahdawis were given a difficult reception. One resident asked why so little had been achieved since the uprising, another complained of rising food prices. An al-Nahda voter said her family needed urgent financial support. The Nahdawi activists parried the criticisms, saying the movement had been given little time and had faced much obstruction from the government administration and from striking trade unionists. They offered telephone numbers for charitable associations who might help poorer families.

At the Hai 9 avril rally the next day, Zied Ladhari presented al-Nahda as embodying sincerity, trust, loyalty, and 'love of the poor', while its opponents were merely seeking positions of power and personal interest. He told the crowd:

Our movement stood against oppression, our movement stood against dictatorship and monopolization, and our movement was standing up when no one dared to stand up in that period, and therefore we say today after being liberated from oppression, we must know how to choose well, to choose people to govern us who will help us and stand with us.[53]

What was presented here was an ethical agenda, a claim to a distinct value system which al-Nahda believed set it apart from its competitors. Ladhari and the other candidates positioned themselves as champions of the poor, of families struggling to feed their children, and of marginalized citizens frustrated by poor local services. As Ladhari said:

After we won the battle against oppression we must today win with al-Nahda and with others the battle against deprivation, and we stand with the oppressed and today we stand with the needy, so that Tunisia can be for us all.

Two days later, Afifa Makhlouf addressed a similar rally in Zaouiat Sousse by saying: 'You know who to choose: the one who will work for you, not the one who will exploit you; the one who will raise you up, not the one who will be arrogant towards you'.[54] Only occasionally was this ethical commitment linked explicitly to religion. At a rally in Hammam Sousse, Faouzi al-Mhiri, a schoolteacher and election candidate, told the crowd:

We are going to reform the educational system, consolidate its values, and take it back to the Arab-Islamic authenticity (*aṣāla*), because we believe that Islam with its great values is the real and essential engine of development, and of goodness and prosperity (*al-ṣalāh wa-l-falāh*).[55]

The emphasis was not on establishing an Islamic order, although most al-Nahda activists admitted that remained a long-term ambition, but rather a community built around an 'authentic' identity that had previously been excluded by secularizing post-colonial regimes. It reflected an effort to maintain an Islamic character to the movement's policies, while trying not to deter non-Islamist voters.

However, the dilution of religious references and the promises of economic change failed to capture a broader electorate. In the legislative election of October 2014, al-Nahda won only 26.5 per cent of the vote nationwide and sixty-nine seats in the new Assembly of the Representatives of the People.[56] It lost a third of its votes nationwide compared to three years earlier.[57] Again, al-Nahda's strongest performance was in the rural, socially conservative southern governorates of Tataouine, Medenine, Gabes, and Kebili, but this time it did less well in the urban areas. Nidaa Tounes won 35.8 per cent of the vote overall and eighty-six seats, with its strongest performance in the central and northern urban coastal constituencies: Monastir, southern Tunis, and Nabeul.

In Sousse, al-Nahda fared worse than average, winning just 24.2 per cent of the vote and retaining only three of the governorate's ten seats.[58]

Nidaa Tounes won a dominant 48.9 per cent and five seats in Sousse; it was their fifth best constituency result overall. Al-Nahda's support was down in all the districts of the governorate, but it suffered its biggest drops in urban centres including downtown Sousse, Kalaa Kebira, and Akouda, even though these had long been sites of Islamist activism. The message of 'consensus' and 'stability' resonated much less with the electorate than the movement had hoped. But there was also evidence emerging of broader disillusionment with political institutions. Turnout fell from 49 per cent in 2011 to just 41 per cent in 2014.[59] Procedurally this may not have mattered, but it did mean that election turnout in Tunisia as it established democratic institutions was just as low as in neighbouring countries that were not yet going through the same transition from authoritarianism. There was an unexpected convergence of public apathy. An Arab Barometer opinion poll in 2016 showed how much confidence in Tunisia's public institutions had fallen. Since 2011 the ratio of citizens trusting the government to a great or medium extent had dropped from 62 per cent to 35 per cent, driven by perceived government failures in managing the economy, creating jobs, and tackling inequality and corruption.[60] Confidence in parliament had dropped from 31 per cent in 2013 to 20 per cent. Trust in political parties was at just 12 per cent.

In the movement's carefully organized campaign in Sousse there were already signs of difference with the non-confrontational position of the leadership in Tunis. Local activists saw the return of former regime figures as a personal threat to their community. They framed themselves again as defenders of the revolution, with only brief allusions to their Islamic distinctiveness, and with a manifesto focused on local technical, economic improvements. However, the failure of al-Nahda in government to answer pressing socio-economic demands was out of the control of the local organization and worked against them.

Politicization

Al-Nahda's leaders responded to electoral defeat by becoming more politicized. By politicization I mean the adoption of a set of behaviours, as for example identified by Nathan Brown, which include dedicating resources to elections, forming party-like structures, crafting platforms, appealing to new constituencies, complying with laws, and participating in officially sanctioned institutions and procedures.[61] Politicization also meant drafting ideas and narratives to frame this behavioural shift both internally to members of the movement and externally to the Tunisian public and the international community. What was innovative, and unlike most Islamist experiences elsewhere, was that instead of dividing itself into party and movement, al-Nahda at its congress in May 2016 made a formal break with its religious, cultural, and social activities, and became solely a political party. Religious, cultural, and social activism was to take place separately, not in an al-Nahda movement but in an array of autonomous associations and charities.

The disappointment of defeat for al-Nahda members in the legislative election was compounded by the leadership's decision not to endorse a candidate in the subsequent presidential election, held over two rounds in November and December 2014. It was another act of caution. The movement did not want to repeat the mistakes of the Muslim Brotherhood in Egypt, which had overreached only to be forced out of power by a populist coup and brutally repressed. At first the al-Nahda leadership promised to back a 'consensus' candidate, but soon opted for studied neutrality, in effect choosing not to challenge the candidacy of the favourite, Essebsi, the Nidaa Tounes leader. In frustration, many Nahdawis voted for Moncef Marzouki, the former president and CPR leader who had expressly appealed for their support. In a second-round run-off on 21 December, Essebsi won the presidency with 56 per cent of the vote. Voting patterns showed Marzouki was strongly supported in the poorer, rural south, where al-Nahda support tended to be deepest. Several al-Nahda activists described their backing for Marzouki as a vote of protest against their own leadership. Nabil, a former prisoner from a religious family and now leader of a local al-Nahda bureau in Sousse, said:

It was a reaction from the base against the choices of the leadership and for the policies decided during the campaign. It wasn't about support for Marzouki, it was a message to the leaders of our movement. It was a message guaranteed to be received from the base to the leaders of the movement.[62]

Nabil went on to resign his position as a bureau leader in January 2015, in exasperation at what he saw as a widening gap between the leadership and the Nahdawi base.

A second frustration followed when the movement leadership lobbied hard to be included in the Nidaa Tounes coalition government, eventually securing a minor role, in which Ladhari was made employment minister, and three al-Nahda deputies were given lesser secretary of state posts.[63] Those Nahdawis advocating entry to the coalition argued it was a vital source of security:

Our long-term goal is to normalize our relationship with state and society, but you cannot do this in opposition. We have had a long tradition of confrontation with the state and if we go into opposition in a volatile situation it will degenerate into a new confrontation. That might mean us facing a new repression, or jail, and perhaps a violent response from our young people.[64]

However, many were angered by the decision to ally with a party that had been so overtly hostile to al-Nahda. In Tunis, the most high-profile protest came when Abdelhamid Jelassi briefly stepped down from the Executive Bureau. In Sousse, Nabil, the bureau leader who resigned, said: 'We could have been in opposition and presented a model of a constructive opposition. That would have allowed us to restructure the movement, to rebuild it on a correct basis.'[65] He blamed the decision to ally with Nidaa Tounes on Ghannouchi directly, and compared it to Ghannouchi's decision in late 1987 to accept Ben Ali after his coup against Bourguiba. 'That wasn't the choice of the base at the time and nor was this,' he said. 'There was a choice by the leadership that was different to the choice of the base.'

To match its actions, the movement leadership shifted its narrative frames. Where in the past it had mounted a challenge to the secularizing ambition of the authoritarian regime, now it proposed the movement follow a non-confrontational 'consensus approach' (*manhaj al-tawāfuq*) for the new cause of a successful democratic transition.[66] This was defensive in that it meant prioritizing political alliances in order to share the burden of government and to avoid the risk of marginalization, even repression, if it sat in opposition. But it was also an effort to harness a social consensus. Al-Nahda presented Tunisian society as one homogenous community with one authentic Arab-Islamic identity. It was, in al-Nahda's view, up to the state to act as guardian over this society, constraining individual freedoms so they did not infringe on the collective religious tradition, hence its concern about attacks on 'the sacred'. Popular will was acknowledged as the foundation of legitimacy but this meant that, if correctly educated about their religion, Tunisians would eventually choose for themselves the implementation of shari'a law.[67]

Consensus was not a neutral concept. It had a problematic history in Tunisia, where it had often been used by Ben Ali as a disciplinary technique which demanded a single identification with the nation.[68] For individual Nahdawis it looked as if their movement, by allying with Nidaa Tounes, was now endorsing and enabling power arrangements and dominant values that were little changed from the years of repression. This was a disconcerting realization. As Gudrun Krämer argues, Islamist movements can enjoy the appeal of purity and autonomy from party politics, which is often seen as a distasteful contest for power. However, integration into political life eats away at this appeal: 'It cannot but compromise the uncorrupted.'[69]

Some Nahdawis again felt the movement's most essential work was being overwhelmed by an obsession with political goals. Although Tunisia had experienced a rise in religiosity since the 2000s, many Nahdawis believed the population still had an inadequate understanding of Islam. They cast the priorities of their project in much the same way their predecessors had in the early 1970s, as if proselytizing needed to start afresh. As one experienced female activist in the Hai Riadh bureau said:

The first thing we must do is *da 'wa*. The movement won't succeed unless it has people who are well trained in *da 'wa*, with a strong belief and who are trained and convinced in Islamic thought. That comes before everything else. Then comes politics. And politics is the means not the end (*wasīla mush ghāya*). It's the way we return to our Islam and apply it in this society. Our objective is not to win the presidency or enter government. No. That's just a tool to help us, to give us freedom to work in society, to spread this Islam, and Islam will be applied again in Tunisia. Because in Tunisia we have come very far from Islam.[70]

Her sense was of politics as providing the apparatus for an open competition of ideas, including competition over Islamization. Proselytizing was to be directed at what she perceived to be superficial understandings of the meaning of the hijab, and at the unexpected spread of Salafist movements and the appeal of ISIS. It was a surprisingly proximate challenge. Several mosques in Sousse had been taken over by Salafist preachers since the uprising, despite government attempts to reassert control. Often individual Nahdawis found themselves arguing with their new Salafist preachers. As one activist said:

We abandoned the mosques, and the Salafists came and took the mosques. They spread extremist ideas that we don't adopt. They used violence, excluding people. They don't believe in allowing opposing thoughts ... The problem in al-Nahda is that we let ourselves become too preoccupied with political work.[71]

There was a sense here of an urgent need to face competitive waves of Islamization and a recognition that al-Nahda's dominance as the primary representative of Islam in society was under challenge. Political power, in this alternative reading, was not seen as the objective but rather provided the structure through which the movement could freely pursue its Islamizing mission in a way denied it for decades.

In practice, this meant many in the al-Nahda community wanted to put their effort into projects of social outreach, either through charitable associations, preaching organizations, or Qur'anic study groups. Several religious charities emerged in 2011, originally to help the thousands of Libyans flooding across the Tunisian border to escape armed conflict. This humanitarian work has been seen as the rise of a 'new Islamic social counter-power', which challenged the traditional social bloc linked to the

Bourguibist nationalist elite.[72] Some of these charities overlapped with the al-Nahda community, including, for example, Attaouen (the Association of Cooperation and Social Connection). Attaouen was established in Sousse in 2010 by Nejib Karoui, a doctor who had been an al-Nahda activist even though his father, Hamid Karoui, was a pillar of the ruling party and prime minister in 1989–99. Karoui had been active in the Islamic Tendency Movement (MTI) student group at the Faculty of Medicine in Tunis in the early 1980s and prayed at his local Sousse mosque, al-Ghazali, with activists like Mohamed Chemli and Hamadi Jebali, for whom he worked as an aide until leaving al-Nahda in 1993. Attaouen began in the late 2000s as an informal enterprise 'driven by religious feelings', Karoui said.[73] A small group of likeminded friends cooperated to distribute food and second-hand clothes to poor communities during Ramadan and the Eid holidays. After 2011 the association grew rapidly. Soon, under pressure from media criticism, Karoui had to defend Attaouen's independence and to insist that employees (though not volunteers) could not contest elections or be known as active members of a political party. As he said:

If we become identified politically, then it's no longer charity but working for political gain and the first objective of having God's reward is lost. And if you ask people for charity and you have a political party, they won't give to you.

He was now critical of al-Nahda which he saw still acting with the inward-looking 'mentality of a sect' and failing to open up to external advice and cooperation. Yet, by 2014 Attaouen had scaled back its operations amid increasing media criticism of the motivations of Islamic charitable organizations. 'Charitable work has weakened a lot recently, because they're going after association after association ... It's the demonization of Islamists, the demonization of al-Nahda,' Karoui said. He was not entirely exaggerating. The climate of the Ben Ali era in which Islamist social outreach had been all but impossible was creeping back. In July 2014, the government suspended more than 150 Islamic associations across the country and shut two radio stations, all for alleged links to terrorism.[74] In the context of the Egyptian coup a year earlier, many Islamists felt vulnerable once more.

One Attaouen branch was run out of a small second-floor office in Hai Riadh and was crowded with rails of used clothes, tables piled with old schoolbooks, and bundles of shoes spread across the floor. Here a group of veiled women cleaned the clothes, repaired the books, and distributed them, along with money, to around 140 poor families in the district. Farida, the office organizer and a hospital nurse, had been active within the MTI community in the 1980s. Though she insisted

Attaouen was 'an association, not an Islamic association', she framed
her work in explicitly religious terms:

Political work is for other people. We say our work is dedicated to God. There are
layers in society: poor, rich, and middle class. In the Qur'an it says the richest
must help the poor. Social justice is in the Qur'an and as a Muslim you apply
the Qur'an.[75]

She had faced criticism from her Nahdawi friends for not taking part in
their political work, but after leaving the movement in the 1990s in order
to keep her job she had decided not to return to al-Nahda after 2011.

I devote myself just to this work, even Nahdawis blamed me for this. I told them,
when I was young I lived for the political work and I loved it and devoted much
time to the MTI and to al-Nahda. Then came the break of the 1990s and
I retreated. I kept my job, I couldn't leave my job, and I hadn't studied just to
stay at home ... I like the al-Nahda movement, but I work independently now.
There are no restrictions or conditions.

Again, here was the search for other dimensions to the religious project
beyond the legalistic agenda offered by al-Nahda, with its focus on formal
politics.

Similar concerns about al-Nahda were evident elsewhere. In the
Qur'anic association in Hammam Sousse, established by Chokri in
2005, work had broadened significantly after the uprising. The association soon spread to two different sites, with around 300 students, young
boys and girls and adult men and women, with classes focusing on
Qur'anic memorization, recitation, and studies of Qur'anic commentaries and Islamic belief and jurisprudence. On the walls of the school
rooms were drawings by the children, and posters listing the five pillars of
Islam, the ninety-nine names of God, and details of Arabic grammatical
rules to be memorized. Chokri explained:

We are trying to build a small society within the bigger society. There is a bigger
society that has alcohol, corruption, nightclubs, and drugs, and we are trying to
build a better society within that bigger society. It's the same project as the
1980s.[76]

For Chokri, the urgency of Qur'anic study lay with the problems caused
by years of poor quality teaching from ineffectual state-appointed imams
in the mosques. That had been replaced, he said, by an 'awakening'
(ṣaḥwa) of religiosity to which al-Nahda as a movement had failed to
respond.

We say as ordinary people that al-Nahda is zero. It's not relevant to us in the way
it was before. It's a civil Islamic project, and that means there should be both
change from the top down and from the bottom up ... But al-Nahda is focusing

more on the political issue than the religious issue at the moment, even though it's a religious movement.

Chokri was especially critical of al-Nahda's alliance with Nidaa Tounes at a time when government ministers were again proposing what he described as the 'neutralizing' of mosques (taḥyīd al-masājid) in a way that the Ben Ali regime had done.

The growing unease at the base of the movement revived the idea of separating al-Nahda into a political party and a religious social movement. It was a question referred to internally as 'the ways of conducting the project' (subul taṣarruf al-mashrū') or, informally, 'joining or splitting' (al-waṣl aw al-faṣl). In this way, those who favoured political work could continue along the path of reinventing al-Nahda as a socially conservative political party that would appeal to all Tunisian citizens. Those who preferred a cultural, social, or religious da'wa project could carry out their activism separately, without having to endorse pragmatic political compromises.

The experience of Islamist movements operating in authoritarian or semi-authoritarian settings shows that though they had eager political ambitions, they were cautious about taking part in a constrained political process. If winning an election was not a realistic outcome, then the rewards of politics were limited. This explains why in a semi-authoritarian context, in which elections might be held but are not fair, Islamist movements invest only cautiously in politics and, as Brown argues, leave themselves 'lines of retreat' to protect their social movements.[77] Islamists followed the approach of 'participation not domination' (mushāraka lā mughāliba), curbing their ambitions at the ballot box to avoid repression, as, for example, in Morocco in 2002 and Egypt before 2011.[78] Other non-Islamist opposition parties developed a similar risk-averse strategy. Given this prudence, we might reasonably expect such caution to persist well into a transition away from authoritarian rule, especially after the brutal repression of the Muslim Brotherhood in Egypt following the 2013 coup. Transitions are inherently unpredictable and often lead not to consolidated democracies but to a 'political gray zone' characterized by 'serious democratic deficits'.[79] A movement structure would therefore continue to offer Islamists a source of shelter and resilience in the uncertainty of a transitional period. Leaders might also struggle to convert a religious social movement, which is forged around personal networks and a collective identity, into a political party, which is open to an array of new members and likely to face the need for pragmatism. We might expect, too, that an election defeat would reinforce for Islamists a wariness of irreversible politicization and that, based on experiences elsewhere, successive defeats might even begin to erode their confidence in the political system.[80]

The case of al-Nahda, however, suggests an alternative theory. During an uncertain transition away from authoritarianism, Islamists can make a deep commitment to politicization if they perceive benefits of legitimacy and security and in order to avoid being marginalized. But this strategy reduces the scale of the original Islamist project and leaves it open to being outflanked by innovative and radical Islamic social movements. Here was an Islamist organization pursuing a costly politicization, which left no 'lines of retreat' to the original social movement.

For al-Nahda this was an easier step to take because its social welfare project was comparatively underdeveloped. Islamist movements are often assumed to have deep social outreach programmes, built on the model of the Egyptian Muslim Brotherhood, with its extensive network of schools, medical clinics, and other social services which have important mobilizing potential.[81] But al-Nahda had a much less significant organized welfare operation, because of the brutal repression of the Ben Ali era and new pressures on religious charitable work in the post-2011 environment. In the transitional period, there were small charity operations, religious study groups, and at least one major da'wa association, all of which had al-Nahda connections, but none of this was yet on the scale usually associated with Islamist movements.[82] This difference helps explain why the movement ultimately chose to reshape itself as a political party. Since it did not have an extensive, historic social welfare operation it had less to lose in opting for politicization. It was comparatively easier for the movement's leaders to focus their energies on formal political work.

There was no clear short-term gain to politicization, given that the 2014 election defeat illustrated the costs of holding office early in a transition. Yet al-Nahda made the case to itself on several fronts. Primarily, it sought broader legitimacy. The movement argued that it had failed to distinguish itself sufficiently in the eyes of the general public from the often-violent Salafist movements which had surged in support after 2011. This was compounded by a popular sense, expressed during weeks of protests in mid-2013, that al-Nahda in government had been either too lax towards the Salafists, or was in some unproven way complicit in their violence. In addition, al-Nahda argued that by presenting itself as Islamist, it implied an unimpeachable integrity of behaviour which no political organization could uphold. It created unrealistic expectations. 'The population expects you to be a saint and to behave without any fault otherwise they will say that you are not proper Islamists, or that Islam is to blame,' as one Nahdawi said.[83] Participation also offered the best source of shelter from the risk of future repression in a still-unconsolidated democracy. Being a formal political actor provided the resources to negotiate with political opponents to avoid isolation, and also to be seen in public to be acting in a professional, law-abiding capacity. This became more important as regional dynamics turned against the Islamists, with the repression of the Brotherhood in Egypt, the growing influence of the conservative United Arab Emirates, and the decline of Qatar, once a key supporter of Islamists in the region. There was also a risk of marginalization in staying outside the political process, which would mean not only an inability to shape legal reforms but the danger of retreat into damaging polarization and, at worst, a return to repression and social exclusion. This risk of marginalization had been similarly identified by Islamist parties in Jordan and Kuwait which had returned to participation in recent years after repeated election boycotts.[84]

However, the strategy of politicization brought new costs. The ground rules for the precise relationship between the party and the religious and cultural activism of its members had yet to be determined. Party officials were no longer allowed to preach in mosques or take leadership positions in religious or charitable associations, though this was yet to be put into practice.[85] Policy decisions had to be taken more quickly because of pressure to respond to new draft bills placed before parliament, including in 2015 an anti-terrorism bill and a bill to amnesty those accused of corruption under the former regime. The new politicization also raised deeper questions.

First, the movement had still to convince the rest of the Tunisian political elite that it was sincere in its strategic adaptation. An earlier plan to divide al-Nahda into a political party and a separate religious movement was shelved, for fear that the public would not believe there had been fundamental change. Al-Nahda was still commonly portrayed as a theocratic threat by its opponents on the left, and criticized by youth activists who had been involved in the uprising for compromising on questions of transitional justice in its consensus-led cooperation with Nidaa Tounes. Politicization did not immediately resolve either of these problems. Instead, it positioned al-Nahda as a conservative force that was ready to make significant concessions to protect the political and business elite. In September 2017 the al-Nahda leadership in parliament supported the return of three former RCD ministers into the cabinet in key positions, and then voted in favour of Essebsi's 'administrative reconciliation' bill to allow public officials and 'others like them' accused of corruption under the former regime to repay stolen money and avoid prosecution.[86] In so doing, al-Nahda introduced a conservative bias into the transition, which held back sweeping redistributive economic reforms and delayed and diluted the parallel transitional justice process.

Second, there were differences of opinion within the membership about politicization. The movement's original intellectual vision was deeply embedded, and not easily discarded. Some feared that separating political work from religious, social, and cultural activism would undermine their concept of the completeness of the Muslim character and might lead to a form of schizophrenia (*infiṣām*). As Youssef, a local bureau leader in Sousse, said:

> The problem is it's a functional separation, but not an intellectual one. The separation can't be intellectual unless we fall into the problem of asking ourselves when are we doing politics and when are we doing *da'wa*. That's why I'm not totally with the idea of separation, because it's a negative idea and it will result in a split character.[87]

Dividing the two implied a failure of the original project, even if the actual relationship between the political and religious missions was never as harmonious as imagined. However, even anxious Nahdawis like Youssef could not deny the urgency of the debate. 'There's a metamorphosis inside the party and we must face it,' he said. 'There is an essential, profound change inside the party.' The movement's original ideology was flexible and adaptable, but not endlessly so. For al-Nahda the principle of the 'comprehensive conception of Islam' (*al-taṣawwur al-shumūlī li-l-islām*), which combined the political and religious in one vision, had been fundamental since the earliest years and was hard to shed.[88]

Third, al-Nahda had still to fashion an intellectual justification for its new identity as a political party. Those favouring politicization argued that since al-Nahda was no longer a movement of underground resistance it needed to present itself as a modern, technocratic political party with policies that appealed to voters well beyond the Islamist core. The project would be secularized to the extent that Islam would be no longer a totalizing principle but instead a moral guide. The movement would not seek, for now at least, to implement shari'a as a strict code of law, but rather to pursue the broader objectives of the shari'a (*maqāṣid al-shari'a*), such as freedom, rights, civility, and equality, a reformist, non-legalistic reading which drew on the earlier work of the Tunisian theologian Mohamed Tahar Ben Achour.[89] Ghannouchi's own philosophical innovation on this, as explained in his much earlier work *Public Liberties in the Islamic State*, was to provide for popular participation in determining what in the shari'a was timeless and fixed and what was open to reinterpretation in changing contexts.[90] Shari'a as a source of legitimacy was unquestionable. However, the comprehension and interpretation of divine principles, *ijtihād*, was not the sole preserve of an individual or an institution but was subject to approval by the community.[91] In Andrew March's words, it was for the people collectively 'to be the decider of how God's sovereignty is brought into the world'.[92]

The accompanying semantic shift from 'Islamists' to 'Muslim democrats' was an attempt to allay criticism by again inviting parallels with Christian Democratic parties in Western Europe.[93] It was an odd comparison to make because it presaged a radical contraction in the scale of al-Nahda's ambition. Christian Democracy had emerged from a societal subcultural movement not unlike that of the early Tunisian Islamist movement. Catholic associations were formed in late nineteenth-century Europe in response to Liberal anticlerical attacks as 'a utopian project of a counterculture and a counter-society hostile to and separate from the Liberal state and society'.[94] In late nineteenth-century Germany, for example, this counterculture involved Catholic charitable associations, workers' associations, annual 'Catholic Day' rallies, and, from the 1890s, trade unions.[95] Once opposed to liberal democracy, these Catholic movements eventually produced political parties which came to play a dominant role in European politics even as their societies became less and less religiously observant. These parties became not only more politicized than the church had first proposed, but also more secularized. They have survived into the present, with great electoral success in Germany in particular, but they are no longer attached to their social movements, nor do their original conservative Christian social values resonate in society as they once did.[96] Al-Nahda's leaders may have been attracted by Christian Democracy's longevity and political successes, but the model it offered was in fact far more secular than the Tunisian movement was yet prepared to countenance for itself.

Al-Nahda's new intellectual justification was not just about diluting the religious ambition of the movement. There was also an effort, however awkward, to synthesize liberal freedoms into the political project in a way that went beyond Islamist movements elsewhere in the region. Al-Nahda endorsed the new constitution, with its many progressive elements, including an array of individual rights as well as the rare protection of freedom of conscience. This was evidence of an emerging if uncertain post-Islamist turn, defined by Bayat as a conceptual reimagining of Islamism to embrace rights rather than duties, plural voices of authority, historicity rather than textual literalness, and individual choice and freedom. He conceives of post-Islamism as 'an endeavor to fuse religiosity and rights, faith and freedom, Islam and liberty'.[97] However, al-Nahda also remained a socially conservative political party, which stood for identity, traditions, and culture, and which placed the family, not the individual, as the most important unit in society. In practice, the articulation of this new project was often rather more prosaic than the post-Islamist ambition implied. Al-Nahda sought to reposition itself as a technocratic provider of solutions in what it saw as a post-ideological age. It was a distinct reorientation of the way the movement framed contention, away from questions of injustice, oppression, and class struggle, as articulated in the MTI's original 1981 manifesto, towards a technocratic politics of consensus. Though al-Nahda's technocratic politics was presented as non-ideological, it had at its heart distinct neoliberal tendencies, with a vision of a light-touch, non-interventionist state and an eagerness to appeal to international financial institutions, which required the conditionalities of austerity, including reductions in subsidies, slimming of the public sector, privatizations, and steps to increase foreign investment.[98] The more the coalition government formed after the 2014 elections pursued these neoliberal economic policies, relying on International Monetary Fund (IMF) loans, cutting subsidies, and raising consumption taxes, the more protest returned to the streets of Tunisia, with hundreds of demonstrations a month recorded nationwide.[99] Ghannouchi now spoke of Islamism as 'correcting its mistakes and preparing for an imminent new phase of better governance'.[100] This new phase was beyond ideology, in his view, because questions of Islamization or secularization of society were no longer relevant. Although al-Nahda would continue to be 'inspired' by the principles of Islam, Ghannouchi said, now it would 'seek to create solutions to the day-to-day problems that Tunisians face rather than preach about the hereafter'.[101] Where there had once been a transcendent comprehensive vision, now the new ideology was a worldly problem-solving technocracy.

*

A focus on the compromises made by the al-Nahda leadership in the months and years after the 2011 uprising has tended to miss the internal dynamics within a movement struggling to rebuild itself and to redefine its project. The evidence from the al-Nahda community in Sousse reveals not only the rapid rebuilding of the movement in the image of the MTI in the 1980s, but also the fragmentation and demobilization of a social movement abruptly shifting from opposition to running a government at a moment of great change. Shadi Hamid argues that Islamist parties elsewhere in the region, at least in authoritarian contexts, have prioritized their large charitable, educational, and preaching activities over electoral success: they 'historically privileged self-preservation over political contestation'.[102] Yet in the transitional context of Tunisia, al-Nahda did the opposite. Here was a movement with much less developed charitable, educational, and preaching arms than other Islamist organizations, and which privileged political contestation over a revival of its *da'wa* operations. It did this in search of legitimacy and security and to avoid marginalization and a return to repression. The structural impact of this decision was to reduce the organization to a political party which was separate from religious, social, and cultural work. But this had an intellectual impact too, forcing individual Nahdawis to reassess what they understood of the movement and their role within it.

Al-Nahda was trying, however inconclusively, to marry the Islamizing ideals of the movement with the ambition for freedom and the complex demands of the new political realities. Such intellectual shifts were in evidence during previous periods of adaptation, and, of course, this adaptation was by no means unique to the Islamists but typical of all parties, secular and leftist too, which worked to accommodate new vocabularies of freedom, democracy, citizenship, and human rights. In the end, al-Nahda sought shelter in a post-ideological discourse of consensus and technocracy.

The long-running tension between politics and preaching came to a head soon after al-Nahda transitioned from opposition force to party of government, with all the pragmatism, compromise, and politicking this entailed. The debate over whether to adopt a structural separation is evidence that ideological adaptation and political pragmatism can come at a significant cost. Adapting to changing political opportunities can bring not just advantages, but also the challenge of fragmentation and demobilization. Members of al-Nahda took individual decisions during this period about how they saw the movement and their role in it, and these decisions were shaped by the actions of the leaders, as well as concern over the hostile media battles that the new landscape of Tunisian politics produced. The defining characteristics of the movement in the period after 2011 were less to do with an innovative post-Islamist ideological evolution, but rather problems of internal instability, individual disillusionment, and unexpected confusion about al-Nahda's own identity.

7 Conclusion

This book began with the question of how best to explain the transformation of al-Nahda's Islamist project. An answer lies in exploring the way the movement has mobilized support, the meanings Nahdawis gave to their actions, and why these meanings changed over time. Making lived experiences the central focus of inquiry has revealed overlapping understandings of the movement's priorities. It demonstrates that the relationship between what Nahdawis called their political work and their preaching work has been awkward and contested. This portrait of al-Nahda reflects the experiences of its ordinary members but stands in contrast to the leadership narrative, often reproduced by scholars, in which the movement is primarily engaged in the pursuit of state power.

When the movement emerged in its first formation, as the Islamic Group in the 1970s, it focused on faith, morality, and behaviour as articulated through a project of *da'wa*. It built an imagined solidarity of shared values, reinforced by a network of charismatic individuals who spread their influence through schools, universities, mosques, and local communities. Even as a political project was developed by some in the movement leadership from the early 1980s, this book has shown just how significant the subculture of faith, morality, and behaviour remained at the local level in Sousse. This subculture reinforced the Islamist community and created new expressions of their collective imagined solidarity. It also proved a highly durable resource in the two decades of repression that were to follow in the 1990s and 2000s. Scholars often ascribe the resilience of Islamist movements to their organizational skills, through the grassroots depth of carefully structured movements, or the reputational advantage of charitable social activities, but Nahdawis could not draw on such resources during the years of repression under Ben Ali. Instead, they drew on a shared experience of brutality in prison and their collective efforts to reclaim dignity within the confines of the prison cell. After prison, they relied on their individual understandings of the Islamist project, the network of ties it created, and discrete activism on the periphery of the movement. But this had unanticipated consequences.

It broadened the differences between those who favoured political participation for reform conducted at the state level and those who preferred a
project of reform directed at society at large. In the years since 2011 these
differences expanded so much that by 2016 al-Nahda felt compelled to
separate its political project, the party, away from its religious, social,
and cultural project. This 'functional specialization', as the movement's
leadership described it, was a strategy to provide legitimacy and security
and to avoid marginalization during the transitional period. But it also
signalled an intellectual crisis, a profound difference of views over what it
meant to be Islamist in the newly democratizing Tunisia. The apparent
ease with which the decision to separate passed at the May 2016 congress,
with 80 per cent of delegate votes, belied tensions, debates, and ambiguities reaching back many years.[1]

At a time when discussions of contemporary Islamist movements too
often slide back into reductive debates about the compatibility of Islam
and democracy, the evidence from the Nahdawis studied in these pages
casts new light on the internal tensions at the heart of the Islamist project.
I am not arguing that there is an inherent pathology within Islamism, nor
that Islamism itself has finally 'failed'. Instead, I consider Islamist movements like al-Nahda to be highly adaptive to their changing environment.
For al-Nahda those adaptations resulted from, and in turn inspired,
competing narratives of meaning within the movement. This narrative
competition produced phases of fragmentation, strategic change, and
intellectual rethinking so that the project was constantly updated. Which
came first: strategic adaptation or intellectual revision? At times strategic
adaptation went hand-in-hand with intellectual revision, as during the
1980s when the movement accepted democratic norms as it pursued
inclusion within the political process. At other times, intellectual rethinking preceded strategic change, as during the years of repression when the
movement acknowledged the cost of its political ambition before it began
to ally with other opposition parties. But since 2011, with a fast-paced
transition away from authoritarianism, strategic pragmatic behaviour has
come before intellectual revision. The religious movement has become
politicized for practical reasons: for legitimacy and security and to avoid
marginalization. The intellectual justification for this strategic shift is still
being written, which is why the movement's ideologues so often explain
their new strategy in the risk-averse lexicon of technocracy.

Most previous studies of the al-Nahda movement and its forerunners,
the Islamic Group, and the Islamic Tendency Movement (MTI), have
focused on elite-level bargaining and confrontation between the movement's leaders and the regime. These leaders are seen as either promot-
ing a cultural challenge to post-independence secularizing regimes or

reacting to the failure of regime-led modernization. Their goal is portrayed as the capture of state power through a political project. However, the evidence from this detailed local study identifies as the primary mechanism of mobilization an innovative project to transform daily practices and understandings of faith, and to build a new identity. It was about ideas, not interests. Individuals were not drawn in by personal calculations about the benefits that might accrue by joining a political movement targeting state power, for Islamists were consistently excluded from the political process and targeted for their activism. Instead, men and women were attracted to the transcendental idea that through correct belief, behaviour, and morality their lives and their society might be transformed. This idea was reinforced through informal but robust networks. Certainly, state-level political ambitions were an element of the overall project for some, but it was the ambition for societal change that drove the movement at the local level. This understanding of the Islamist project aligns with those who seek out the often less visible, daily lived practice of religious faith in other contexts, what has been described elsewhere as 'silent movement work on everyday practices'.[2]

This silent work began with mosque discussion circles but quickly spread to study groups, sports events, and a focus on morality and ethical behaviour to remedy what activists perceived to be a spiritual vacuum in society. In later years these practices crystallized into a distinct subculture that forged new patterns of marriage, music, and prayer, and in which individuals gave each other financial and practical assistance even as they found themselves straining relations with their own families. The era of repression under the Ben Ali regime in the 1990s and the 2000s dismantled the subcultural community, but it reinforced a sense of the moral and ethical project because this was the only remaining outlet for Islamist expression. Nahdawis reimagined the project as individuals and sought sanctuary in morality and correct comportment in line with religious commitments like prayer and fasting. This is why Youssef, the former prisoner from Hammam Sousse, described Nahdawis as 'living Islam in our daily lives', and why Nabil, the ex-prisoner and former bureau leader from Sousse, talked of drawing on their 'stock' of religious morals. After the 2011 uprising, there was a concerted attempt to recreate the process of cultivation, education, and training that had existed in the 1980s before the crackdown, but these efforts were swamped by the challenges the movement faced as it took part in the formal political process for the first time, winning and then relinquishing political power.

We can think of the way social movements make meanings through three broad mechanisms. They frame contentious politics by creating an interpretative scheme of the outside world for their followers. They construct collective identities, which includes setting boundaries between 'us' and 'them'. They reflect, capture, and shape emotions.[3] Certainly, al-Nahda drew on all three of these mechanisms, but it also shaped a particular pattern of behaviour, forged by shared practices of faith and morality. This notion of daily practice is particularly relevant in the case of Islamist or piety movements but remains understated in the social movement literature.[4] The most important way in which the al-Nahda movement and its forerunners forged their collective project was through an idealized understanding of correct behaviour drawing on a renewed attention to faith and prayer. Religious faith, in other words, played a central, ideational role. This, in turn, contributed to framing the competition for an 'authentic' Arab-Islamic identity against secularizing authoritarian regimes, or to constructing a collective identity in a subcultural community, or to shaping emotions of commitment, fellowship, defiance, and the self-purification of starting life anew. However, it was the daily practices that came first.

Al-Nahda's work on societal transformation was different to the formal political project but it was not apolitical. Through daily practices it challenged prevailing norms of behaviour, ritual, and dress. Changing daily behaviour was part of a broader political struggle in a context in which the state constantly intervened and regulated social and religious norms. After 2011, Nahdawis frequently remarked how their society had grown more religious, how contemporary wedding ceremonies often resembled the 'Islamic' marriages they had first introduced four decades earlier, and how the preamble of the 2014 constitution made explicit reference for the first time to the 'teachings of Islam' and 'our Arab-Islamic identity'. This is not to ascribe these changes solely to al-Nahda's societal project, for there are many other reasons that explain public religiosity in contemporary Tunisian society. Instead, it is to demonstrate that the movement saw itself as locked in an ongoing competition to transform society. In part, this was a competition with the state, because both the Bourguiba and Ben Ali regimes appropriated religious institutions and discourse, claiming the sole right to interpret Islam in an effort to monopolize religious symbolism. When Bourguiba intervened in 1981 to try to enforce the Ramadan fast by closing cafes, this was in competition with the newly emerging Islamist trend. When Ben Ali made his superficial changes after the coup, returning some autonomy to the Zaytuna mosque-university and allowing state radio and television to broadcast the call to prayer, this too was in competition with the Islamist movement. This competition also explains the often highly polarized debates between Islamists and secularists in the post-2011 transition. As Malika Zeghal argues, these debates were not about what form the new state structure should take, since all agreed on a republican electoral democracy. Instead they were about 'ways of life' and Tunisians' different concepts of freedom, belief, and conduct.[5] When these debates were engulfed by questions of identity, it was not some superficial distraction from more tangible political questions but rather the continuation of long-running symbolic competition. For, as Sami Zemni writes, these 'symbolic discussions are political battles over historical memory'.[6]

This chapter highlights the prominent themes that emerge from this research and demonstrates how they explain the transformations of al-Nahda. First, it looks at how other Islamist movements in the region have dealt with similar structural changes and what lessons they might offer for al-Nahda's future.

Islamist Lessons

Although it may be tempting to see the experience of al-Nahda as a rather particular case which seems to lie outside universalist theories of Islamism, I do not find this helpful. What has struck me throughout is how comparable are the transformations experienced by al-Nahda and other Islamist movements in the region. These movements all drew on the same literature and organizational strategies of the Egyptian Muslim Brotherhood and engaged in similar social and political struggles against semi-authoritarian regimes. All have tackled questions over the definition and role of the shari'a, the articulation of an Islamist vision, the development of a subculture, and the organizational balance between religious movement and political party. Like al-Nahda, many Islamist movements also survived episodes of severe regime repression, including in Syria, Egypt, Jordan, and the Gulf. Even the more recent problematic of naming, whether these movements should identify themselves as Islamist, or as a civil party with an Islamic reference, or as Muslim democrats, is a common challenge shared across the region. All Islamist movements observe each other's experiences; many read and follow the work of Ghannouchi, and in turn al-Nahda has sought advice from Islamists outside Tunisia.[7]

Islamist movements confront challenges faced by all political parties, whether religious or not. In semi-authoritarian systems Islamists are often considered to enjoy political advantages over other opposition forces, whether through the provision of social services, organizational capacity, ideological hegemony, or a reputation for good governance.[8] In the context of a transition, however, Islamist movements find themselves subject to the familiar contingencies of party competition and the shifting loyalties of the electorate. For example, parties that win founding elections in transitions rarely gain a second consecutive term, as al-Nahda found to its cost in October 2014.[9] Islamists are just as likely as any other party to fail to meet the heightened expectations typical of a new political opening or to fall short in fulfilling their campaign promises.[10] In founding elections Islamists can use their deep connections with voters to convince them they will pursue economic policies on behalf of the poor, but, as Tarek Masoud argues, over time other parties will take advantage of new open media access to diminish the Islamist informational advantage.[11] Islamist electoral advantage is therefore likely to be limited to the founding election as they find that the ideological hegemony they once enjoyed weakens in the face of newly energized political debate. The impact of social welfare provision on voter preferences may not be very pronounced, as we saw with al-Nahda, which was unable to engage in social welfare outreach under the Ben Ali regime and which continued to be restricted in this arena even after 2011 because of media criticism and a crackdown on religious associations. One assessment of the performance of Islamic political parties across many countries shows how few seats they tend to win in elections.[12] A pattern emerges: the best performances come in breakthrough elections offering relatively fair competition after years of repression; for example, in Jordan in 1989, Algeria in 1991, Bahrain in 2002, Iraq in 2005, Palestine in 2006, and Tunisia and Egypt in 2011–12. However, these were often merely brief political openings. Where relatively open elections have become routine, Islamic parties have been shown to receive fewer votes over time.[13]

The comparison with other Islamist movements helps identify varied responses to common challenges, including over the question of relations between political work and preaching. Political opportunities and institutional context are essential in deciding when and how Islamist movements create political parties. In Jordan, after martial law was lifted and a new political parties law introduced in 1992, the Muslim Brotherhood chose to create a new body, the Islamic Action Front (IAF), to compete in future elections. Similarly in Morocco, the Islamist movement Reform and Renewal, which had long pressed for a political role, was finally permitted entry into the political process at a time of opening in 1996 after it was given royal permission to take over another political party to create the Party of Justice and Development (PJD). In Kuwait, the Brotherhood established a political bloc, the Islamic Constitutional Movement (ICM), in March 1991 to take advantage of new post-conflict opportunities after Iraqi troops had been expelled by Western military intervention. By contrast, other movements engaged in elections without forming political parties because they operated under different institutional constraints. When the Palestinian movement Hamas chose to take part in legislative elections in January 2006 (after succeeding in municipal elections a year earlier), it created an electoral list, Change and Reform, but no separate party. Entering elections was a long-debated step to take advantage of the new political opportunity after the death of Yasser Arafat in 2004, the withdrawal of Israeli settlers and soldiers from Gaza in 2005, and the fading relevance of the Oslo accords.[14] But Hamas maintained its movement structure, which provided the particular flexibility and resilience it needed in the context of the ongoing Israeli military occupation. Egypt's Muslim Brotherhood, much like al-Nahda, retained its political and preaching projects intertwined within one organization until after the 2011 uprisings. The Brotherhood had taken part in electoral politics since the early 1980s but had also experienced several rounds of repression, which taught it to be cautious about politicization and to rely on a deep movement structure for shelter at a time of crackdown. Whether or not an Islamist movement might be granted formal inclusion in the political process depended on institutional settings: on balance, republican-authoritarian regimes were less likely to allow in Islamists for fear of losing power, while monarchies, which positioned themselves above the political fray, might be more open to inclusion.[15]

In some cases, these newly formed political parties grew in importance until they appeared to overshadow the original movement. Morocco's PJD offers the best example of this process. The party and its associated movement, which was later renamed the Movement of Unity and Reform, were theoretically distinct at first, with separate newspapers and separate criteria for membership (the movement laid down moral and religious criteria while the party did not). However, over time the party came to dominate. In the wake of the 2003 Casablanca terrorist attacks a much sharper division between party and movement developed, as both tried to avoid accusations of extremism. It was not that the party became entirely autonomous from the movement, but rather, in Avi Spiegel's view, that the movement and its authority 'has slowly dissolved into the party'.[16] This has its strategic uses. It allowed the party to deploy the movement when needed and to make space for controlled internal protest. Most of all, it helped the party build its base by attracting those more interested in religion than politics, while also keeping control over this religiously oriented activism.[17] Future party leaders were those who had already proven their activism in the movement.

Alternatively, the Islamist party may remain largely indistinguishable from the movement and function as leverage in a contest between the movement and a semi-authoritarian regime. In Jordan, after the

Brotherhood had performed well in the first elections in 1989, the monarchy changed the electoral law to limit IAF gains in the 1993 elections. The IAF subsequently boycotted the 1997 elections in protest at the monarchy's peace treaty with Israel as well as new curbs on freedoms of expression and assembly. It then took part in votes in 2003 and 2007 but boycotted in 2010 and 2013, signalling there was nothing to be gained by electoral participation under the regime's highly constrained rules. In Kuwait, the ICM boycotted elections in December 2012 and June 2013 in protest at the electoral system imposed by the emir and a sense that the government had become the source of political deadlock.[18] But both the IAF and the ICM eventually made the calculation that there was too much to lose by remaining marginalized outside the political process and both returned to participation.[19] The Jordanian IAF took part in elections in September 2016, winning 11 out of parliament's 130 seats, fewer than it had hoped for but enough to rebuild its political profile. The Kuwaiti ICM ran in elections in November 2016, winning four of the five seats it contested.

By contrast, the case of Egypt demonstrates how power can shift from the movement to the party and back to the movement in the face of a return to repression. With the fall of President Hosni Mubarak, the Brotherhood quickly established the Freedom and Justice Party (FJP), which was presented as a party that would be open to Egyptians of all faiths and fully independent from the movement.[20] In fact, the relationship between the FJP and the Muslim Brotherhood was very close: it was the Brotherhood's Consultative Council that chose the party's top leadership, including its president Muhammad Morsi, and Brothers were soon told that the FJP was the only political party they could join.[21] Over time, though, the weight of energy and activism shifted from the movement towards the political party until the 2013 coup, when the party was formally dissolved by the regime. The long-term effect of repression is uncertain, although the Muslim Brotherhood may now come to look more like the diverse social movement it was in the 1970s.[22] One senior Brotherhood figure argues that, when the opportunity for political and social activism returns, the movement should 'totally disengage' from 'any partisan competitive work' and leave formal political activity to independent political parties with their own platforms and policies.[23] As all Islamist movements realized when creating parties, the participatory experiment carried risks and if it failed, then the movement could provide shelter when repression returned.

There is much debate about the effect of political participation on Islamist ideology. As Carrie Wickham notes, it is not enough to argue that Islamists change merely because of strategic adaptation without acknowledging the 'potentially transformative effects of participation' on their ideological commitments and how they define the broader purposes of the movement.[24] She argues that through participation Islamists place a greater stress on democracy and the expansion of public freedoms, not in order to deceive but because it meets their interests. The benefit of political gain encourages pragmatism in rhetoric and action, as we saw with al-Nahda's decisions to make alliances with secular parties for the cause of democratic reform and to postpone the implementation of the shari'a. With this behavioural change comes intellectual change, which, as we saw with al-Nahda, may involve reformist readings of Islam, like the *maqāṣid al-shari'a*, and the incorporation of a human rights discourse into the Islamist vocabulary. This intellectual change was reflected in the careful way these Islamist parties now described themselves. Like al-Nahda, Morocco's PJD defined itself not as Islamist but as 'a party with an Islamic reference'; Egypt's FJP similarly called itself 'a civil party with an Islamic frame of reference'. Turkey's Justice and Development Party (AKP) said it represented 'conservative democrats', which echoed in al-Nahda's later choice of the name 'Muslim democrats'. Yet this sequence of change between behaviour and ideology is itself problematic. It is difficult to discern when behaviours are merely rational, strategic responses to opportunities and when they are the embodiment of an ideological commitment, and whether there is a substantive difference between the two.[25]

Political participation could also incur organizational division. Egypt's Muslim Brotherhood experienced this in 1996 with the splintering off of the more reformist al-Wasat party. The split emerged from long-running tensions between Brotherhood's old guard figures and their internal critics, who were frustrated by the ideological rigidity of their elders. Old guard leaders were furious at the split and the embarrassing exposure of internal critiques, even though al-Wasat was never legalized and never emerged as a significant challenger.[26] The old guard responded by tightening control with stronger demands for loyalty and obedience and by reaffirming a commitment to the original *da'wa* project. Another, even more serious split, developed after the 2013 coup, between established leaders among the Brotherhood, who sought to cling to the movement's nonviolent, gradualist, conciliatory methods, and a younger generation, who hungered for a decisive, revolutionary response to unprecedented repression.[27] They disagreed publicly on whether there should be discussions with the Egyptian regime, the importance of continued protests, and even on the role of violence. The Jordanian Brotherhood also suffered from a similar series of internal rifts. In 2001, a small number of the IAF's most progressive leaders split off to form their own al-Wasat party. The split was apparently in opposition to the Front's boycott of the 1997 election but also, in Wickham's analysis, in frustration at the failure of the IAF to develop its independence as a political party separate from the Brotherhood movement, which continued to impose ideological and behavioural conformity.[28] Again since 2013, the Jordanian Brotherhood has faced a new and more serious split, emerging from the long-running divide between Jordanian East Bankers and Palestinian-Jordanians within the movement. Several East Bankers led the Zamzam Initiative in late 2013 calling for internal reform and a less confrontational approach to the Jordanian regime. They were expelled from the Brotherhood but then in 2015 won government approval to establish a rival, the Muslim Brotherhood Society, with the encouragement of the palace. This represented a major split in the original Brotherhood organization, which lost its legal recognition and some of its financial resources. Despite the Islamist reputation for tightly controlled, disciplined organizations, in fact splits over political programmes and strategies are not uncommon.

What is particularly striking in light of the Tunisian case is how often Islamist political parties in the region have acted pragmatically, searched for consensus, and advocated programmes that were technocratic rather than ideological. Often the pragmatic self-limiting compromises required of the Islamists are disproportionate to the political influence they enjoy.[29] In Kuwait, a concern for stability since the 2003 Iraq war and the 2011 uprisings has encouraged Islamists to favour compromise and gradual reform over a stricter Islamist social agenda.[30] ICM figures spoke of their loyalty to the ruling family and their preference for reform over change, including a gradualist approach to the implementation of the shari'a and cooperation with other opposition movements. This mirrors the PJD, which was reluctant to criticize the Moroccan monarchy, capturing this delicate balance in the early years of political participation with the telling phrase: 'We are the opposition *of* His Majesty, not the opposition *to* His Majesty'.[31] The PJD gradually improved its electoral performance by focusing not on religious questions but on issues of unemployment, corruption, and increasing the minimum wage.[32] Eventually its leader Abdelilah Benkirane won the premiership in November 2011. Yet the PJD's caution was wise. Its newly won power proved insubstantial and highly dependent on the continued support of the monarchy.[33] Eventually, Benkirane was removed by the king when he became too popular and adversarial; he was replaced by another PJD figure seen as more pliable. Even though the Moroccan monarchical context was very different to the post-2011 Tunisian transition, the PJD's caution, its pragmatic attention to economic problems, and its willingness to compromise for the higher goal of survival is strikingly similar to the posture adopted by al-Nahda, with its consensus approach and its repeated conciliation towards the former regime elite.

Between Politics and Preaching

This book has demonstrated the surprisingly contested relationship between al-Nahda's political ambitions for control of the state and its preaching project, the social, cultural, and Islamizing mission of da'wa outreach. This challenges the movement's own 'comprehensive' understanding of its project as combining both elements in one innovative proposition. Instead, the evidence in these pages reveals that a structural and intellectual tension was present in the movement from the early 1980s, when some in the leadership first pursued politicization. This tension was shaped by the leadership's confrontation with the Ben Ali regime in the late 1980s and the long period of repression that followed. It finally came to a head as the movement rebuilt itself for the post-2011 transition from authoritarianism. The primary fractures within the movement were not between 'hardliners' and 'moderates', or between a younger generation and veterans, or between those who remained in Tunisia during the repression and those who escaped into exile. Instead, individuals tended to divide between those who favoured politics and those who favoured preaching, depending how they understood and had experienced the identity of their movement. This debate was foremost in the minds of the Nahdawis I met in Sousse during the fieldwork for this book in 2013–15.

The separation between politics and preaching that we see in al-Nahda appears to mirror Roy's failure of political Islam thesis, in which he sees Islamist movements splitting into normalized nationalist political parties advocating elections, coalitions, and democracy on the one hand, and morality-focused activism in the private domain, which he calls 'neofundamentalism', on the other.[34] The experiences of al-Nahda that I have explored here do support Roy's essential argument that the unification of the religious and the political was no more than an 'Islamist myth' because the idealized Islamic state was never achieved, thereby leaving the religious and political spheres autonomous.[35] However, Roy's framework of a 'drift' from state-seeking Islamism to society-focused neofundamentalism does not capture the experience of al-Nahda.[36] First, it suggests that at some stage there is a tipping-point between the comprehensive Islamist mission of the past, and, once that has 'failed', the new era characterized by the political-neofundamentalist split. The evidence from the Tunisian case, however, is that even from its very start in

1981 the comprehensiveness of the Islamist mission was contested within the organization. The political and the preaching wings coexisted awkwardly for more than three decades before the formal rupture. Second, the binary split that Roy describes does not capture the full range of fragmentation that took place within the Tunisian movement. Some were clearly drawn to a political project of competing as a national political party in a civil, democratic system, while some, in line with Roy, were drawn back to the original project of morality-focused activism. However, the Tunisian case shows others still clung to the original comprehensive idea of the project and tried to be active in both trends. Others conceived of a political project that was strategically much more oppositional than the movement's consensus-seeking political leaders. Instead, they championed the secular goals of the uprising, including social justice, regional equality of development, and accountability for past crimes, issues that had little to do with Islamization. Still others demobilized, leaving (or choosing not to rejoin) the movement in order to be active not in formal politics but in civil society groups that were defined not by a religious zeal, but by a different discourse of human rights, or local cultural development. Further fragmentation is likely to follow in the years ahead once the split between party and religious activities has settled and it has become clear where the real balance of power now lies. Third, Roy's framework explicitly considers the political project in terms of state capture, rather than acknowledging that the societal *da'wa* project is also political. Islamists, like other activists, compete in a 'struggle over people's imaginations—habits of the mind, the heart, and of public space that help shape people's ideas of the common good'.[37] This struggle is just as political as running for election.

How can we explain this contested relationship between politics and preaching? When the MTI proposed its 'comprehensive conception of Islam' in 1981 it was an idealistic vision. Even in that first press conference, the movement admitted that this proposition was made up of different strands: the primary goal was cultural, social, and intellectual before it was political. However much the movement hoped to weave all these threads together, it was clear from the start that this was a utopian formulation. It was also an effect of power, in that the movement was compelled to enter political competition with the state because of the state's modernizing, secularizing interventions in the social life of its citizens. But this was at odds with the movement's initial shari'a-driven project, which is why there was so little detail about what Islamist political institutions would look like. The political project meant striving to establish some form of Islamic state, but there was never any precise explanation of how the authoritarian post-independence Tunisian state might be re-engineered in an Islamic configuration. This is not to argue that the proposition of Islamism was so inchoate as to be without substance. Instead, it is to pay detailed attention to the inherent friction that lay within what was an ideal project from the outset and to track that friction over time.

Although the movement maintained a political ambition since the early 1980s, it barely took part in the political process until after the 2011 uprising, apart from discreet negotiations with the Mohamed Mzali premiership in the early 1980s and its fateful participation in the April 1989 elections. The comprehensive project was not rigorously tested in practice until after 2011. Once al-Nahda was allowed entry into competitive pluralism with the elections of October 2011, it was very quickly confronted by the contradictions inherent in its plan. Soon the question of separating the political and the religious emerged as the central debate within al-Nahda, eventually culminating in a structural transformation.

Yet, the comprehensive project was not merely idealistic but also useful in its ambiguity in those early years. This plasticity allowed the movement to maximize its mobilizing potential, drawing in as wide a range of supporters as possible and presenting itself as engaged in a broad array of interests beyond the question of identity and religion to also encompass democratic, social, economic, and even class aspirations. This accounts for its explicit alignment in 1981 with the 'oppressed' and the idea of a fair distribution of wealth, as well as its appeal at that early stage to labour unions.[38] Such broad appeal was necessary given that the movement saw itself in direct competition not just with rival opposition parties, but with the modernizing post-independence regime as well. The dual project allowed the movement to mobilize informal networks at the local level with one discourse, while trying to engage in competition with the political elite and the national media using another. The pursuit of legalization was an effort to avoid being pushed to the margins. It allowed individuals with different priorities and different understandings of the challenges ahead to coexist within one organization.

The contest within the movement between political and preaching ambitions represents a form of political adaptation, in which the movement reflected on its experience and drew lessons. This is what has been characterized elsewhere as 'political learning', defined as the modification of beliefs or tactics as a result of crises, frustrations, and dramatic changes in environment.[39] This is not to presume that the movement always drew the 'right' lessons from its experience, nor to impose on its historical trajectory a normative, teleological reading in which it 'evolved' from religious movement to opposition force to democratic actor (even though the movement often uses the concept of evolution in precisely this way in its own discourse). Rather, I argue that Islamists, like any other social movement, change their strategic aims and alter course in their activism depending on changing contexts and varied interpretations of past actions. Importantly, there was no one collective lesson learned. Instead different trends within al-Nahda learned different lessons from the repression of the early 1990s. Movement leaders, who had proposed reconciling with the Ben Ali regime, were motivated to compromise their Islamizing ambitions after 2011 for fear of a return to repression. They saw political pragmatism and inclusion in coalition government, whatever the cost, as the strongest protection against a return to exclusion. However, others took a different path. In the 2000s, inside Tunisia, they worked with non-Islamists in human rights associations or in other opposition parties to challenge the authoritarian regime with a cross-party, rights-based discourse. They often continued such civil society work after 2011. So, for some in the movement, the effect of repression and social exclusion was to encourage a new interpretation of the political project that reached beyond al-Nahda to embrace a wider discourse of human rights and cultural values. Many others, of course, stayed away from all political and civil society activity altogether under Ben Ali because of the punishing weight of repression and social exclusion. For them, the lesson of the confrontation was that the political ambitions of their leaders had damaged the Islamist subculture. In their isolation they reimagined what it meant to be Islamist when it was no longer possible to organize as a group. For many it meant returning as individuals to the movement's original project of morality and correct behaviour. The different conclusions drawn by separate trends within the movement help explain why the differences between politics and preaching remained so animated within the movement.

Resilience Under Repression

A second aim of this book has been to uncover the sources of al-Nahda's resilience during the years of repression. The paradox of al-Nahda is that it re-emerged surprisingly quickly in the weeks after the fall of Ben Ali despite two decades of jail, exile, and social exclusion. The movement had not been able to rely on those elements elsewhere considered vital to Islamist resilience, including a structured movement, activism in professional associations, and grassroots welfare activities. Instead, what was most important was the movement's robust networks and the way individuals adapted their idea of the Islamist project. This may signal unexpected opportunities for those Islamist movements in Egypt and

Jordan which since 2013 have had their ability to provide social services severely curtailed.

Nahdawis were not simply recipients of state-mandated prison terms and social exclusion. In prison, even as the authorities suffocated the Nahdawi prisoners through a range of coercive practices, activists found the space to discuss their experiences. There were disagreements about why their movement had entered into confrontation, but these also served to restore independence of mind and freedom of spirit, and to keep the idea of the Islamist project alive. The prison cell also became a site of resistance, from which individuals could reclaim their dignity in the face of the humiliation meted out by the carceral regime. Family visits, though burdensome, allowed relatives to mix, share stories, and offer mutual comfort. These connections kept alive the social ties that had bound the community together so tightly before the years of repression.

After prison, when Nahdawis found themselves facing social exclusion and a newly inferior social status, they were forced to rethink for themselves what their Islamist belonging meant to them as individuals. The associational work that did take place, in human rights groups or other political parties, happened at the periphery of the movement and served to pull al-Nahda in new directions, encouraging cross-party activism and a new human rights discourse. At the same time, a fresh generation of young men and women were drawn to the Islamist project either through parental influence or on personal spiritual quests. Though these new supporters were modest in number, their debates, particularly with the nascent Salafist movement, and their strong opposition to the Ben Ali regime injected fresh energy into the movement. These new elements emerged at a time when the cautious rump leadership was pushing for reconciliation with the authorities and slowly beginning to regroup. Al-Nahda had disappeared as a structured hierarchical organization, but it remained as a collection of ideas of Islamism, even as the movement disaggregated into its diverse components.

What continued to bind these individuals together in their project was an informal but robust series of networks. These networks were first built in study circles at mosques in the 1970s, and in school dormitories or on university campuses, hence the pocket of Islamist support in the faculties of medicine and law in Sousse. Individual teachers and charismatic preachers helped strengthen these bonds. They explain why pockets of Islamist support emerged in particular schools in Sousse, like the Lycée de Garçons, or in particular nearby villages, like Chorbane, the small rural village that produced half a dozen prominent Islamist figures. Men and women from within these networks sometimes married each other, further cementing community ties. These local level networks came before the structural organization of the movement. They represented concrete steps that led from shared daily practices into a community building project. Studying one local community of activists over a long historical time frame has shown just how resilient those social ties remained over several decades, even as individuals within the networks disagreed on the movement's tactics, strategies, and identity. These networks perpetuated the shared vision of the societal project, a vision that proved remarkably durable from the early 1970s and into the post-2011 environment.

Most importantly, network ties survived two decades of repression. This book argues that the key to the movement's survival was not the formal hierarchy, the schematic *organigramme* so often studied and mapped, of local cells, regional leaders, a national Consultative Council, and an Executive Bureau. Instead, resilience began with the connective tissue of informal networks which had been formed in earlier years at school, or in mosques, or in local communities. It was these networks that provided the basis for the early efforts at reorganization that began to emerge in the late 2000s, and which enabled communication between al-Nahda leaders elsewhere in the country and the local networks in Sousse. These networks suddenly became visible again in the rapid rebuilding of the movement in the weeks after January 2011.

Networks were created around shared values, daily practice, and a collective identity, rather than through formal organizational hierarchies. Such social interaction has now been acknowledged as playing a role in social movements as a site of creation and change and in forging the dynamics of contentious politics.[40] As Sidney Tarrow puts it, interpersonal networks serve as connective structures which build movement identities, offer opportunities for individuals to participate, and shape individual preferences. They operate as 'the sites for the normative pressures and solidary incentives out of which movements emerge and are sustained'.[41] To build on this, the case of al-Nahda in Sousse demonstrates the significance of daily practice as a way to make meanings and shows how flexible these networks can be. Close personal ties endured despite individual differences of opinion about the strategy of the al-Nahda project. Those former members who chose not to rejoin the movement after it was legally authorized in 2011 were not rejected from these networks. The networks were flexible enough, at least in the short term, to accommodate a range of strategic differences because they united together behind a shared experience, including a shared experience of repression, as well as the original Islamizing mission. This explains why Tahar, the former Nahdawi who in 2014 was working in a civil society association, could say of his decision not to rejoin the movement: 'I respect al-Nahda and at heart I'm with them but I'm not a member'. However, these networks were not immune from difficulty. In the post-2011 environment their members were increasingly middle aged and continued to draw on their earlier experience from the 1970s and 1980s. They struggled to replicate their networks among a younger generation, for whom the experience of subculture community building under the Bourguiba regime carried little resonance. The younger generation lacked, as one Nahdawi said, the sense of 'familial belonging'.[42] The formerly resilient networks were ageing, drawing on their old reserves, and struggling to regenerate themselves. This book demonstrates that though interpersonal networks may play a vital role in movement cohesion, they are also likely to be time-limited. Dense social networks may be hard to reproduce from one generation to the next.

Those Nahdawis who remained in Tunisia under Ben Ali were subject to harsh prison sentences and severe social exclusion once they returned home. Yet, there is evidence of resilience, built on the persistence of the idea of the Islamist project, reinforced by social networks and activism on the periphery of the movement. This resilience explains why al-Nahda was able to return so quickly in 2011 after what had appeared to be a two-decade absence. However, the new circumstances that suddenly erupted in the wake of the popular uprising brought not just the opportunity to rebuild, but also the challenge to adapt.

Adapting by Separating

The case of al-Nahda demonstrates how an Islamist organization makes strategic and intellectual adaptations as its surrounding political and social environment changes. These adaptations show flexibility but they are limited by dense networks of belonging and they incur costs, particularly to the stability of the organization and the coherence of its vision. Until the repression of the 1990s, the movement had managed to combine its political and preaching activism in one organization, though as I have demonstrated there were always tensions in this project. This ambiguity resisted those efforts to categorize Islamist movements by their attitude to the state, in which statists are seen as having ambitions to acquire state power, while non-statists either avoid politics or have a vision of a community not bound to the modern nation state. A better explanation of the logic behind the organization's structural ambiguity would be to consider the movement of the 1980s as reflecting not some transnational Muslim Brotherhood organizational model, but rather the mirror image of the structure of Tunisia's own ruling party.[43] In what

Michel Camau and Vincent Geisser call an 'unconscious imitation', the Islamists built a movement with branch organizations across the country, centralized around a president, and reaching into social sectors that in many ways mimicked the ruling party of Bourguiba and Ben Ali. This accommodated the movement's twin ambitions of capturing power and reforming society, and reflected again the extent of competition under-way with the regime. It demonstrates too how forms of resistance can, surprisingly, reflect the ways people have experienced power them-selves.[44] When al-Nahda rebuilt itself after the fall of Ben Ali in 2011, it revived the organization by again using that single political-preaching structure and thus operated under the ambiguous name the Party of the Movement of al-Nahda. However, because of the unprecedented demands of the democratic transition, the political work again over-whelmed efforts to revive the programmes of da'wa outreach. Some charitable, preaching, and Qur'anic associations were loosely linked to the movement, but al-Nahda had not successfully recreated the grass-roots organization that existed in the 1980s. Soon the question of separ-ation emerged, and in al-Nahda's most challenging adaptation yet, it decided in May 2016 to reconstruct itself as a conservative political party which was separate from social, religious, and cultural activism.

The newly described political project began as a strategic pragmatic shift; the intellectual adaptation was more difficult for the movement to articulate. At the moment of specialization as a party, Ghannouchi explained that the Islamist project had been defined in earlier years by its challenge to dictatorship and to what he called 'secularist extremism'.[45] Those twin threats, in his view, had now passed, therefore Ghannouchi concluded: 'There is no longer a justification for political Islam in Tunisia'. Al-Nahda gave a more detailed account of this new stance in its concluding statement to the 2016 congress:

The party of the al-Nahda movement has in practice gone beyond all the justifications used by those who consider it part of what is called 'political Islam' and this widely used label does not express the reality of its current identity nor does it reflect the substance of its future project. Al-Nahda considers that its work is within an authentic effort to form a broad trend of 'Muslim democrats', who reject any contradiction between the values of Islam and the values of modernity.[46]

Here we find a self-reflexive movement explicitly rejecting the labels applied to it by scholars and political rivals, labels long acknowledged as unhelpful constructs caught in a 'forgotten swamp' of analytical con-fusion.[47] Though al-Nahda was portraying itself as unthreatening, this was also an effort to reimagine what it meant to be an Islamist movement that competed within a democratic, pluralist system for control over a

civil, not theocratic, state and that did not seek the immediate implementation of the shariʿa. It was the latest stage in a long intellectual debate
that reached back to Lourimi's proposition of a 'battle of renewal' and
beyond to the writings of Ben Achour and Bennabi.

An evolving vocabulary accompanied the conceptual shift. Soon after
2011 Ghannouchi described al-Nahda as no longer Islamist but rather a
'civil party with an Islamic reference'.[48] Others talked of 'a national party
that is the heir to a movement of religious, political and social reform'.[49]
By 2016, Ghannouchi and others were using the broad term 'Muslim
democrats'.[50] They positioned themselves as the antithesis of violent
Islamic groups who threatened Tunisian security, a framing that recalled
how movement leaders had previously tried to offer themselves as a
bulwark against violent Salafists in the late 2000s. The movement
insisted its intellectual shift did not mean the 'secularization' of
al-Nahda, though that was precisely what some Nahdawis feared.[51]
The Islamic reference would remain in the political project, but it was
now defined through al-Nahda's '*maqāṣidī* understanding of the Islamic
reference', referring to the idea of the broader objectives of the shariʿa
(*maqāṣid al-shariʿa*).[52] Al-Nahda defined the Islamic reference in the
most general terms. It was a 'programme of reform' (*manhaj li-l-iṣlāḥ*)
and a 'guiding force' (*quwwa tawjīhiyya*), but one that was still linked to
the holy texts through a revivalist reading (*qirāʾa tajdīdiyya wa ijtihādiyya*)
of the Qurʾan and Sunna.[53]

The concept of post-Islamism can go some way to explain the challenges the movement faced in composing its new intellectual vision after
2011. Al-Nahda's adaptation did not divest it of an Islamic reference, but
rather recast the role of Islam and asserted a cultural Islamic identity in
its discourse. This is a reading of post-Islamism which goes beyond Roy's
'failure' thesis to highlight the ideological revision which was underway,
even if the outcome was uncertain. Since it was a process of 'experimen-
tation' there was still much ambiguity, but a secular outcome was not yet
inevitable.[54] Bayat notes that the post-Islamist turn remains largely
untested in relation to minority rights, gender rights, and freedom of
thought, religion, and lifestyle.[55] For al-Nahda, the years after the fall of
Ben Ali were a moment of rethinking, testing, and refining. The debates
among the movement's political leaders centred on the question of what
it meant to adopt religious values as references and markers of cultural
identity while not enforcing them as explicit principles of law. But the
new al-Nahda was still struggling to write an intellectual programme
that went beyond a problem-solving technocratic identity, the prioritizing of pragmatism over ideology, and broad allusions to an Islamic
reference.

Al-Nahda had yet to convince the rest of the Tunisian political elite and electorate of the sincerity of its strategic adaptation. This concern was why it had given up on an earlier plan to divide itself into party and movement, which would have been more in line with Islamist strategies elsewhere in the region. Not having a movement in reserve meant al-Nahda no longer had a shelter from any potential future repression. There were also still differences of opinion within the membership about politicization. Much was still to be negotiated about the relative weight and influence between the party and religious or cultural activities and how easily individual Nahdawis would be able to cross between the two in their work. Some senior figures resigned from the movement within weeks of the May 2016 congress. Mohamed Taher Chokri, the head of the movement's Sidi Bouzid regional bureau, left in protest at what he called 'clan-like' manoeuvrings among the senior leadership during the conference.[56] Others who were unhappy with al-Nahda's decision to ally with Nidaa Tounes chose a lower profile. From early 2017, Abdelhamid Jelassi, who had been a vice president of al-Nahda after 2011, now sat only as a member of the Consultative Council and was no longer in the Executive or Political Bureaux. He spoke out about his concern that al-Nahda's position in the coalition government was not one of parity with Nidaa Tounes but merely supplementary, and that this unprecedented alliance risked becoming a 'deal of the gullible' (ṣafqat al-mughaffalīn).[57] Though al-Nahda enjoyed a wide range of expertise among its ranks, including ministers, elected deputies, and activists, Jelassi argued the movement was failing to manage its internal resources properly, leaving 'a kind of vacuum'. 'The minimal investment in these resources causes us concern about the future of al-Nahda and its project,' he said.

The organizational separation of the political and preaching projects in 2016 was the culmination of many years of internal debate and disagreement, dating back to well before the democratic transition. It was the latest effort at adaptation: a structural decision to allay the criticisms of political rivals and to reimagine what it meant to draw on an Islamic reference for a political project. It was as ambitious as it was ambiguous. Elsewhere in the region, Islamist political parties have often come to dominate and dilute the influence of their movements as political ambitions came to the fore. This may signal the future direction for al-Nahda too, and at least initially the weight of power in terms of key appointments appeared to remain firmly within al-Nahda the party. Yet finding the balance between ambitions for politics and preaching is a fraught process, as this book has demonstrated. The tension between the two trends is ever present, waxing and waning with the changing political context. The creation of political parties by Islamist movements is another act of strategic and intellectual adaptation to changing political circumstances and a desire for legitimacy and protection in uncertain times. The subsequent trajectory of these parties depends on lessons drawn from their own experiences, the resilience of informal networks, and the unanticipated outcomes of participation in the political process.

Notes

1 Introduction

1 Frédéric Bobin, 'Rached Ghannouchi: "Il n'y a plus de justification à l'islam politique en Tunisie"', *Le Monde*, Paris, 19 May 2016.

2 Rachid Ghannouchi, 'Kalimat al-Shaykh Rashid al-Ghannushi fi Iftitah Ashghal al-Mu'tamar al-'Ashir li-l-Haraka [The Speech of Shaykh Rachid Ghannouchi at the Opening of the Tenth Congress of the Movement]', *Al-Fajr*, Tunis, 22 May 2016.

3 Harakat al-Ittijah al-Islami, 'al-Bayan al-Ta'sisi li-Harakat al-Ittijah al-Islami [The Founding Statement of the Islamic Tendency Movement]', in *Bayanat Dhikra al-Ta'sis li-Harakat al-Nahda al-Tunisiyya [Statements Commemorating the Foundation of the Tunisian al-Nahda Movement]* (Tunis: Harakat al-Nahda, 2012), 15.

4 Michel Camau and Vincent Geisser, *Le Syndrome Autoritaire: Politique en Tunisie de Bourguiba à Ben Ali* (Paris: Presses de Sciences Po, 2003), 267.

5 Some still see Tunisia as exceptional, for example: Safwan M. Masri, *Tunisia: An Arab Anomaly* (New York, NY: Columbia University Press, 2017).

6 On 26 June 2015, thirty-eight people, including thirty British tourists, were killed by a gunman on a Sousse beach. Earlier that year, on 18 March, twenty-two people, mostly foreign tourists, were killed in a similar attack at the Bardo Museum in Tunis. Much Western analysis of contemporary Tunisian politics has been shaped by such attacks, as well as the startling fact that some 6,000 young Tunisians were estimated to have travelled to Syria to fight with extremist groups by late 2015. Farah Samti and Carlotta Gall, 'Tunisia Attack Kills at Least 38 at Beach Resort Hotel', *New York Times*, New York, NY, 26 June 2015; Soufan Group, 'Foreign Fighters: An Updated Assessment of the Flow of Foreign Fighters into Syria and Iraq' (New York, NY: The Soufan Group, December 2015).

7 François Burgat, *Face to Face with Political Islam* (London: IB Tauris, 2003), 3.

8 Burgat, *Face to Face*, 4.

9 Olivier Roy, *The Failure of Political Islam*, translated by Carol Volk (London: IB Tauris, 1994), 13–15; Dale Eickelman and James Piscatori, *Muslim Politics*, 2nd edn (Princeton, NJ/Oxford: Princeton University Press, 2004), 46–57;

Wael B. Hallaq, *The Impossible State: Islam, Politics, and Modernity's Moral Predicament* (New York, NY: Columbia University Press, 2014), 48–70.

10 Bassam Tibi, *Islamism and Islam* (New Haven, CT/London: Yale University Press, 2012), 1–2.

11 Roy, *The Failure of Political Islam*, xi; Olivier Roy, *Globalised Islam: The Search for a New Ummah* (London: Hurst, 2004), 58.

12 Roy, *The Failure of Political Islam*, ix.

13 Frédéric Volpi, *Political Islam Observed* (London: Hurst, 2010), 11.

14 Esen Kirdiş, 'Between Movement and Party: Islamic Movements in Morocco and the Decision to Enter Party Politics', *Politics, Religion & Ideology* 16:1 (2015): 69.

15 Frédéric Volpi and Ewan Stein, 'Islamism and the State after the Arab Uprisings: Between People Power and State Power', *Democratization* 22:2 (2015).

16 Roy, *The Failure of Political Islam*, ix.

17 I take this definition largely from: Volpi, *Political Islam Observed*, 14.

18 Faisal Devji and Zaheer Kazmi, 'Introduction', in *Islam after Liberalism*, eds. Faisal Devji and Zaheer Kazmi (London: Hurst, 2017), 5–6; Faisal Devji, 'Islamism as Anti-Politics', *Political Theology Today*, 2 August 2013, www.politicaltheology.com/blog/.

19 Roy, *The Failure of Political Islam*, 60–74.

20 Saba Mahmood, *Politics of Piety: The Islamic Revival and the Feminist Subject* (Princeton, NJ: Princeton University Press, 2005), 73–4.

21 Cihan Tuğal, 'Transforming Everyday Life: Islamism and Social Movement Theory', *Theory and Society* 38:5 (2009): 428–9.

22 Salwa Ismail, *Rethinking Islamist Politics: Culture, the State and Islamism* (London: IB Tauris, 2006), 168.

23 Talal Asad, *Formations of the Secular: Christianity, Islam, Modernity* (Stanford, CA: Stanford University Press, 2003), 199.

24 Eickelman and Piscatori, *Muslim Politics*, 5.

25 Nathan J. Brown, *When Victory Is Not an Option: Islamist Movements in Arab Politics* (Ithaca, NY/London: Cornell University Press, 2012), 5–6.

26 Asef Bayat, 'Islamism and Social Movement Theory', *Third World Quarterly* 26:6 (2005): 895.

27 Bayat, 'Islamism and Social Movement Theory', 903.

28 See, for example: Azzam Tamimi, *Rachid Ghannouchi: A Democrat within Islamism* (Oxford: Oxford University Press, 2001).

29 For example: Alfred Stepan, 'Tunisia's Transition and the Twin Tolerations', *Journal of Democracy* 23:2 (2012). Duncan Pickard, 'Al-Nahda: Moderation and Compromise in Tunisia's Constitutional Bargain', in *Political and Constitutional Transitions in North Africa: Actors and Factors*, eds. Justin O. Frosini and Francesco Biagi (London/New York, NY: Routledge, 2015); Amel Boubekeur, 'Islamists, Secularists and Old Regime Elites in Tunisia: Bargained Competition', *Mediterranean Politics* 21:1 (2015); Olivier Roy, 'The Transformation of the Arab World', *Journal of Democracy* 23:3 (2012).

30 Michelle Pace and Francesco Cavatorta, 'The Arab Uprisings in Theoretical Perspective—An Introduction', *Mediterranean Politics* 17:2 (2012): 127.

31 Jillian Schwedler, *Faith in Moderation: Islamist Parties in Jordan and Yemen* (Cambridge: Cambridge University Press, 2006), 5.

32 Jenny White, *Islamist Mobilization in Turkey: A Study in Vernacular Politics* (Seattle, WA/London: University of Washington Press, 2002), 25–6.

33 Sidney Tarrow, *Power in Movement: Social Movements and Contentious Politics* (Cambridge/New York, NY: Cambridge University Press, 2011), 9.

34 Doug McAdam, John D. McCarthy, and Mayer N. Zald, eds., *Comparative Perspectives on Social Movements: Political Opportunities, Mobilizing Structures, and Cultural Framings* (Cambridge: Cambridge University Press, 1996), 2–7; Charles Tilly, *The Contentious French* (Cambridge, MA: Belknap Press, 1986), 4.

35 For example: Jeff Goodwin, James M. Jasper, and Francesca Polletta, eds., *Passionate Politics: Emotions and Social Movements* (Chicago, IL: University of Chicago Press, 2001); Doug McAdam, Sidney G. Tarrow, and Charles Tilly, *Dynamics of Contention* (Cambridge: Cambridge University Press, 2001), 22; Ronald R. Aminzade and Doug McAdam, 'Emotions and Contentious Politics', in *Silence and Voice in the Study of Contentious Politics*, eds. Ronald R. Aminzade, et al. (New York, NY: Cambridge University Press, 2001); Charles Kurzman, 'Meaning-Making in Social Movements', *Anthropological Quarterly* 81:1 (2008).

36 This was a leader of Egypt's Muslim Brotherhood: Amr Darrag, 'Politics or Piety? Why the Muslim Brotherhood Engages in Social Service Provision', in *Rethinking Political Islam*, eds. Shadi Hamid and William McCants (New York, NY: Oxford University Press, 2017), 223.

37 Christian Smith, 'Correcting a Curious Neglect, or Bringing Religion Back In', in *Disruptive Religion: The Force of Faith in Social-Movement Activism*, ed. Christian Smith (New York, NY/London: Routledge, 1996), 4.

38 Smith, 'Correcting a Curious Neglect', 6.

39 Bayat, 'Islamism and Social Movement Theory', 904.

40 Wendy Wolford, *This Land Is Ours Now: Social Mobilization and the Meanings of Land in Brazil* (Durham, NC: Duke University Press, 2010), 10.

41 Bayat, 'Islamism and Social Movement Theory', 904.

42 Dorothy Holland, Gretchen Fox, and Vinci Daro, 'Social Movements and Collective Identity: A Decentered, Dialogic View', *Anthropological Quarterly* 81:1 (2008): 99.

43 Tunisia was semi-authoritarian because even though there were regular elections, there was no chance that any party other than Ben Ali's Democratic Constitutional Rally (RCD) would win power. Legal opposition parties were allotted a few seats in the assembly. Several political movements, including al-Nahda, were never even legally authorized.

44 Béatrice Hibou, *The Force of Obedience: The Political Economy of Repression in Tunisia*, translated by Andrew Brown (Cambridge: Polity Press, 2011), 18.

45 Including revealing new work on al-Nahda, notably: Anne Wolf, *Political Islam in Tunisia: The History of Ennahda* (London: Hurst, 2017).

46 Harry F. Wolcott, *Ethnography: A Way of Seeing* (Lanham, MD/Plymouth: AltaMira Press, 2008), 69.

47 Patrick Biernacki and Dan Waldorf, 'Snowball Sampling: Problems and Techniques of Chain Referral Sampling', *Sociological Methods & Research* 10:2 (1981).

48 Melani Cammett, 'Political Ethnography in Deeply Divided Societies', *Qualitative Methods* 4:2 (2006).

49 Jan Kubick, 'Ethnography of Politics: Foundations, Applications, Prospects', in *Political Ethnography: What Immersion Contributes to the Study of Power*, ed. Edward Schatz (Chicago, IL: University of Chicago Press, 2009), 31.

50 Lorraine Bayard de Volo and Edward Schatz, 'From the Inside Out: Ethnographic Methods in Political Research', *Political Science and Politics* 37:2 (2004).

2 Morality, Behaviour, and Networks

1 Abdallah, former MTI member; born in 1952, imprisoned 1981–83. Interviewed in Sousse, 11 March and 9 September 2014.

2 Smith, 'Correcting a Curious Neglect', 5–7; Carrie Rosefsky Wickham, *Mobilizing Islam: Religion, Activism, and Political Change in Egypt* (New York, NY: Columbia University Press, 2002), 13; Cihan Tuğal, 'Islamism in Turkey: Beyond Instrument and Meaning', *Economy and Society* 31:1 (2002): 95; Eva Bellin, 'Faith in Politics: New Trends in the Study of Religion and Politics', *World Politics* 60:2 (2008): 345.

3 Ghannouchi told Burgat he was an Arab nationalist until June 1966, at which point he realized: 'I had believed in an Arabism for which I was prepared to die but which was in fact opposed to the Islam which had nourished me and of which I was proud.' Burgat, *Face to Face*, 36.

4 Historically the Sousse governorate included the cities of Monastir and Mahdia in an area of around 2,400 square miles until a 1974 law split the region into the three governorates that exist today: Sousse, Monastir, and Mahdia.

5 At the moment of independence, around 4,000 European families each owned farms an average of 200 hectares in size, while about 5,000 Tunisia families each owned farms an average of 80 hectares each. Both groups used modern farming techniques, but another 450,000 Tunisian families owned small farms of just seven hectares each: Abdelkader Zghal, 'Les Effets de la Modernisation de l'Agriculture sur la Stratification Sociale dans les Campagnes Tunisiennes', *Cahiers Internationaux de Sociologie* 38 (1965); Charles Micaud, Leon Carl Brown, and Clement Henry Moore, *Tunisia: The Politics of Modernisation* (London: Pall Mall Press, 1964), 81.

6 Clement Henry Moore, *Tunisia since Independence: The Dynamics of One-Party Government* (Berkeley, CA: University of California Press, 1965), 25.

7 Jacques Berque, *French North Africa: The Maghrib between Two World Wars*, translated by Jean Stewart (London: Faber & Faber, 1967), 147; Moore, *Tunisia since Independence*, 14.

8 Hamza Meddeb, 'Peripheral Vision: How Europe Can Help Preserve Tunisia's Fragile Democracy' (London: European Council on Foreign Relations, January 2017), 2.

9 World Bank, 'The Unfinished Revolution: Bringing Opportunity, Good Jobs and Greater Wealth to All Tunisians' (Washington, DC: May 2014), 282.

10 Tunisia's Institut National de la Statistique (INS) considers those aged 15 or above to be of working age. INS 'Sousse: À travers le Recensement Général de la Population et de l'Habitat 2014' (Tunis: 2014), 44.

11 INS 'Estimation de la population par commune au 1er janvier 2013' (Tunis: 2013); INS 'Estimation de la population par gouvernorat au 1er janvier 2013' (Tunis: 2013).

12 Sadri Khiari and Béatrice Hibou, 'La Révolution Tunisienne ne vient pas de nulle part', *Politique Africaine* 1:121 (2011): 25; cited in: Michael J. Willis, 'Revolt for Dignity: Tunisia's Revolution and Civil Resistance', in *Civil Resistance in the Arab Spring: Triumphs and Disasters*, eds. Adam Roberts, et al. (Oxford: Oxford University Press, 2016), 31.

13 Vincent Geisser and Éric Gobe, 'Un si long règne ... Le régime de Ben Ali vingt ans après', *L'Année du Maghreb* IV (2008): 5–6.

14 Seventeen Sousse hotels closed after the attack and the number of tourists visiting Sousse dropped 35 per cent in the first half of 2016: 'Sousse terrorist attack has caused closure of 17 hotels, 35% drop in tourists (official)', *Agence Tunis Afrique Press*, Tunis, 25 June 2016.

15 Abdelkader Fahem, 'Un exemple de relations villes—campagne: Sousse et le Sahel tunisien', *Revue Tunisienne de Sciences Sociales* 15: December (1968): 287.

16 Taoufik Monastiri, 'Tunisie: Chronique Sociale et Culturelle', *Annuaire de l'Afrique du Nord* XI (1972): 435–7.

17 Fahem, 'Un exemple', 284.

18 Fahem, 'Un exemple', 295. The wider governorate was home to 511,000 Tunisians in 1966, around a tenth of the national population, up 15 per cent from the previous decade.

19 Fahem, 'Un exemple', 293–4.

20 Hédi Bouslama, 'Le Gouvernorat de Sousse en Voie de Developpement: Bulletin économique de la Chambre de Commerce du Centre' (Sousse: Chambre de Commerce du Centre, 1972), 8–9.

21 E. Badri, 'M. Mohamed Ennaceur: Tourisme et industries, le Sahel amorce un nouveau départ sous le signe de l'unité régionale', *La Presse*, Tunis, 2 March 1973. The career of Mohamed Ennaceur, who was born in El-Jem, in the Sahel, in 1934, illustrates a common trajectory of the Sahelian administrative elite. Educated in Tunis and Paris, he was appointed governor of Sousse and was twice minister for social affairs under Bourguiba. Under Ben Ali he was assigned to the Tunisian mission to the UN in Geneva and then worked as a private sector consultant. He returned to political life after the 2011 uprising, serving again as minister for social affairs in 2011. He joined the Nidaa Tounes party in early 2014 as vice-president, won the election in the Mahdia constituency in October 2014, and, at the age of 80, was appointed speaker of the new parliament.

22 'Gouvernorat de Sousse: Réalisations 1973', *Bulletin Économique de la Chambre de Commerce du Centre* 64 (1973): 5.

23 Farmers protested against the cooperatives in the town of Ouerdanin, in what is today the governorate of Monastir, in January 1969: Lars Rudebeck, 'Developmental Pressure and Political Limits: A Tunisian Example', *The Journal of Modern African Studies* 8:2 (1970): 190.

24 Christopher Alexander, *Tunisia: Stability and Reform in the Modern Maghreb* (Abingdon: Routledge, 2010), 76.

25 Gregory White, *A Comparative Political Economy of Tunisia and Morocco: On the Outside of Europe Looking In* (New York, NY: State University of New

York Press, 2001), 93; 'Loi no. 72–38 du 27 avril 1972, portant création d'un régime particulier pour les industries produisant pour l'exportation' (Tunis: Republic of Tunisia, 1972).

26 'Gouvernorat de Sousse'.

27 Moore, *Tunisia since Independence*, 41.

28 Marguerite Rollinde, 'Les émeutes en Tunisie: un défi à l'État?', in *Émeutes et mouvements sociaux au Maghreb: Perspective comparée*, eds. Didier Le Saout and Marguerite Rollinde (Paris: Karthala, 1999), 113.

29 'Sousse: Poursuite du procès des syndicalistes impliqués dans les événements du 26 janvier', *L'Action*, Tunis, 2 August 1978; Rollinde, 'Les émeutes en Tunisie', 114.

30 See, for example: Wickham, *Mobilizing Islam*; Mahmood, *Politics of Piety*, 3; Aaron Rock-Singer, 'A Pious Public: Islamic Magazines and Revival in Egypt, 1976–1981', *British Journal of Middle Eastern Studies* 42:4 (2015).

31 Abdelkader Zghal, 'The Reactivation of Tradition in a Post-Traditional Society', *Daedalus* 102:1 (1973).

32 John P. Entelis, 'Ideological Change and an Emerging Counter-Culture in Tunisian Politics', *The Journal of Modern African Studies* 12:4 (1974): 559.

33 Mark Tessler, 'Political Change and the Islamic Revival in Tunisia', *The Maghreb Review* 5:1 (1980).

34 'Reflets de la vie quotidienne', *Jeune Afrique*, Paris, 20 February 1976, 33.

35 François Burgat, *The Islamic Movement in North Africa*, translated by William Dowell (Austin, TX: Center for Middle Eastern Studies, University of Texas at Austin, 1993), 208.

36 Souhayr Belhassen, 'L'islam contestataire en Tunisie', *Jeune Afrique*, Paris, 14 March 1979.

37 Camau and Geisser, *Le Syndrome Autoritaire*, 277.

38 Mohamed Elbaki Hermassi, 'La société tunisienne au miroir islamiste', *Maghreb Machrek* 103 (1984): 47–8; Emad Eldin Shahin, *Political Ascent: Contemporary Islamic Movements in North Africa* (Boulder, CO: Westview, 1997), 72.

39 The act of *da'wa* was carried out by small units of the Tablighi Jamaat who would visit villages and call on Muslims to: recite and understand the *shahāda*, the Muslim profession of faith; say the *ṣalāt*, the ritual prayer; perform *dhikr*, the ritual remembrance of God; be respectful to fellow Muslims; volunteer for *da'wa* work; and to do these tasks honestly and sincerely. Mumtaz Ahmad, 'Islamic Fundamentalism in South Asia: The Jamaat-i-Islami and the Tablighi Jamaat of South Asia', in *Fundamentalisms Observed*, eds. Martin E. Marty and R. Scott Appleby (Chicago, IL/London: University of Chicago Press, 1994), 513–15.

40 Tamimi, *Rachid Ghannouchi*, 24–5; Wolf, *Political Islam*, 34–5.

41 Ahmad, 'Islamic Fundamentalism in South Asia', 517.

42 Douglas Magnuson, 'Islamic Reform in Contemporary Tunisia: Unity and Diversity', in *Tunisia: The Political Economy of Reform*, ed. I. William Zartman (Boulder, CO: Lynne Rienner, 1991), 172–6.

43 Yahya, former al-Nahda member; born in 1952, imprisoned 1987, 1991–95. Interviewed in Sousse, 27 November 2013.

44 Habib, local al-Nahda member; born in 1951, imprisoned 1987. In hiding 1992–99. Interviewed in Sousse, 28 November 2013.

45 Mohamed Elhachmi Hamdi, *The Politicisation of Islam: A Case Study of Tunisia* (Boulder, CO/Oxford: Westview Press, 1998), 20.

46 Abdallah, Author interview.

47 Rachid Ghannouchi, *Min Tajribat al-Haraka al-Islamiyya fi Tunis* [*On the Experience of the Islamic Movement in Tunisia*] (Beirut: Dar al-Mojtahed, 2011), 52.

48 Rachid Ghannouchi, speech at an al-Nahda rally in Sousse, 11 October 2014.

49 See, for example: Hermassi, 'La société tunisienne', 43.

50 There was a religiously conservative trend within the Neo-Destour, and several children of Bourguibist Destourians became Nahdawis. Camau and Geisser, *Le Syndrome Autoritaire*, 275–6.

51 Khairi, Senior al-Nahda leader; born in 1962, imprisoned 1991–2007. Interviewed in Tunis, 9 October 2014.

52 Ali Nouir (1943–2000) later taught mathematics in Medenine, where one of his pupils was Ali Laarayedh, a senior al-Nahda leader who was prime minister in 2013–14. Nouir was jailed in 1981, 1987–88, and 1991–94, and then died of ill-health in 2000. See: Lotfi al-Amaduni, 'Safahat min Tarikhu wa-Nidalhu fi Dhikra Rahil al-Ustadh Ali Nuwir [Pages from History and the Struggle in Remembrance of the Late Teacher Ali Nouir]', *Al-Fajr*, Tunis, 15 April 2016.

53 Bayat, 'Islamism and Social Movement Theory', 904.

54 Wahiduddin Khan, *God Arises* (Riyadh: International Islamic Publishing House, 2005 [1966]), 294.

55 Zaytuna had been a centre of Islamic teaching since the mid-eighth century, but was marginalized during the French Protectorate. From 1912 to 1951 Zaytuna offered three levels of diploma, the lower levels of which were taught through several Zaytuna schools across the country: aptitude (*al-ahliyya*), proficiency (*al-tahsil*), and scholarship (*al-'ilmiyya*). From 1951 the system was modified so that the proficiency degree was divided into two parts and was equivalent to a baccalaureate. From 1958, under Bourguiba's reforms, Zaytuna was integrated into the public education system and then from March 1961 Zaytuna lost its independence and was incorporated into the new University of Tunis as the small Faculty of Shari'a and Theology. At the time of the 1958 reforms there were 16,000 students and 500 academic staff at Zaytuna. Moore, *Tunisia since Independence*, 54.

56 Shahin, *Political Ascent*, 72; Burgat, *The Islamic Movement*, 4.

57 Chapter 32, verse 19. All Qur'anic Translations Are Taken from: Seyyed Hossein Nasr, ed. *The Study Quran: A New Translation and Commentary* (New York, NY: HarperOne, 2015).

58 Susan Waltz, 'Islamist Appeal in Tunisia', *Middle East Journal* 40:4 (1986): 665.

59 Sahbi, local al-Nahda leader; born in 1958; imprisoned 1983. Interviewed in Chott Meriem, 20 and 21 August 2014.

60 Janine A. Clark, *Islam, Charity, and Activism: Middle-Class Networks and Social Welfare in Egypt, Jordan, and Yemen* (Bloomington, IN: Indiana University Press, 2004), 14.

61 Malika Zeghal, 'Public Institutions of Religious Education in Egypt and Tunisia', in *Trajectories of Education in the Arab World: Legacies and Challenges*, ed. Osama Abi-Mershed (Abingdon: Routledge, 2010), 117.

62 Zeghal, 'Public institutions', 117.

63 Khelif (1917–2006) became a member of the official Higher Islamic Council in 1989 and stood as a candidate for the ruling party in the April 1989 elections, heading the list for Kairouan. His candidacy was part of a regime effort to co-opt the religious revival. Later Khelif gave Qur'anic classes on the Saudi-based Iqraa satellite television channel. Mohamed Kerrou, 'La Grande Mosquée de Kairouan: L'imam, la ville et le pouvoir', *Revue des mondes musulmans et de la Méditerranée* 125: July (2009); Franck Frégosi, 'La régulation institutionelle de l'islam en Tunisie: entre audace moderniste et tutelle étatique' (Paris: Institut Français des Relations Internationales, November 2003), 27.

64 Michaël Ayari, *Le Prix de l'Engagement Politique dans la Tunisie Autoritaire: Gauchistes et islamistes sous Bourguiba et Ben Ali (1957–2011)* (Tunis/Paris: Édition Karthala et IRMC, 2016), 138.

65 Camau and Geisser, *Le Syndrome Autoritaire*, 272.

66 Hassan al-Banna (1906–49), a schoolteacher, founded the Egyptian Society of Muslim Brothers in 1928; Hassan al-Hudaybi (1891–1973) was the Brotherhood's second leader in the period 1951–73; and Mohammed al-Ghazali (1917–96), was an Egyptian cleric and scholar. Abdedayem Noumi, former local al-Nahda member; born in 1957, imprisoned 1991–99. Interviewed in Sousse, 25 June 2013, 25 January, 11 September, and 5 October 2014, 12 May 2015.

67 'Entre-Nous', *Tunis Hebdo*, Tunis, 7 January 1980.

68 Noumi, author interview.

69 Khairi, author interview.

70 Gilles Kepel, *Jihad: The Trail of Political Islam* (London: IB Tauris, 2002), 66.

71 Khairi, author interview.

72 Waltz, 'Islamist Appeal in Tunisia', 654.

73 Fethi, regional al-Nahda leader; born in 1956, imprisoned 1987–88. Interviewed in Monastir, 29 May 2015.

74 Souad Ladhari, local al-Nahda member; born in 1959, abroad 1981–96. Interviewed in Chott Meriem, 9 June 2014.

75 'Hend Chelbi: La femme musulmane doit conserver son authenticité', *Le Temps*, Tunis, 3 October 1975.

76 Camau and Geisser, *Le Syndrome Autoritaire*, 282.

77 Asad, *Formations of the Secular*, 200. I have written elsewhere in more detail about the complex nature of state secularism under Bourguiba and Ben Ali: Rory McCarthy, 'Re-Thinking Secularism in Post-Independence Tunisia', *The Journal of North African Studies* 19:5 (2014).

78 Franck Frégosi, 'Bourguiba et la régulation institutionelle de l'Islam: les contours audacieux d'un gallicanisme politique à la tunisienne', in *Habib Bourguiba: La trace et l'héritage*, eds. Michel Camau and Vincent Geisser (Paris: Karthala, 2004), 96.

79 '544 Shabban Yashrakuna fi Musabaqat Wilayat Susa [544 Young People Participate in a Competition of the Sousse Governorate]', *al-'Amal*, Tunis, 28 August 1977.

80 'Sousse: Projection du film "Le Message"', *Le Temps*, Tunis, 7 January 1978.
81 Jalila Hafsia, 'Espoir et Renouveau à Sousse, Perle de Culture Enchantée', *La Presse*, Tunis, 10 April 1979.
82 Magnuson, 'Islamic Reform', 170.
83 Burgat, *The Islamic Movement*, 185.
84 Hamdi, *The Politicisation of Islam*, 21.
85 Abdul Qadir Slama, 'Al-Iftitahiyya [The Editorial]', *Al-Ma'rifa*, Year 1: No 1 (September) 1972.
86 Yusuf al-Qaradawi (born 1926) is an Egyptian theologian; Sayyid Qutb (1906–66) was an Egyptian Islamist writer executed for plotting against the Egyptian President Gamal Abdel Nasser; his brother Muhammad Qutb (1919–2014) was an Islamist author. Muhammad Qutb, 'Mudhakkirat al-Du'aa [A Reminder for the Preachers]', *Al-Ma'rifa*, Tunis, Year 2: No 10 (June) 1975.
87 Rachid Ghannouchi, 'Al-Isti'mar Yakhruj min al-Ardh li-Yatasallal al-Ra's [Colonialism left the land to infiltrate the head]', *Al-Ma'rifa*, Tunis, Year 1: No 3 (November–December) 1972.
88 Rachid Ghannouchi, 'Ma Huwa al-Takhalluf? [What is backwardness?]', *Al-Ma'rifa*, Tunis, Year 1: No 9 1973, 39.
89 'Al-Hibi [The Hippy]', *Al-Ma'rifa*, Tunis, Year 3: No 1 1975, 7.
90 Abdallah, author interview.
91 Abdallah, author interview.
92 Youssef, local al-Nahda leader; born in 1961, imprisoned 1993–95. Interviewed in Hammam Sousse, 20 March 2014, 21 May 2015.
93 Youssef, author interview.
94 Abul Ala Maududi (1903–79) was an Indian-born Islamist who founded the Jamaat-e-Islami; Muhammad Baqir al-Sadr (1935–80) was an Iraqi theologian and philosopher; and Ruhollah Khomeini (1902–89) was an Iranian ayatollah and leader of the 1979 revolution. Riadh, Regional al-Nahda leader. Born in 1957. In hiding 1987. Interviewed in M'saken, 24 June 2014.
95 Rachid Ghannouchi, 'Al-Thawra al-Iraniyya Thawra Islamiyya [The Iranian Revolution is an Islamic Revolution]', *Al-Ma'rifa*, Tunis, Year 5: No 3 (February) 1979, 3.
96 Rachid Ghannouchi, 'Qadat al-Haraka al-Islamiyya al-Mu'asira [The leaders of the modern Islamic movement]', *Al-Ma'rifa*, Tunis, Year 5: No 4 (April) 1979, 15.
97 Wolf, *Political Islam*, 46–7.
98 Wolf, *Political Islam*, 42–4.
99 Saleh, local al-Nahda member; born in 1958, imprisoned 1987, 1991–94. Interviewed in Akouda, 10 and 24 June 2014.

3 Rethinking Politicization

1 Hassan, local al-Nahda leader; born in 1963, imprisoned 1986–87, 1991–93. Interviewed in Kalaa Seghira, 13 February 2014.
2 See, for example: François Burgat, *The Islamic Movement*; Shahin, *Political Ascent*; Mohamed Elhachmi Hamdi, *The Politicisation of Islam*; Alaya Allani,

'The Islamists in Tunisia between Confrontation and Participation: 1980–2008', *The Journal of North African Studies* 14:2 (2009).

3 Burgat, *The Islamic Movement*, 183.

4 Allani, 'The Islamists in Tunisia', 257.

5 'Interview Transcript: Rachid Ghannouchi', *Financial Times*, London, 18 January 2011.

6 Anouar al-Jamaoui, 'Nurid Hukm al-Balad bi-Tafwid min al-Sha'b [We Want a Government of the Country with a Popular Mandate]', *Al-Fajr*, Tunis, 26 October 2012.

7 Harakat al-Ittijah al-Islami, 'al-Nadwa al-Suhufiyya al-Awwala li-Harakat al-Ittijah al-Islami [The First Press Conference of the Islamic Tendency Movement]', in *Bayanat Dhikra al-Ta'sis li-Harakat al-Nahda al-Tunisiyya* [*Statements Commemorating the Foundation of the Tunisian al-Nahda Movement*] (Tunis: Harakat al-Nahda, 2012), 19.

8 Camau and Geisser, *Le Syndrome Autoritaire*, 287.

9 Ghannouchi, 'Al-Thawra al-Iraniyya', 4.

10 Ghannouchi, *Min Tajribat*, 55. The word 'oppressed' (*al-mustaḍ'afīn*) has a particular resonance. It is used in the Qur'an and Sunna in the context of empowering the powerless and thereby constituting a notion of Islamic justice. It was used politically by Ali Shariati, the Iranian intellectual, who argued that true Islam was committed to social justice in resisting oppressive forces: Khaled Abou El Fadl, 'Qur'anic Ethics and Islamic Law', *Journal of Islamic Ethics* 1:1–2 (2017): 24; William Montgomery Watt, *Islamic Fundamentalism and Modernity* (Abingdon: Routledge, 2013), 134.

11 Issa Ben Dhiaf, 'Chronique politique Tunisie', *Annuaire de l'Afrique du Nord* XIX (1980): 583.

12 Issa Ben Dhiaf, 'Chronique politique Tunisie', *Annuaire de l'Afrique du Nord* XX (1981): 591; Mohamed Boughzala and Azzam Mahjob, 'Chronique économique Tunisie', *Annuaire de l'Afrique du Nord* XIX (1980): 663.

13 Ben Dhiaf, 'Chronique politique (1981)', 586–8.

14 Ben Dhiaf, 'Chronique politique (1981)'; Jaleleddine Rouis, *al-Khasa'is al-Tanzimiyya wa-l-Haykaliyya li-l-Haraka al-Islamiyya fi Tunis—al-'Amal al-Jama'i* [*Organisational and Structural Characteristics of the Islamist Movement in Tunisia—Collective Action*] (Tunis: Manshurat Karem al-Sharif, 2014), 18; Eva Bellin, 'Civil Society in Formation: Tunisia', in *Civil Society in the Middle East. Volume 1*, ed. Augustus Richard Norton (Leiden/New York, NY/Köln: Brill, 1995), 133.

15 Harakat al-Ittijah al-Islami, 'al-Bayan al-Ta'sisi'.

16 In the early 1990s, well after al-Nahda had formally committed to operating within a civil state, Ghannouchi still advocated the establishment of an 'Islamic government' for which the supreme legislative authority was the shari'a, from which scholars would deduce laws and regulations for judges. Political power would rest with the Muslim community, through a system of 'mandatory consultation'. Rachid Ghannouchi, 'The Participation of Islamists in a Non-Islamic Government', in *Power-Sharing Islam?*, ed. Azzam Tamimi (London: Liberty for Muslim World, 1993), 55.

17 Harakat al-Ittijah al-Islami, 'Ijtima' al-Hay'a al-Ta'sisiyya'.

18 Tamimi, *Rachid Ghannouchi*, 58.

19 Hermassi, 'La société tunisienne', 43.

20 Souhayr Belhassen and Abdelaziz Dahmani, 'Sur le Moyen-Orient la Tunisie a su prendre une position d'avant-garde—Une interview de Hedi Nouira, Premier ministre tunisien', *Jeune Afrique*, Paris, 18 April 1979.

21 'Ramadan: Les cafés et les commerces de restauration fermeront durant le jour', *La Presse*, Tunis, 4 July 1981; Ben Dhiaf, 'Chronique politique (1981)', 623.

22 'Debat sur la tolerance', *Le Maghreb*, Tunis, 18 July 1981.

23 Ben Dhiaf, 'Chronique politique (1981)', 597–8.

24 The Tunisian Communist Party was founded in 1934 as a branch of the French Communist Party. It was legalized in 1981, then dropped its attachment to Marxist-Leninism in 1992 and became the Movement of Renewal, known as Ettajdid. It should not be confused with the Tunisian Workers' Communist Party (PCOT), which was founded in 1986 and which remained illegal until 2011. In 2012 the PCOT changed its name to the Workers' Party.

25 UPI 'M. Mzali à l'agence UPI: Tous les Tunisiens présentent un front uni contre l'osbcurantisme et l'intolérance', *La Presse*, Tunis, 18 July 1981; 'M. Mzali aux Imams: Protéger les mosquées contre le terrorisme intellectuel', *La Presse*, Tunis, 31 July 1981.

26 Case no. 12183, Appeal Court of Tunis (3 October 1981).

27 'Loi no. 59–154 du 7 novembre 1959, relative aux associations' (Tunis: Republic of Tunisia, 1959).

28 Case no. 12183.

29 Mahmoud, former MTI member; born in 1952, imprisoned 1983. Interviewed in Sousse, 13 February 2014.

30 Kamel Ben Younes, *al-Islamiyyun wa-l-'Ilmaniyyun fi Tunis: Min al-sujun wa-l-idtihad ila tadaddi hukm al-bilad* [*The Islamists and the Secularists in Tunisia: From Prisons and Persecution to the Challenge of Ruling the Country*] (Tunis: Bareq, 2012), 119.

31 Ben Younes, *al-Islamiyyun wa-l-'Ilmaniyyun*, 82.

32 Nadia al-Turki, 'al-Jebali fi Mudhakkirathu li-l-Sharq al-Awsat: Kuntu shabban masisan bidun tawajjuh Islami [Jebali in his Recollections to Asharq al-Awsat: I was a politicized young man without an Islamist orientation]', *Asharq al-Awsat*, London, 7 July 2014.

33 Rouis, *al-Khasa'is al-Tanzimiyya*, 20.

34 Rouis, *al-Khasa'is al-Tanzimiyya*, 21.

35 Harakat al-Ittijah al-Islami, 'Bayan hawla Tashkil al-Maktab al-Tanfidhi al-Jadid li-Harakat al-Ittijah al-Islami [Statement on the formation of a new Executive Bureau of the Islamic Tendency Movement]' (Tunis: 19 January 1983).

36 Souhayr Belhassen, 'Un coup à droite, un coup à gauche', *Jeune Afrique*, Paris, 5 August 1981.

37 Abdelfattah, local al-Nahda leader; born in 1963, imprisoned 1987, 1992–93. Interviewed in Akouda, 14 August 2014.

38 Issa Ben Dhiaf, 'Chronique Tunisie', *Annuaire de l'Afrique du Nord* XXI (1982): 712.

39 Among the prominent al-Nahda members from beyond Sousse who came to the city to study at the Faculty of Law in the late 1980s were: Habib Khedher, rapporteur for the constitution in the 2011–14 assembly; Farida Labidi, a member of al-Nahda's political bureau in 2014; Samir Dilou, a minister for human rights in 2011–14; as well as several deputies who sat in the 2011–14 assembly and the parliament elected in 2014, including Amel Ghouil, Adel Ben Attia, and Dalila Babba.

40 Ajmi Lourimi, senior al-Nahda leader; born in 1962, imprisoned 1991–2007. Interviewed in Tunis, 20 July 2011.

41 Camau and Geisser, *Le Syndrome Autoritaire*, 290.

42 Jean-Philippe Bras, 'Chronique Tunisie', *Annuaire de l'Afrique du Nord* XXIV (1985): 708.

43 Ben Younes, *al-Islamiyyun wa-l-'Ilmaniyyun*, 95–6.

44 Laarayedh, an engineer from Medenine, in southern Tunisia, had studied at the merchant marine school in Sousse in 1977–80. Later, he became interior minister in 2011–13 and prime minister in 2013–14. Rouis, *al-Khasa'is al-Tanzimiyya*, 25.

45 The Democratic Patriots eventually became a legal political party in 2011. Their leader, Chokri Belaïd, was assassinated in Tunis on 6 February 2013. Ben Dhiaf, 'Chronique Tunisie (1982)', 687.

46 James M. Jasper, *The Art of Moral Protest: Culture, Biography, and Creativity in Social Movements* (Chicago, IL/London: University of Chicago Press, 1997), 106.

47 Jamel, regional al-Nahda leader; born in 1966, imprisoned 1991–99. Interviewed in Sousse, 27 August and 9 September 2014.

48 Sahbi, author interview.

49 Hermassi, 'La société tunisienne', 42.

50 Diego Gambetta and Steffen Hertog, *Engineers of Jihad: The Curious Connection between Violent Extremism and Education* (Princeton, NJ: Princeton University Press, 2016), 74–5.

51 Gambetta and Hertog, *Engineers of Jihad*, 128–58.

52 My research was not constructed as a representative quantitative survey, however of the 85 Nahdawis interviewed, I have details of university education for 77. Of those, 70 attended university: 40 studied non-scientific subjects (law, social sciences, theology, humanities, Arabic); 28 studied scientific subjects (medicine, engineering, general sciences); 2 went into teacher training, which could draw on non-scientific or scientific education. There were 16 law graduates, 10 medics, and 9 engineers.

53 New work on contemporary Egyptian Islamists has demonstrated that it is not that young Islamist activists are overwhelmingly students of engineering and medicine, but rather that political activism tends to attract students with higher grades who have studied science, a subject for which the university entrance examination is more prestigious. Thus 'political activism attracts elite students': Neil Ketchley and Michael Biggs, 'The Educational Contexts of Islamist Activism: Elite Students and Religious Institutions in Egypt', *Mobilization: An International Quarterly* 22:1 (2017): 58.

54 Éric Gobe, 'The Tunisian Bar to the Test of Authoritarianism: Professional and Political Movements in Ben Ali's Tunisia (1990–2007)', *The Journal of North African Studies* 15:3 (2010): 334.

55 Youssef, author interview.

56 Gsouma Gsouma, 'Mujaz fi Tarikh al-Haraka al-Siyasiyya dhat al-Huwiyya al-'Arabiyya al-Islamiyya bi-Tunis [A Summary of the History of the Political Movement with an Arab-Islamic identity in Tunisia]', in *Harakat al-Nahda al-Tunisiyya: Min al-Sujun wa-l-Manafi ila Surrat al-Hukm* [*The Tunisian al-Nahda Movement: From Prisons and Exile to the Centre of Government*], ed. Abdedayem Noumi (Tunis: Matba'a al-Buraq, 2011), 21.

57 The date is Martyrs' Day in Tunisia in remembrance of a nationalist protest during the French protectorate demanding political reform.

58 The student council (*al-Majlis al-'Ilmi* or *le Conseil Scientifique*) was an annually elected body in each university faculty that gathered representatives of students and teaching staff. Election results indicated the strength of rival political factions among students.

59 Abdelfattah, author interview.

60 Ali Shariati (1933–77) was an Iranian scholar whose ideas were taken up during the Iranian revolution; Malek Bennabi (1905–73) was an Algerian philosopher, whose work influenced Ghannouchi. While in prison in 1981–84, Ghannouchi translated a Bennabi essay on Islam and democracy, which argued that Islam inspires in man a democratic attitude. Tamimi, *Rachid Ghannouchi*, 63. On Bennabi, see also: François Burgat, *Islamism in the Shadow of al-Qaeda*, translated by Patrick Hutchinson (Austin, TX: University of Texas Press, 2008), 10–12, 33–4.

61 Rachid, regional al-Nahda leader; born in 1960, imprisoned 1987, 1991–2002. Interviewed in Sousse, 23 January, 7 February, and 2 June, 2014.

62 Hedi, local al-Nahda leader; born in 1968, imprisoned 1991–95. Interviewed in Kalaa Kebira, 12 June and 12 August 2014.

63 Rachid, author interview.

64 Harakat al-Nahda, 'al-Qanun al-Asasi li-Harakat al-Nahda [The Basic Law of the al-Nahda Movement]', in *Bayanat Dhikra al-Ta'sis li-Harakat al-Nahda al-Tunisiyya* [*Statements Commemorating the Foundation of the Tunisian al-Nahda Movement*] (Tunis: Harakat al-Nahda, 2012).

65 Abdelkader Zghal, 'The New Strategy of the Movement of the Islamic Way: Manipulation or Expression of Political Culture?', in *Tunisia: The Political Economy of Reform*, ed. I. William Zartman (Boulder, CO: Lynne Rienner, 1991), 217.

66 Saleh, local al-Nahda member; born in 1958, imprisoned 1987, 1991–94. Interviewed in Akouda, 10 and 24 June 2014.

67 Linda Jones, 'Portrait of Rashid al-Ghannoushi', *Middle East Report* 153 (1988): 20.

68 Christopher Alexander, 'Opportunities, Organizations, and Ideas: Islamists and Workers in Tunisia and Algeria', *International Journal of Middle East Studies* 32:4 (2000): 466.

69 Sayida, local al-Nahda leader; born in 1960, interviewed in Chott Meriem, 21 August 2014.

70 Farida, former al-Nahda member; born in 1972, interviewed in Hai Riadh, 22 September 2014.

71 Farida, author interview.

72 Hafedh, local al-Nahda member; born in 1955, imprisoned 1987, 1991–93. Interviewed in Kalaa Seghira, 9 June 2014.

73 Hafedh, author interview.

74 Nabil Douik, local al-Nahda member; born in 1966, interviewed in Sousse, 15 May 2015.

75 Abdelhamid, local al-Nahda leader; born in 1961, imprisoned 1987, 1991–94. Interviewed in Hammam Sousse, 13 April 2014.

76 Nira Yuval-Davis, 'Belonging and the Politics of Belonging', *Patterns of Prejudice* 40:3 (2006).

77 White, *A Comparative Political Economy*, 118.

78 The Personal Status Code was a progressive set of family laws introduced by Bourguiba in August 1956 banning polygamy, ending the male right of repudiation, and giving women the right to divorce and to approve arranged marriages. Burgat, *The Islamic Movement*, 196; Abdellatif al-Furati, 'Hadith Khass maʿ al-Shakyh Rashid al-Ghannushi [A Special Interview with Shaykh Rachid Ghannouchi]', *Al-Sabah*, Tunis, 17 July 1988.

79 'Bourguiba: Il est inadmissible que l'Université soit transformée en un forum pour des obscurantistes', *La Presse*, Tunis, 20 February 1987.

80 Asma Larif-Béatrix, 'Chroniques intérieures: Tunisie', *Annuaire de l'Afrique du Nord* XXVI (1987): 649. Abdelhamid Jelassi, *Hisad al-Ghuyyab: al-Yad al-Saghira la Takdhib [The Harvest of the Absent: The Small Hand Does Not Lie]* (Tunis: Maktabat Tunis, 2016), 70.

81 Elbaki Hermassi, 'The Islamicist Movement and November 7', in *Tunisia: The Political Economy of Reform*, ed. I. William Zartman (Boulder, CO: Lynne Rienner, 1991), 195.

82 Walid, regional al-Nahda leader; born in 1963, imprisoned 1987, 1991–2006. Interviewed in Sousse, 21 April and 30 September 2014; 29 May 2015.

83 Bechir, local al-Nahda leader; born in 1968, imprisoned 1991–93. Interviewed in Sousse, 9 February 2014.

84 Jamel, author interview.

85 'Le reseau Khomeinyst', *La Presse*, Tunis, 28 March 1987.

86 Hermassi, 'The Islamicist Movement', 195.

87 'Tunisie: le procès des islamistes. L'avocat général requiert la peine de mort', *Le Monde*, Paris, 15 September 1987.

88 'Tunisie: le procès des intégristes. Les islamistes du MTI menacent de réagir 'face à la tyrannie'', *Le Monde*, Paris, 11 September 1987.

89 Burgat, *The Islamic Movement*, 224–8; Camau and Geisser, *Le Syndrome Autoritaire*, 292; Wolf, *Political Islam*, 64–6.

90 Walid, author interview.

91 AFP, 'Tunisie: La déclaration du successeur', *Le Monde*, Paris, 8 November 1987; Nicolas Beau and Jean-Pierre Tuquoi, *Notre Ami Ben Ali: L'envers du 'miracle tunisien'* (Paris: La Découverte, 2011), 44–5.

92 Hermassi, 'The Islamicist Movement', 198.

93 Several opposition parties were formally authorized including the Progressive Socialist Rally (RSP) of Nejib Chebbi (which later became the Progressive Democratic Party and then the Republican Party); the Social Party for Progress (PSP) of Mounir Beji (which later became the Social Liberal Party);

and the Arab nationalist Unionist Democratic Union (UDU) of Abderrahmane Tlili. 'Loi organique no. 88–32 du mai 1988 organisant les partis politiques', (Tunis: Republic of Tunisia, 1988); 'Proclamation du Pacte Nationale: Une étape éminente dans l'histoire de la Tunisie', *La Presse*, Tunis, 8 November 1988.

94 Harakat al-Nahda, 'al-Qanun al-Asasi'.

95 I. William Zartman, 'The Conduct of Political Reform: the Path toward Democracy', in *Tunisia: The Political Economy of Reform*, ed. I. William Zartman (Boulder, CO: Lynne Rienner, 1991), 22.

96 Zartman, 'The Conduct of Political Reform', 23.

97 François Soudan, 'Tunisie: La stratégie des islamistes', *Jeune Afrique*, Paris, 19 April 1989.

98 Abdelbaki Hermassi, 'The Rise and Fall of the Islamist Movement in Tunisia', in *The Islamist Dilemma: The Political Role of Islamist Movements in the Contemporary Arab World*, ed. Laura Guazzone (Reading: Ithaca, 1995), 115.

99 Abdelfattah, Author interview.

100 Mortadha Labidi, regional PCOT leader, born in 1952, interviewed in Sousse, 1 May 2014.

101 This is according to the official figures: 'Tous les résultats des législatives', *La Presse*, Tunis, 4 April 1989.

102 Soudan, 'Tunisie: La stratégie des islamistes', 37.

103 'Le scrutin a été tout à fait régulier', *La Presse*, Tunis, 4 April 1989.

104 'Ben Ali: "Je veillerai a l'intérêt de la patrie"', *La Presse*, Tunis, 4 April 1989.

105 Burgat, *The Islamic Movement*, 237.

106 'Ben Ali s'adresse à la Nation: Programme pour une Étape Nouvelle', *La Presse*, Tunis, 8 November 1989.

107 Rachid Ghannouchi, 'Al-Fajr Musahama fi al-Hall [Al-Fajr is Participating in the Solution]', *Al-Fajr*, Tunis, 21 April 1990.

108 Charfi had been a leader of the leftist Group of Studies and Socialist Action in Tunisia (GEAST) movement, for which he was jailed in 1968, and was an outspoken opponent of the al-Nahda project. 'The Islamists soon accused me of "draining the springs". I made sure to dry up their recruitment. They're right!': Sophie Bessis and François Soudan, 'Mohamed Charfi: Mon combat contre les islamistes', *Jeune Afrique*, Paris, 30 April 1990, 20. The Egyptian Muslim Brotherhood faced an identically named policy, see: Darrag, 'Politics or Piety?', 222.

109 'Al-Nata'ij al-Kamila li-Intikhabat Majalis al-Kulliyyat [The Complete Results for College Council Elections]', *Al-Fajr*, Tunis, 21 April 1990, 9.

110 Manoubi Marouki, 'Tunisie: débat sur la démocratisation. Les huits propositions de l'opposition', *Jeune Afrique*, Paris, 21–27 November 1990, 33.

111 Zakya Daoud, 'Chronique Tunisienne', *Annuaire de l'Afrique du Nord* XXVIII (1989): 790.

112 Sahbi, author interview.

113 Leadership of the movement was passed from one senior figure to another as the repression intensified. Between August 1987 and the end of 1991, there were ten different leaders of the movement. Mohamed Daifallah, 'Min

al-Sirriyya ila al-Mahjar ila al-'Alan [From Secrecy to Exile to Going Public]', *Al-Fajr*, Tunis, 20 May 2016.

114 Hermassi, 'The Rise and Fall', 121. Abdelbaki Hermassi, the Tunisian scholar quoted here, joined Ben Ali's government as culture minister from 1996 and was appointed foreign minister in 2004–5.

115 Charles Kurzman, 'Structural Opportunity and Perceived Opportunity in Social-Movement Theory: The Iranian Revolution of 1979', *American Sociological Review* 61:1 (1996).

116 'Khatir: Masjid Yatahawwal ila Shu'ba [Urgent: A mosque is turned into a party office]', *Al-Fajr*, Tunis, 21 April 1990.

117 Amnesty International, 'Tunisia: Prolonged Incommunicado Detention and Torture', (London: 4 March 1992), 18.

4 Confronting Prison

1 Hamadi Jebali, former senior al-Nahda leader; born in 1949, imprisoned 1989–2006. Interviewed in Oxford, 14 and 15 May, and Tunis, 24 September 2013.

2 Christopher Alexander, 'Back from the Democratic Brink: Authoritarianism and Civil Society in Tunisia', *Middle East Report* 205 (1997): 35.

3 Emma Murphy, *Economic and Political Change in Tunisia: From Bourguiba to Ben Ali* (Basingstoke: Macmillan, 1999), 199.

4 Graham Usher, 'The Reawakening of Nahda in Tunisia', *Middle East Research and Information Project*, Washington, DC, 30 April 2011.

5 Aryeh Neier, 'Confining Dissent: The Political Prison', in *The Oxford History of the Prison: The Practice of Punishment in Western Society*, eds. Norval Morris and David J. Rothman (New York, NY/Oxford: Oxford University Press, 1995), 424.

6 Sune Haugbolle, 'Imprisonment, Truth Telling and Historical Memory in Syria', *Mediterranean Politics* 13:2 (2008): 264–5.

7 White, *A Comparative Political Economy*, 170.

8 Laleh Khalili and Jillian Schwedler, eds., *Policing and Prisons in the Middle East: Formations of Coercion* (London: Hurst, 2010), 1.

9 Murphy, *Economic and Political Change*, 193.

10 Clement Henry, 'Tunisia's "Sweet Little" Regime', in *Worst of the Worst: Dealing with Repressive and Rogue Nations*, ed. Robert I. Rotberg (Washington, DC: Brookings Institution Press, 2007), 301–2; Derek Lutterbeck, 'Tool of Rule: The Tunisian Police under Ben Ali', *The Journal of North African Studies* 20:5 (2015): 815.

11 Roy Walmsley, 'World Prison Population List, 6th edn' (London: International Centre for Prison Studies, King's College, 2005).

12 The Brotherhood in turn took this name from the experience of Ahmad Ibn Hanbal, the jurist jailed in Baghdad in the eighth century, in order to portray prison as a test of faith and perseverance before God: John Calvert, *Sayyid Qutb and the Origins of Radical Islamism* (London: Hurst, 2010), 197.

13 'Loi no. 87–79 du 29 décembre 1987, portant suppression de la cour de sûreté de l'État' (Tunis: Republic of Tunisia, 1987); 'Loi no. 87–70 du

26 novembre 1987, portant modification de certains articles du code de procédure pénale' (Tunis: Republic of Tunisia, 1987).

14 Amnesty International, 'Tunisia: Prolonged Incommunicado Detention', 3.

15 Noureddine Sraieb, 'Tunisie—Chronique Intérieure 1993', *Annuaire de l'Afrique du Nord* XXXII (1993): 621.

16 Tarek Osman, *Islamism: What It Means for the Middle East and the West* (New Haven, CT/London: Yale University Press, 2016), 29.

17 Esmail Nashif, *Palestinian Political Prisoners: Identity and Community* (Abingdon/New York, NY: Routledge, 2008), 203.

18 Amnesty International, 'Tunisia: Prolonged Incommunicado Detention', 8; Jebali, author interview.

19 By 2003 around 1,000 were thought to be in exile, most in Britain, France, Belgium, Holland, Germany, Switzerland, and Canada: Camau and Geisser, *Le Syndrome Autoritaire*, 305.

20 Human Rights Watch, 'Tunisia: Military Courts That Sentenced Islamist Leaders Violated Basic Fair-Trial Norms' (New York, NY: October 1992); Amnesty International, 'Tunisia: Heavy sentences after unfair trials' (London: 19 October 1992).

21 Case no. 9058, Criminal Circuit Court of Appeal for Sousse (20 April 1993).

22 As in 1981, this second charge referred to a breach of the 1959 law relating to associations: 'Loi no. 59–154'.

23 Lynn Welchman, 'Trying Times in Tunis: Notes from a Purposeful Observer', in *Narratives of Truth in Islamic Law*, eds. Baudouin Dupret, Barbara Drieskens, and Annelies Moors (London: IB Tauris, 2008), 185.

24 Welchman, 'Trying Times in Tunis', 191–2.

25 Hamza, local al-Nahda member; born in 1964, imprisoned 1987, 1991–93. Interviewed in Kalaa Kebira, 29 January, and 4 June 2014.

26 Jelassi, *Hisad al-Ghuyyab*, 168–9.

27 The Islamic Salvation Front (al-Jabha al-Islamiyya li-l-Inqadh, or FIS) had swept municipal elections in Algeria in June 1990. Key FIS leaders were arrested by the army in June 1991, but the group went on to win the first round of parliamentary elections in December 1991 before the military stepped in to stage a coup the following month.

28 The pseudonym given to the author by the human rights activists who published his account was Abdelwahab Sdiri, a combination of the names of two al-Nahda prisoners who died in prison in 2002: Abdelwahab Boussaa, who died after a four-month hunger strike, and Lakhdhar Sdiri, who died from lack of medical care. Abdelwahab Sdiri, *Dans cinq ans il n'y aura plus de Coran: Un prisonnier tunisien témoigne*, translated by Luiza Toscane (Paris: Éditions Paris-Méditerranée, 2003), 78–80.

29 Amnesty International, 'In the Name of Security: Routine Abuses in Tunisia', (London: 23 June 2008), 16.

30 Amnesty International, 'In the Name of Security', 16; Doris H. Gray, 'Tunisia after the Uprising: Islamist and Secular Quests for Women's Rights', *Mediterranean Politics* 17:3 (2012): 295; Doris H. Gray and Terry Coonan, 'Notes from the Field: Silence Kills! Women and the Transitional Justice Process in Post-Revolutionary Tunisia', *International Journal of Transitional Justice* 7:2 (2013): 354.

31 Jamel, author interview.
32 Hassan, author interview.
33 Abdelbaki Hermassi, 'Montée et déclin du mouvement islamiste en Tunisie', *Confluences Méditerranée* 12:Autumn (1994): 33.
34 For a reading of al-Nahda as having violent tendencies, see: Michael Collins Dunn, 'The An-Nahda Movement in Tunisia: From Renaissance to Revolution', in *Islamism and Secularism in North Africa*, ed. John Ruedy (London: Macmillan, 1994). For the Algerian comparison, see: Michael J. Willis, *Politics and Power in the Maghreb: Algeria, Tunisia and Morocco from Independence to the Arab Spring* (London: Hurst, 2012), 176–7.
35 Harakat al-Nahda, 'Shuhada' al-Haraka [The Martyrs of the Movement]', www.webcitation.org/6fl0OzT2k.
36 Rachid, author interview.
37 Solidarité tunisienne & Comité de défense des prisonniers politiques en Tunisie, *Les prisonniers à caractère spécial ou la tragédie des prisonniers politiques en Tunisie* (Aubervilliers: Solidarité tunisienne, 2003).
38 Human Rights Watch, 'Tunisia: Long-Term Solitary Confinement of Political Prisoners' (New York, NY: July 2004), 1–2.
39 Sdiri, *Dans cinq ans*, 68; Noumi, author interview.
40 Jamel, author interview.
41 Jamel, author interview.
42 'Raf' Iltibas [A Clarification]', *Al-Sabah*, Tunis, 14 October 1993.
43 'Tabarra' wa-Iltizam [A Declaration of Innocence and Commitment]', *Al-Sabah*, Tunis, 14 September 1993.
44 'Tabarra' [A Declaration of Innocence]', *Al-Sabah*, Tunis, 17 March 1993.
45 Hibou, *The Force of Obedience*, 7.
46 Nabil, local al-Nahda leader; born in 1972, imprisoned in 2007. Interviewed in Sousse, 21 and 28 November 2013, 21 March 2014, 20 May 2015.
47 Earlier accounts of prison repression show some similarities to the treatment of Nahdawis. See, for example: Gilbert Naccache, *Cristal* (Tunis: Les Éditions Mots Passants, 2011 [1982]).
48 Harakat al-Nahda, 'Bayan al-Dhikra al-Khamisa 'Ashar'.
49 Harakat al-Nahda, 'Bayan al-Dhikra al-Khamisa 'Ashar', 62.
50 Harakat al-Nahda, 'Bayan al-Dhikra al-Khamisa 'Ashar', 85.
51 The mention of 'excesses' and of Bab Souika does not seem to appear in the version of this document published by al-Nahda in a collection of historic party documents in 2012, a time when the movement faced constant media suspicion over its commitment to democracy. However, it does appear in an online version of the statement published on an opposition website in 2010, shortly before the fall of Ben Ali, when, as we will see, the movement was trying to reconcile with the regime. Harakat al-Nahda, ''Ayyinat min Muraji'at Harakat al-Nahda [Samples of the Reviews of the al-Nahda movement]', *al-Hiwar.net*, 11 June 2010.
52 Jebali, author interview.
53 Camau and Geisser, *Le Syndrome Autoritaire*, 306.
54 Karkar (1948–2012) had gone into exile in 1987, and was granted political asylum in France in 1988. In 1993 he was put under house arrest in Paris

until October 2011. Camau and Geisser, *Le Syndrome Autoritaire*, 307–8; Wolf, *Political Islam*, 94.

55 Hermassi, 'The Islamicist Movement', 203.
56 Murphy, *Economic and Political Change*, 200–1.
57 Tamimi, *Rachid Ghannouchi*, 72.
58 See, for example: Alfred Stepan and Juan J. Linz, 'Democratization Theory and the "Arab Spring"', *Journal of Democracy* 24:2 (2013).
59 Bechir, author interview.
60 Michael J. Willis, 'Morocco's Islamists and the Legislative Elections of 2002: The Strange Case of the Party that Did Not Want to Win', *Mediterranean Politics* 9:1 (2004); Brown, *When Victory Is Not an Option*, 25; Günes Murat Tezcür, 'The Moderation Theory Revisited: The Case of Islamic Political Actors', *Party Politics* 16:1 (2010).
61 Rachid, author interview.
62 Jelassi, *Hisad al-Ghuyyab*, 173.
63 Walid, author interview.
64 Salah Nouir, regional al-Nahda leader; born in 1950, imprisoned 1981–84, 1987, 1991–95. Interviewed in Hai Riadh, 6 December 2013.
65 Hibou, *The Force of Obedience*, 291.
66 Allen Feldman, *Formations of Violence: The Narrative of the Body and Political Terror in Northern Ireland* (Chicago, IL: University of Chicago Press, 1991), 219; Banu Bargu, *Starve and Immolate: The Politics of Human Weapons* (New York, NY: Columbia University Press, 2014), 313.
67 Bargu, *Starve and Immolate*, 32, 311.
68 Feldman, *Formations of Violence*, 220.
69 Mehdi, regional al-Nahda leader; born in 1972, imprisoned 1991–99. Interviewed in Sousse, 19 January and 13 August 2014.
70 Jamel, author interview.
71 James M. Jasper, 'Emotions and Social Movements: Twenty Years of Theory and Research', *Annual Review of Sociology* 37:1 (2011): 287.
72 Sdiri, *Dans cinq ans*, 124.
73 Jelassi, *Hisad al-Ghuyyab*, 232.
74 Jelassi, *Hisad al-Ghuyyab*, 237.
75 Sdiri, *Dans cinq ans*, 125.
76 Solidarité tunisienne & Comité de défense des prisonniers politiques en Tunisie, *Les prisonniers à caractère spécial*.
77 Human Rights Watch, 'Tunisia: Long-term Solitary Confinement', 20.
78 Rachid, author interview.
79 Rachid, author interview.
80 Jelassi, *Hisad al-Ghuyyab*, 232.
81 Human Rights Watch, 'Tunisia: Long-Term Solitary Confinement', 12.
82 Human Rights Watch, 'Tunisia: Long-Term Solitary Confinement', 12.
83 Jebali was also allowed a television in his solitary confinement cell by 2004 but it was tuned to broadcast only *Canal Tunis*, the state channel. Human Rights Watch, 'Tunisia. Crushing the Person, Crushing a Movement: The Solitary Confinement of Political Prisoners' (New York, NY: April 2005), 17–18. Human Rights Watch, 'Tunisia: Long-Term Solitary Confinement', 17.

84 Taoufik Ben Brik, *Une si douce dictature: Chroniques tunisiennes 1991–2000* (Tunis: RMR Editions, 2011).

85 Richard Lawless, 'Tunisia: History', in *The Middle East and North Africa 2003*, ed. Joanne Maher (London/New York, NY: Europa Publications, 2003), 1076.

86 Hibou, *The Force of Obedience*, 291.

87 Jamel, author interview.

88 Jelassi, *Hisad al-Ghuyyab*, 26.

89 Khawla al-Naqati, "Abd al-Hamid al-Jilasi kama Lam Yatahaddath min Qabl [Abdelhamid Jelassi as he has never spoken before]', *al-Fajr*, Tunis, 15 April 2016.

90 Rachid, author interview.

91 Naccache, *Cristal*, 15, 46.

92 Richard English, *Armed Struggle: A History of the IRA* (London: Macmillan, 2003), 235–6.

93 Monia Ibrahim, 'Sousse le 16 mai 2004', *Tunisnews*, 7 August 2004.

94 Ibrahim, 'Sousse le 16 mai 2004'.

95 Gray and Coonan, 'Notes from the Field', 350–1.

96 Gray and Coonan, 'Notes from the Field', 353.

97 Amnesty International, 'Tunisia: Repression Thrives on Impunity' (London: 2 November 1995), 17–18.

98 Amnesty International, 'Tunisia: Women Victims of Harassment, Torture and Imprisonment' (London: 2 June 1993).

99 Noumi, author interview.

100 Abdelfattah, author interview.

101 Abdelfattah, author interview.

102 Kawther, local al-Nahda leader; born in 1962. Interviewed in Hai Riadh, 11 September 2014.

103 *Mulūkhiyya* is a slow-cooked stew eaten across the region and made with green jute leaves. *'Uṣbān* is a North African sausage made with rice, herbs, and lamb.

104 Solidarité tunisienne & Comité de défense des prisonniers politiques en Tunisie, *Les prisonniers à caractère spécial*.

105 Gray, 'Tunisia after the Uprising', 292, 298.

106 Kawther, author interview.

107 Jelassi, *Hisad al-Ghuyyab*, 273.

5 Beyond Social Exclusion

1 Hamza, author interview.

2 Around 400–500 prisoners were released early in 1999, including many Nahdawis. Other early releases followed in November 2004, November 2005, and February 2006. Abdelaziz Barrouhi, 'Le sens des libérations', *Jeune Afrique*, Paris, 5 March 2006.

3 Mohiddine Lagha, former regional leader of the LTDH; born in 1955, interviewed in Sousse, 29 April 2014.

4 Labidi, author interview.

5 Ismail, *Rethinking Islamist Politics*, 138, 159.
6 Hibou, *The Force of Obedience*, 6.
7 Hibou, *The Force of Obedience*, 213–66.
8 Larbi Sadiki, 'Political Liberalization in Bin Ali's Tunisia: Façade Democracy', *Democratization* 9:4 (2002): 126.
9 Hibou, *The Force of Obedience*, 8.
10 Article 26.
11 Articles 23 and 5.
12 Rachid, author interview.
13 Hafedh, author interview.
14 Bechir, author interview.
15 Nouir, author interview.
16 Murad, local al-Nahda member; born in 1981, interviewed in Sousse, 6 and 13 March 2014.
17 Jean-François Julliard and Hajar Smouni, 'Quand la police tunisienne surveille les journalistes', *Nawaat*, Tunis, 3 December 2006.
18 Public sector work in Tunisia made up 59.1 per cent of all formal employment. Roberta Gatti *et al.*, 'Jobs for Shared Prosperity: Time for Action in the Middle East and North Africa' (Washington, DC: World Bank, 2013), 148.
19 Hafedh, author interview.
20 Nacer Ould Mammar, 'Face à la crise, Leoni Tunisie Groupe se replie sur ses bases', *Kapitalis*, 2012, 2 August 2012.
21 James C. Scott, *Weapons of the Weak: Everyday Forms of Peasant Resistance* (New Haven, CT/London: Yale University Press, 1985), 29.
22 Hamza, author interview.
23 Kamel, regional al-Nahda leader; born in 1953, imprisoned 1987–88, 1991–93. Interviewed in Sousse, 12 June 2014.
24 Youssef, author interview.
25 Nabil, author interview.
26 Clement Henry Moore and Robert Springborg, *Globalization and the Politics of Economic Development in the Middle East* (Cambridge/New York, NY: Cambridge University Press, 2001), 225–6.
27 Patrick Haenni, *L'islam de marché: L'autre révolution conservatrice* (Paris: Éditions du Seuil, 2005), 10–11.
28 Rikke Hostrup Haugbølle and Francesco Cavatorta, 'Beyond Ghannouchi: Islamism and Social Change in Tunisia', *Middle East Report* 262 (2012): 22–4; Rikke Hostrup Haugbølle, 'New Expressions of Islam in Tunisia: An Ethnographic Approach', *The Journal of North African Studies* 20:3 (2015).
29 Rikke Hostrup Haugbølle and Francesco Cavatorta, '"Vive La Grand Famille des Media Tunisiens" Media Reform, Authoritarian Resilience and Societal Responses in Tunisia', *The Journal of North African Studies* 17:1 (2012): 104.
30 Gregory Starrett, *Putting Islam to Work: Education, Politics, and Religious Tranformation in Egypt* (Berkeley & Los Angeles, CA/London: University of California Press, 1998), 4–20.
31 Chokri, former al-Nahda member; born in 1971, imprisoned 1991–92. Interviewed in Hammam Sousse, 15 May 2015.
32 Chokri, author interview.

33 Sayida, author interview.

34 Samy Ghorbal, 'Le Retour du Voile', *Jeune Afrique*, Paris, 28 July 2003; Vincent Geisser and Éric Gobe, '"La question de 'l'authenticité tunisienne": valeur refuge d'un régime à bout de souffle?', *L'Année du Maghreb* III (2007); Haugbølle, 'New Expressions of Islam', 329–30.

35 'Wazir al-Shu'un al-Diniyya li-l-Shuruq: Harisuna 'ala al-Tasaddi li-Zawahir al-Ta'ifiyya [Minister for Religious Affairs tells al-Chourouk: We are keen to address the phenomenon of sectarianism]', *al-Chourouk*, Tunis, 4 January 2006.

36 Sayida, author interview.

37 Kawther, author interview.

38 Mahmood, *Politics of Piety*, 50–1.

39 Talal Asad, *Genealogies of Religion: Discipline and Reasons of Power in Christianity and Islam* (Baltimore, MD: Johns Hopkins University Press, 1993), 62; Ahmad, 'Islamic Fundamentalism in South Asia', 515.

40 Mahmood, *Politics of Piety*, 51.

41 Nejib, regional al-Nahda leader; born in 1985, interviewed in Sousse, 16 June 2014.

42 Nejib, author interview.

43 Amr Khalid was the best known of a new generation of lay preachers in Egypt, who in television broadcasts from 1999 offered what Bayat described as 'an active piety which is thick in rituals and scriptures and thin in politics'. Asef Bayat, 'Piety, Privilege and Egyptian Youth', *ISIM Newsletter* 10 (2002).

44 Faouzi, regional al-Nahda leader; born in 1985, imprisoned in 2004. Interviewed in Sousse, 11 March 2014.

45 The anti-terrorism law followed an al-Qa'ida attack on a synagogue in Djerba in 2002 that left twenty-one people dead. Around 3,000 people were believed to have been arrested under the new law, often for growing beards, wearing religious clothing, consulting prohibited internet sites or 'disturbing public order'. 'Loi no. 2003–75 du 10 décembre 2003, relative au soutien des efforts internationaux de lutte contre le terrorism et à la répression du blanchiment d'argent' (Tunis: Republic of Tunisia, 2003); Human Rights Watch, 'Tunisia's Repressive Laws: The Reform Agenda' (New York, NY: November 2011), 42–3.

46 Moncef Ben Salem (1953–2015) was imprisoned in 1987–89 and in 1990–93. He went on to be minister of higher education in the first al-Nahda government.

47 Faouzi, author interview.

48 Jourchi was one of the Progressive Islamists who had left the Islamic Group in the late 1970s. He went on to work as a journalist and author and was also involved in Tunis with the 18 October Collective in 2005. See: Salaheddine Jourchi, 'The State and Identity: The Relationship between Religion and Politics – Tunisia as an example', *Contemporary Arab Affairs* 6:3 (2013).

49 Nouri, senior al-Nahda leader; born in 1983, interviewed in Sousse, 15 April 2014.

50 Jean-Pierre Stroobants, 'Vie et mort des assassins de Massoud', *Le Monde*, Paris, 19 April 2005.

51 Ten of the main group of twenty-nine convicted over the incident were from Sousse: Alison Pargeter, 'Radicalisation in Tunisia', in *Islamist Radicalisation in North Africa: Politics and Process*, ed. George Joffé (Abingdon/New York, NY: Routledge, 2012), 85–92; Geisser and Gobe, 'Un si long règne', 5–6.

52 Ayman al-Zawahiri (born 1951) is an Egyptian Islamist radical who was a key organizer in Egyptian Islamic jihad and who then became head of al-Qaʿida in 2011.

53 Nouri, author interview.

54 The word *raʿāyā* literally means a flock of animals tended by a shepherd. Ettakatol was a small social democratic opposition party set up in 1994 but given legal authorization only in 2002. It was established and led by Mustapha Ben Jaafar, a doctor from Tunis, and later went into coalition government with al-Nahda in 2011–14.

55 Nouri, author interview.

56 Hibou, *The Force of Obedience*, 131.

57 Nabil, author interview.

58 Jawhara Tiss, elected al-Nahda deputy representing Tataouine; born in 1985. Interviewed in Tunis, 2 July 2013; Wolf, *Political Islam*, 119–21.

59 Larbi Chouikha and Éric Gobe, 'Les organisations de défense des droits de l'Homme dans la formule politique tunisienne: acteurs de l'opposition ou faire-valoir du régime?', *L'Année du Maghreb* V (2009).

60 Sadri Khiari, 'Le Renouveau du Mouvement Democratique Tunisien: Paradoxes et Ambivalences', in *La Tunisie de Ben Ali: La société contre le régime*, ed. Olfa Lamloum and Bernard Ravenel (Paris: L'Harmattan, 2002).

61 The CPR later went into coalition government with al-Nahda in 2011–14.

62 Zied, former al-Nahda member; born in 1973, imprisoned 1991–92. Interviewed in Sousse, 3 September 2014.

63 Abderraouf Ayadi *et al.*, 'Appel de Tunis', *Tunezine.com*, Tunis, 17 June 2003.

64 Ameur Laraiedh, 'Revendications et combat pour les libertés en Tunisie: vers un pacte national de l'opposition', *Annuaire de l'Afrique du Nord* XII (2003): 329–31.

65 Ridha Kéfi, 'La question divise la gauche et l'extrême gauche depuis la libération de nombreux dirigeants d'Ennahdha ... Que faire des islamistes?', *Jeune Afrique*, Paris, 7 May 2006; 'Notre voie vers la démocratie' (Tunis: Collectif du 18 octobre pour les droits et les libertés en Tunisie, 23 November 2007).

66 Moncef, local PDP member; born in 1973, interviewed in Sousse, 25 April 2014.

67 The PDP newspaper *al-Maoukif* reported similar strikes across in the country in Sfax, Kairouan, Gafsa, Jendouba, Bizerte, Beja, Nabeul, Siliana, Mahdia, Medenine and Kasserine: 'Idrabat Musanida wa ʿItisamat fi al-Jihat [Supportive strikes and sit-ins in the regions]', *al-Maoukif*, Tunis, 4 November 2005.

68 Moncef, author interview.

69 Nasser Ben Romdhane, regional PCOT leader; interviewed in Sousse, 7 May 2014.

70 Tahar, former al-Nahda member; born in 1965, forcibly conscripted 1987, 1989. Interviewed in Sousse, 14 April, 25 August, and 16 October 2014.

71 The movement's ten congresses were held in: Manouba, in Tunis, in August 1979; Sousse in April 1981; Suleiman in October 1984; Tunis in December 1986; Sfax in March 1988; Switzerland in December 1995; Holland in April 2001; London in May 2007; Tunis in July 2012; and Hammamet in May 2016. Daifallah, 'Min al-Sirriyya'.

72 Ettajdid was previously the Tunisian Communist Party, which was authorized in 1981.

73 Rachid, author interview.

74 Jebali was one of 1,298 prisoners freed that day, including seventy from al-Nahda. The release came shortly after a highly critical report about prison conditions was submitted by the International Committee of the Red Cross to the Tunisian interior ministry. Barrouhi, 'Le sens des libérations'.

75 Jebali, author interview.

76 Jelassi, *Hisad al-Ghuyyab*, 54.

77 David Ballard, 'An-Nahdha Leader Jebali: Moderate Islamism is the Future' (US Embassy Tunis via Wikileaks, 6 September 2006).

78 Barrouhi, 'Le sens des libérations'.

79 Mohamed al-Hamrouni, 'Laysa Waridan 'Indana al-Taraju' 'an Huquq al-Mar'a wa-Innama al-Matruh Tawsi'ha [For us it is not a question of retracting women's rights, but of expanding them]', *al-Maoukif*, Tunis, 22 December 2006.

80 The Tunisian ambassador to Switzerland, Afif Hendaoui, reportedly met with a group of al-Nahda leaders in exile, including Ameur Laarayedh, in Berne in 2004. Shortly afterwards some senior al-Nahda figures were released from jail in Tunisia, including Laarayedh's brother, Ali. Ridha Kéfi, 'La participation des intégristes au processus politique divise l'opposition ... Que faire des islamistes?', *Jeune Afrique*, Paris, 22 January 2006.

81 Vincent Geisser and Éric Gobe, 'Des fissures dans la 'Maison Tunisie'? Le régime de Ben Ali face aux mobilisations protestataires', *L'Année du Maghreb* II (2005–06).

82 A few exiled Nahdawis were eventually allowed home, including Abdelmajid Najar, a theologian born in 1945 in Medenine. He returned to Tunis in May 2010 and also called for 'political reconciliation'. Alexis Arieff, 'Tunisia: Recent Developments and Policy Issues' (Washington, DC: Congressional Research Service, 18 January 2011): 5.

83 Geisser and Gobe, 'Des fissures dans la 'Maison Tunisie'?'.

84 Camau and Geisser, *Le Syndrome Autoritaire*, 313.

85 Geisser and Gobe, 'Un si long règne', 8–9.

86 Ajmi Lourimi, 'A'tabar anna 18 Uktubir Ahamm Mahatta Siyasiyya [I Consider 18 October the Most Important Political Stage]', *Mouatinoun*, Tunis, 5 December 2007.

87 Lourimi, 'A'tabar anna 18 Uktubir Ahamm Mahatta'.

88 Abdelhamid Jelassi, 'Qira'a 'Abd al-Hamid al-Jilasi li-l-Waqi' ba'da 17 Sana min al-Sijn [Abdelhamid Jelassi's assessment of the facts after seventeen years imprisonment]', *Assabil Online*, Tunis, 8 December 2007.

89 Ajmi Lourimi, 'al-Islamiyyun wa-l-Sulta fi Tunis [The Islamists and the Regime in Tunisia]', in *al-Islamiyya fi Tunis* [*Islamism in Tunisia*] (Dubai: al-Mesbar Studies and Research Center, 2009).

90 Ajmi Lourimi, 'Hal Yamlik al-Islamiyyun Mashruʿan? [Do the Islamists have a project?]', *al-ʿArab al-Qatariyya*, Doha 2010.

91 Schwedler, *Faith in Moderation*, 150.

92 Francesco Cavatorta and Fabio Merone, 'Moderation through Exclusion? The Journey of the Tunisian Ennahda from Fundamentalist to Conservative Party', *Democratization* 20:5 (2013): 871.

93 Sahbi, author interview.

6 Rebuilding and Fragmenting

1 Rachid, author interview.

2 'La Commission Bouderbala présente son rapport final', *Leaders*, Tunis, 4 May 2012.

3 Harakat al-Nahda, 'al-Bayan al-Taʾsisi li-Harakat al-Nahda [The Founding Statement of the al-Nahda Movement]' (Tunis: 7 February 2011).

4 For example: Stepan, 'Tunisia's Transition'; Alaya Allani, 'The Post-Revolution Tunisian Constituent Assembly: Controversy over Powers and Prerogatives', *The Journal of North African Studies* 18:1 (2013); Monica L. Marks, 'Convince, Coerce, or Compromise? Ennahda's Approach to Tunisia's Constitution', (Doha: Brookings Doha Center, February 2014); Pickard, 'Al-Nahda: Moderation and Compromise', 30; Kasper Ly Netterstrøm, 'The Islamists' Compromise in Tunisia', *Journal of Democracy* 26:4 (2015); Boubekeur, 'Islamists, Secularists and Old Regime Elites'.

5 Volpi and Stein, 'Islamism and the State'.

6 Francesco Cavatorta and Fabio Merone, 'Post-Islamism, Ideological Evolution and "la *tunisianité* " of the Tunisian Islamist Party *al-Nahda* ', *Journal of Political Ideologies* 20:1 (2015): 32.

7 Malika Zeghal, 'Competing Ways of Life: Islamism, Secularism and Public Order in the Tunisian Transition', *Constellations* 20:2 (2013): 259.

8 al-Jamaoui, 'Nurid Hukm al-Balad'; Bobin, 'Rached Ghannouchi'.

9 Fabio Merone, 'Enduring Class Struggle in Tunisia: The Fight for Identity beyond Political Islam', *British Journal of Middle Eastern Studies* 42:1 (2015): 82.

10 Hedi, author interview.

11 The notion of 'gains made in the country' (*makāsib al-bilād*) is purposefully vague but appears to refer to those laws and institutions that were then regarded as widely accepted and defended in Tunisian society, including those achieved during the 2011 uprising, such as ending authoritarian rule. Most secularist and leftist politicians would have considered, for example, the Personal Status Code as among those 'gains'. By 2011 the movement said publicly it would not seek to change the Code. Nabil, author interview.

12 Harakat al-Nahda, 'Al-Nizam al-Asasi [The Basic Law]' (Tunis: 21–22 May 2016).

13 Notably the Muslim Brotherhood in Egypt for whom the goal of such 'cultivation' was to reform the individual in order 'to produce a new kind of person: the Muslim Brother': Hazem Kandil, *Inside the Brotherhood* (Cambridge: Polity, 2015), 6.

14 Nabil, author interview.

15 Fatima, local al-Nahda member; born in 1955, interviewed in Sousse, 20 June 2014.

16 Hizb al-Tahrir, founded in Tunisia in the 1980s and given brief legal authorization in 2012–15, was the Tunisian branch of the international organization of the same name which advocated for an Islamic caliphate by way of a coup and which opposed the democratic political process. Nouri, author interview.

17 Habib Mellakh, *Chroniques du Manoubistan* (Tunis: Cérès Éditions, 2013).

18 Harakat al-Nahda, 'Bayan Harakat al-Nahda al-Islamiyya baʿd Istiqala al-Sayyid Mohamed al-Ghannouchi [Statement of the Islamic al-Nahda movement after the resignation of Mr Mohamed Ghannouchi]' (Tunis: 27 February 2011).

19 Samir Dilou, senior al-Nahda leader; born in 1966, imprisoned 1991–2001. Interviewed in Tunis, 16 August 2011.

20 Harakat al-Nahda, *Barnamaj Harakat al-Nahda: Min ajl Tunis al-Hurriyya wa-l-ʿAdala wa-l-Tanmiyya* [*The Programme of the al-Nahda Movement: For a Tunisia of Freedom, Justice and Development*] (Tunis: Harakat al-Nahda, 2011), 3.

21 Harakat al-Nahda, 'Mashruʿ Dustur al-Jumhuriyya al-Tunisiyya [Draft of the Constitution of the Tunisian Republic]' (Tunis: Harakat al-Nahda, 2012).

22 Al-Asaad Ben Ahmad, 'We Fought for Freedom Not Sharia Law', *Al-Ahram Weekly*, Cairo, 5–11 April 2012.

23 I have written in more detail on the debates over the drafting of this constitutional provision here: Rory McCarthy, 'Protecting the Sacred: Tunisia's Islamist Movement Ennahdha and the Challenge of Free Speech', *British Journal of Middle Eastern Studies* 42:4 (2015).

24 Harakat al-Nahda, *al-Bayan al-Khitami li-l-Muʾtamar al-Tasiʿ li-Harakat al-Nahda* [*The Concluding Statement of the Ninth Congress of the al-Nahda Movement*] (Tunis: Harakat al-Nahda, 2012), 7.

25 al-Bawsala, 'Vote sur l'article 167 de la proposition de loi organique relative aux élections et référendums' (Tunis: 30 April 2014).

26 Marc Lynch, 'In Uncharted Waters: Islamist Parties beyond Egypt's Muslim Brotherhood' (Washington, DC: Carnegie Endowment for International Peace, December 2016), 15.

27 Rachid Ghannouchi, 'Kalimat Raʾis Harakat al-Nahda al-Shaykh Rashid al-Ghannushi Khilal al-Nadwa al-Suhufiyya [The Speech of al-Nahda President Shaykh Rachid al-Ghannouchi at the Press Conference]', Tunis, 15 August 2013.

28 Belaïd was an elected deputy from the Movement of Democratic Patriots. Brahmi was a Nasserist politician who led the People's Movement.

29 One al-Nahda minister, Samir Dilou, admitted in September 2012 that the movement had initially showed 'a certain laxity' in hoping to address the Salafist threat through dialogue and not force: Dominique Lagarde and

Camille Le Tallec, 'Tunisie: "Nous avons fait preuve d'un certain laxisme face aux salafistes"', *L'Express*, Paris, 21 September 2012.

30 The prize was awarded in October 2015 to the National Dialogue Quartet: the trade union UGTT, the employers' union UTICA (Tunisian Confederation of Industry, Trade and Handicrafts), the human rights group LTDH, and the Tunisian Order of Lawyers: 'The Nobel Peace Prize for 2015' (Oslo: The Norwegian Nobel Committee, 10 October 2015).

31 Hedi, author interview.

32 Bobin, 'Rached Ghannouchi'.

33 Khalid, local al-Nahda member; born in 1987, interviewed in Hai Riadh, 11 February and 2 March 2014.

34 Samia, local al-Nahda member; born in 1990, interviewed in Hammam Sousse, 11 March 2014.

35 Charles Tilly and Sidney Tarrow, *Contentious Politics*, 2nd edn (Oxford: Oxford University Press, 2015), 131.

36 Tahar, author interview.

37 Femen was a group of women activists, originating in the Ukraine, who staged topless demonstrations against patriarchal power structures. In May 2013 a young Tunisian women, Amina Sboui, also known as Amina Tyler, was arrested for a Femen protest. 'Tunisie: ouverture du procès d'Amina', *Le Monde*, Paris, 30 May 2013.

38 Noumi, author interview.

39 Hamadi Jebali, 'Bayan wa-I'lam [Statement and Notification]', *Facebook.com*, Sousse, 11 December 2014.

40 Lila Blaise, 'Interview de Riadh Chaïbi, démissionnaire d'Ennahdha', *Huffpostmaghreb.com*, Tunis, 9 December 2013.

41 al-Bawsala, 'Vote sur un amendement no. 42 de l'article premier' (Tunis: 4 January 2014).

42 al-Bawsala, 'Vote sur un amendement de l'article 6: Supprimer la liberté de "conscience"' (Tunis: 4 January 2014).

43 al-Bawsala, 'Vote sur l'article 167'.

44 Walid, author interview.

45 'Le coordinateur régional de Nidaa Tounes à Sousse explique les raisons de sa démission', *AfricanManager.com*, Tunis, 29 December 2013.

46 Hamza Meddeb, 'The Streets, the Ballot Box and Consensus: High-Stakes Elections in Tunisia' (Oslo: Norwegian Peacebuilding Resource Centre, October 2014), 2; Boubekeur, 'Islamists, Secularists and Old Regime Elites', 15.

47 Zied Ladhari, Televised election broadcast on al-Wataniyya, 8 October 2014.

48 Avi Max Spiegel, 'Morocco', in *Rethinking Political Islam*, eds. Shadi Hamid and William McCants (New York, NY: Oxford University Press, 2017), 58–9.

49 See Arab Barometer Wave III at www.arabbarometer.org/content/online-data-analysis.

50 The title derives from chapter 17, verse 34: 'And fulfill the pact; surely the pact is called to account'. Harakat al-Nahda, *Barnamaj Harakat al-Nahda*, 4.

51 Not only did Essebsi dress in similar style to Bourguiba, with a dark suit and dark sunglasses, but he began his presidential election campaign in November

2014 with a televised pilgrimage to Bourguiba's mausoleum in Monastir, where he was filmed bowed in contemplation over the independence leader's tomb.

52 Qais, local al-Nahda member; born in 1993, interviewed in Sousse, 13 October 2014.

53 Zied Ladhari, speech at an al-Nahda rally in Hai 9 Avril, Sousse, 15 October 2014.

54 Afifa Makhlouf, speech at an al-Nahda rally in Zaouiat Sousse, 17 October 2014.

55 Faouzi al-Mhiri, speech at an al-Nahda rally in Hammam Sousse, 18 October 2014.

56 ISIE 'Taqrir al-Hay'a al-'Ulya al-Mustaqilla li-l-Intikhabat hawla al-Intikhabat al-Tashri'iyya wa-l-Ri'asiyya 2014 [Report of the Independent High Authority for the Elections on the Legislative and Presidential Elections of 2014]' (Tunis: ISIE, March 2015), 334.

57 Al-Nahda's vote count fell from 1,498,905 in October 2011 to 947,058 in October 2014.

58 The candidates Zied Ladhari, Monia Ibrahim, and Ajmi Lourimi were re-elected.

59 This is the ratio of actual voters to eligible voters (the voting eligible population turnout) using the 2011 figure for eligible voters because none was given for 2014.

60 Michael Robbins, 'Tunisia Five Years after the Revolution: Findings from the Arab Barometer' (Arab Barometer, 15 May 2016), 8–9.

61 Brown, *When Victory Is Not an Option*, 5–6.

62 Nabil, author interview.

63 In a reshuffle in August 2016 under the new Prime Minister Youssef Chahed, al-Nahda increased its cabinet representation to three ministers (of trade, employment, and communication technologies). After a second reshuffle in September 2017, al-Nahda had four ministries (development, investment and international cooperation; industry and commerce; communication technologies; and economic reforms).

64 Lotfi Zitoun, senior al-Nahda leader; interviewed in Tunis, 21 September 2016.

65 Nabil, author interview.

66 Khawla al-Naqati, 'Awlawiyyatna fi al-Marhala al-Qadima [Our Priorities in the Coming Stage]', *Al-Fajr*, Tunis, 3 October 2014.

67 Nadia Marzouki, 'From Resistance to Governance: The Category of Civility in the Political Theory of Tunisian Islamists', in *The Making of the Tunisian Revolution: Contexts, Architects, Prospects*, ed. Nouri Gana (Edinburgh: Edinburgh University Press, 2013), 217.

68 Hibou, *The Force of Obedience*, 205–6.

69 Gudrun Krämer, 'Integration of the Integrists: A Comparative Study of Egypt, Jordan and Tunisia', in *Democracy without Democrats?*, ed. Ghassan Salamé (London: IB Tauris, 1994), 205.

70 Kawther, author interview.

71 Sahbi, author interview.

72 Evie Soli and Fabio Merone, 'Tunisia: The Islamic Associative System as a Social Counter-Power', *openDemocracy*, London, 23 October 2013.

73 Nejib Karoui, head of Attaouen and former al-Nahda member; born in 1962. Interviewed in Sousse, 18 May 2015.

74 Human Rights Watch, 'Tunisia: Suspension of Associations Arbitrary' (New York, NY: 13 August 2014).

75 Farida, author interview.

76 Chokri, author interview.

77 Brown, *When Victory Is Not an Option*, 160.

78 Willis, 'Morocco's Islamists'; Mona El-Ghobashy, 'The Metamorphosis of the Egyptian Muslim Brothers', *International Journal of Middle East Studies* 37:3 (2005): 387; Shadi Hamid, 'Arab Islamist Parties: Losing on Purpose?', *Journal of Democracy* 22:1 (2011): 74–5.

79 Thomas Carothers, 'The End of the Transition Paradigm', *Journal of Democracy* 13:1 (2002): 9.

80 Christopher J. Anderson *et al.*, *Losers' Consent: Elections and Democratic Legitimacy* (Oxford/New York, NY: Oxford University Press, 2005), 184.

81 Clark, *Islam, Charity, and Activism*; Steven Brooke, 'From Medicine to Mobilization: Social Service Provision and the Islamist Reputational Advantage', *Perspectives on Politics* 15:1 (2017).

82 The major *da'wa* association was the Association of *Da'wa* and Reform (Jam'iyyat al-Da'wa wa-l-Islah), established after 2011 and whose leaders included two prominent Nahdawi figures, Habib Ellouze and Sadok Chourou. Both Ellouze and Chourou had briefly led al-Nahda during the crackdown in the late 1980s and early 1990s, and both sat as elected al-Nahda deputies in the Constituent Assembly in 2011–14, though neither ran for re-election in October 2014.

83 Zitoun, author interview.

84 Lynch, 'In Uncharted Waters', 8.

85 Rached Ghannouchi, 'From Political Islam to Muslim Democracy: The Ennahda Party and the Future of Tunisia', *Foreign Affairs* 95:5 (2016): 63.

86 The bill was formally titled Draft Law No.49/2015 on Exceptional Measures Relating to Economic and Financial Reconciliation and was passed on 13 September 2017, with a narrow majority of 117 votes in favour (out of a possible 217). During the revisions of the draft, it was renamed the Administrative Reconciliation bill.

87 Youssef, author interview.

88 Harakat al-Ittijah al-Islami, 'al-Bayan al-Ta'sisi'.

89 For more on the ideological influence of Ben Achour (1879–1973), see: Cavatorta and Merone, 'Post-Islamism', 35; Muhammed al-Tahir Ibn Ashur, *Ibn Ashur: Treatise on Maqāṣid al-Sharī'ah* (Herndon, VA/London: International Institute of Islamic Thought, 2011).

90 Rachid Ghannouchi, *al-Hurriyat al-'Amma fi al-Dawla al-Islamiyya* [*Public Liberties in the Islamic State*] (Beirut: Markaz Dirasat al-Wahda al-Arabiyya, 1993).

91 Tamimi, *Rachid Ghannouchi*, 99.

92 Andrew F. March, 'Geneaologies of Sovereignty in Islamic Political Theology', *Social Research* 80:1 (2013): 313–4.

93 This was not a new comparison. Even in the early 1990s, during the crackdown against al-Nahda, such parallels were under discussion in Tunisia. See, for example, this interview with Mohamed Charfi, the then education minister and a critic of al-Nahda: Bessis and Soudan, 'Mohamed Charfi: Mon combat', 22.

94 Stathis N. Kalyvas, *The Rise of Christian Democracy in Europe* (Ithaca, NY/London: Cornell University Press, 1996), 67.

95 Karl-Egon Lönne, 'Germany', in *Political Catholicism in Europe, 1918–1965*, eds. Tom Buchanan and Martin Conway (Oxford: Oxford University Press, 1996), 156; Klaus Tenfelde, 'Civil Society and the Middle Classes in Nineteenth-Century Germany', in *Civil Society before Democracy: Lessons from Nineteenth-Century Europe*, eds. Nancy Bermeo and Philip Nord (Lanham, MD: Rowman & Littlefield, 2000), 97.

96 Olivier Roy, 'Political Islam after the Arab Spring', *Foreign Affairs* 96:6 (2017).

97 Asef Bayat, *Making Islam Democratic: Social Movements and the Post-Islamist Turn* (Stanford, CA: Stanford University Press, 2007), 11.

98 al-Naqati, 'Awlawiyyatna'; Katerina Dalacoura, 'Islamism and Neoliberalism in the Aftermath of the 2011 Arab Uprisings: The Freedom and Justice Party in Egypt and Nahda in Tunisia', in *Neoliberal Governmentality and the Future of the State in The Middle East and North Africa*, ed. Emel Akçali (Basingstoke: Palgrave Macmillan, 2016).

99 The first IMF Stand-By Arrangement following the 2011 uprising (indeed since 2001) was signed in June 2013 and was worth $1.74 billion. It was followed by a four-year Extended Fund Facility in May 2016 worth $2.9 billion. Monthly protests were recorded by the Forum Tunisien pour les Droits Économiques et Sociaux, see: www.ftdes.net.

100 Rachid Ghannouchi, 'Mada Misdaq Da'wa Fashal al-Islam al-Siyasi? [How Credible is the Claim that Political Islam has Failed?]', *aljazeera.net*, Doha, 24 October 2013.

101 Ghannouchi, 'From Political Islam', 64.

102 Shadi Hamid, *Temptations of Power: Islamists and Illiberal Democracy in a New Middle East* (New York, NY: Oxford University Press, 2014), 116.

7 Conclusion

1 Almost all the decisions at the congress, including Ghannouchi's re-election, were passed with similarly large majorities after months of work to build a consensus. However, there was a much closer vote on the question of whether the congress should elect the Executive Bureau or whether Ghannouchi should appoint the bureau at will. Ghannouchi won the vote with a slim 52 per cent majority. Harakat al-Nahda, 'Nata'ij al-Taswit 'ala al-Lawa'ih fi al-Yawm al-Akhir min Ashgal al-Mu'tamar al-'Amm al-'Ashir [Results of the Votes on the Statutes on the Last Day of Work at the Tenth Congress]', Tunis, 22 May 2016; Abdelkrim Dermech, 'Abdellatif El Mekki à La Presse: "Il est temps d'évaluer l'expérience de partenariat au pouvoir avec Nida Tounes"', *La Presse*, Tunis, 19 March 2017.

2 Mahmood, *Politics of Piety*; Ismail, *Rethinking Islamist Politics*; Tuğal, 'Transforming Everyday Life', 451.

3 Tarrow, *Power in Movement*, 142–3.

4 For exceptions, see: Smith, 'Correcting a Curious Neglect'; Tuğal, 'Transforming Everyday Life'.

5 Zeghal, 'Competing Ways of Life', 255.

6 Sami Zemni, 'The Extraordinary Politics of the Tunisian Revolution: The Process of Constitution Making', *Mediterranean Politics* 20:1 (2015): 3.

7 Jordan's Muslim Brotherhood drew on Ghannouchi's thinking when it made the case for political participation and later when it looked for direction in the challenging post-2011 environment. In the run up to the 2016 congress, al-Nahda invited Islamist leaders from across the Arab world to give advice on party-movement relations. Schwedler, *Faith in Moderation*, 157; Lynch, 'In Uncharted Waters', 16.

8 Melani Cammett and Pauline Jones Luong, 'Is There an Islamist Political Advantage?', *Annual Review of Political Science* 17 (2014): 199.

9 Philippe C. Schmitter, 'Twenty-Five Years, Fifteen Findings', *Journal of Democracy* 21:1 (2010): 24.

10 Jillian Schwedler, 'A Paradox of Democracy? Islamist Participation in Elections', *Middle East Report* 209 (1998): 28.

11 Tarek Masoud, *Counting Islam: Religion, Class, and Elections in Egypt* (New York, NY: Cambridge University Press, 2014), 7.

12 Charles Kurzman and Didem Türkoğlu, 'Do Muslims Vote Islamic Now?', *Journal of Democracy* 26:4 (2015): 101.

13 Kurzman and Türkoğlu, 'Do Muslims Vote Islamic Now?', 101.

14 Beverley Milton-Edwards and Stephen Farrell, *Hamas: The Islamic Resistance Movement* (Cambridge: Polity, 2010), 230–59.

15 Holger Albrecht and Eva Wegner, 'Autocrats and Islamists: Contenders and containment in Egypt and Morocco', *The Journal of North African Studies* 11:2 (2006).

16 Avi Max Spiegel, *Young Islam: The New Politics of Religion in Morocco and the Arab World* (Princeton, NJ/Oxford: Princeton University Press, 2015), 179.

17 Spiegel, 'Morocco', 60.

18 Courtney Freer, 'Kuwait', in *Rethinking Political Islam*, eds. Shadi Hamid and William McCants (New York, NY: Oxford University Press, 2017), 144.

19 Lynch, 'In Uncharted Waters', 8.

20 Carrie Rosefsky Wickham, *The Muslim Brotherhood: Evolution of an Islamist Movement* (Princeton, NJ/Oxford: Princeton University Press, 2013), 174–5.

21 Wickham, *The Muslim Brotherhood*, 177.

22 Nathan J. Brown, 'A Struggle for Power: Islamism and Democracy', *The Middle East Journal* 69:3 (2015): 467.

23 Darrag, 'Politics or Piety?', 225.

24 Wickham, *The Muslim Brotherhood*, 8.

25 Jillian Schwedler, 'Can Islamists Become Moderates? Rethinking the Inclusion-Moderation Hypothesis', *World Politics* 63:2 (2011): 371.

26 Wickham, *The Muslim Brotherhood*, 81.

27 Nathan J. Brown and Michele Dunne, 'Unprecedented Pressures, Uncharted Course for Egypt's Muslim Brotherhood' (Washington, DC: Carnegie Endowment for International Peace, July 2015).

28 Wickham, *The Muslim Brotherhood*, 214.

29 Lynch, 'In Uncharted Waters', 15.

30 Freer, 'Kuwait', 132.

31 Michael J. Willis, 'Between *alternance* and the *Makhzen*: *At-Tawhid wa Al-Islah's* entry into Moroccan politics', *The Journal of North African Studies* 4:3 (1999): 76–7.

32 Spiegel, 'Morocco', 58–9.

33 Mohammed Masbah, 'His Majesty's Islamists: The Moroccan Experience' (Beirut: Carnegie Middle East Center, 23 March 2015).

34 Roy, *The Failure of Political Islam*.

35 Roy, *Globalised Islam*, 3.

36 Roy, *The Failure of Political Islam*, 75.

37 Eickelman and Piscatori, *Muslim Politics*, xv.

38 Harakat al-Ittijah al-Islami, 'al-Bayan al-Ta'sisi'; Alexander, 'Opportunities, Organizations, and Ideas', 471–2.

39 Nancy Bermeo, 'Democracy and the Lessons of Dictatorship', *Comparative Politics* 24:3 (1992): 274.

40 McAdam, Tarrow, and Tilly, *Dynamics of Contention*, 22.

41 Tarrow, *Power in Movement*, 124.

42 Nabil, author interview.

43 Camau and Geisser, *Le Syndrome Autoritaire*, 284.

44 Charles Tripp, *The Power and the People: Paths of Resistance in the Middle East* (Cambridge: Cambridge University Press, 2013), 14.

45 Bobin, 'Rached Ghannouchi'.

46 Harakat al-Nahda, 'al-Bayan al-Khitami li-l-Mu'tamar al-'Amm al-'Ashir li-Harakat al-Nahda [The Concluding Statement of the Tenth General Congress of the al-Nahda Movement]' (Tunis: 25 May 2016).

47 Guilain Denoeux, 'The Forgotten Swamp: Navigating Political Islam', *Middle East Policy* IX:2 (2002): 56; Sadik al-Azm, 'Islamic Fundamentalism Reconsidered: A Critical Outline of Problems, Ideas and Approaches, Part I', *South Asia Bulletin* XIII:1 & 2 (1993).

48 al-Jamaoui, 'Nurid Hukm al-Balad'.

49 Khawla al-Naqati, 'Ma Zilna fi Marhala Intiqaliyya [We are Still in a Transitional Stage]', *Al-Fajr*, Tunis, 6 November 2015.

50 Sayida Ounissi, 'Ennahda from Within: Islamists or 'Muslim Democrats'?', in *Rethinking Political Islam*, eds. Shadi Hamid and William McCants (New York, NY: Oxford University Press, 2016).

51 Lotfi Zitoun, 'Lutfi Zaytun: Al-Nahda al-Jadid … 'Almana am Tunasa? [Lotfi Zeitoun: The New Nahda … Secularizing or Tunisianizing?]', *Al-Jadid*, Tunis, 29 March 2016.

52 Harakat al-Nahda, 'al-Bayan al-Khitami li-l-Mu'tamar al-'Amm al-'Ashir'.

53 Harakat al-Nahda, 'al-Bayan al-Khitami li-l-Mu'tamar al-'Amm al-'Ashir'.

54 Michaelle Browers, 'Rethinking Post-Islamism and the Study of Changes in Islamist Ideology', in *Rethinking Islamist Politics*, ed. Marc Lynch (Washington, DC: Project on Middle East Political Science, 2014), 16.

55 Asef Bayat, ed. *Post-Islamism: The Changing Faces of Political Islam* (New York, NY: Oxford University Press, 2013), 27.

56 'Démission du secrétaire général du bureau régional d'Ennahdha à Sidi Bouzid', *Business News*, 5 June 2016.

57 Mongi Khadhraoui, "Abd al-Hamid al-Jilasi al-qiyadi fi al-Nahda li-l-Shuruq: Tahaluf al-Nahda wa-l-Nida' . . . safqat al-mughaffalin [Al-Nahda leader Abdelhamid Jelassi to al-Chourouk: The Nahda-Nidaa Alliance is . . . the deal of the gullible]', *Al-Chourouk*, Tunis, 22 September 2016.

Bibliography

INTERVIEWS

Abdallah. Former MTI member. Born in 1952. Imprisoned 1981–83. Interviewed in Sousse, 11 March and 9 September 2014.

Abdelfattah. Local al-Nahda leader. Born in 1963. Imprisoned 1987, 1992–93. Interviewed in Akouda, 14 August 2014.

Abdelhamid. Local al-Nahda leader. Born in 1961. Imprisoned 1987, 1991–94. Interviewed in Hammam Sousse, 13 April 2014.

Bechir. Local al-Nahda leader. Born in 1968. Imprisoned 1991–93. Interviewed in Sousse, 9 February 2014.

Ben Romdhane, Nasser. Regional PCOT leader. Interviewed in Sousse, 7 May 2014.

Chokri. Former al-Nahda member. Born in 1971. Imprisoned 1991–92. Interviewed in Hammam Sousse, 15 May 2015.

Dilou, Samir. Senior al-Nahda leader. Born in 1966. Imprisoned 1991–2001. Interviewed in Tunis, 16 August 2011.

Douik, Nabil. Local al-Nahda member. Born in 1966. Interviewed in Sousse, 15 May 2015.

Faouzi. Regional al-Nahda leader. Born in 1985. Imprisoned 2004. Interviewed in Sousse, 11 March 2014.

Farida. Former al-Nahda member. Born in 1972. Interviewed in Hai Riadh, 22 September 2014.

Fatima. Local al-Nahda member. Born in 1955. Interviewed in Sousse, 20 June 2014.

Fethi. Regional al-Nahda leader. Born in 1956. Imprisoned 1987–88. Interviewed in Monastir, 29 May 2015.

Habib. Local al-Nahda member. Born in 1951. Imprisoned 1987. In hiding 1992–99. Interviewed in Sousse, 28 November 2013.

Hafedh. Local al-Nahda member. Born in 1955. Imprisoned 1987, 1991–93. Interviewed in Kalaa Seghira, 9 June 2014.

Hamza. Local al-Nahda member. Born in 1964. Imprisoned 1987, 1991–93. Interviewed in Kalaa Kebira, 29 January and 4 June 2014.

Hassan. Local al-Nahda leader. Born in 1963. Imprisoned 1986–87, 1991–93. Interviewed in Kalaa Seghira, 13 February 2014.

Hedi. Local al-Nahda leader. Born in 1968. Imprisoned 1991–95. Interviewed in Kalaa Kebira, 12 June and 12 August 2014.

Jamel. Regional al-Nahda leader. Born in 1966. Imprisoned 1991–99. Interviewed in Sousse, 27 August and 9 September 2014.

Jebali, Hamadi. Former senior al-Nahda leader. Born in 1949. Imprisoned 1989–2006. Interviewed in Oxford, 14 and 15 May and Tunis, 24 September 2013.

Kamel. Regional al-Nahda leader. Born in 1953. Imprisoned 1987–88, 1991–93. Interviewed in Sousse, 12 June 2014.

Karoui, Nejib. Head of Attaouen and former al-Nahda member. Born in 1962. Interviewed in Sousse, 18 May 2015.

Kawther. Local al-Nahda leader. Born in 1962. Interviewed in Hai Riadh, 11 September 2014.

Khairi. Senior al-Nahda leader. Born in 1962. Imprisoned 1991–2007. Interviewed in Tunis, 9 October 2014.

Khalid. Local al-Nahda member. Born in 1987. Interviewed in Hai Riadh, 11 February and 2 March 2014.

Labidi, Mortadha. Regional PCOT leader. Born in 1952. Interviewed in Sousse, 1 May 2014.

Ladhari, Souad. Local al-Nahda member. Born in 1959. Abroad 1981–96. Interviewed in Chott Meriem, 9 June 2014.

Lagha, Mohiddine. Former regional leader of the LTDH. Born in 1955. Interviewed in Sousse, 29 April 2014.

Lourimi, Ajmi. Senior al-Nahda leader. Born in 1962. Imprisoned 1991–2007. Interviewed in Tunis, 20 July 2011.

Mahmoud. Former MTI member. Born in 1952. Imprisoned 1983. Interviewed in Sousse, 13 February 2014.

Mehdi. Regional al-Nahda leader. Born in 1972. Imprisoned 1991–99. Interviewed in Sousse, 19 January and 13 August 2014.

Moncef. Local PDP member. Born in 1973. Interviewed in Sousse, 25 April 2014.

Murad. Local al-Nahda member. Born in 1981. Interviewed in Sousse, 6 and 13 March 2014.

Nabil. Local al-Nahda leader. Born in 1972. Imprisoned in 2007. Interviewed in Sousse, 21 and 28 November 2013, 21 March 2014, 20 May 2015.

Nejib. Regional al-Nahda leader. Born in 1985. Interviewed in Sousse, 16 June 2014.

Nouir, Salah. Regional al-Nahda leader. Born in 1950. Imprisoned 1981–84, 1987, 1991–95. Interviewed in Hai Riadh, 6 December 2013.

Noumi, Abdedayem. Former local al-Nahda member. Born in 1957. Imprisoned 1991–99. Interviewed in Sousse, 25 June 2013, 25 January, 11 September and 5 October 2014, 12 May 2015.

Nouri. Senior al-Nahda leader. Born in 1983. Interviewed in Sousse, 15 April 2014.

Qais. Local al-Nahda member. Born in 1993. Interviewed in Sousse, 13 October 2014.

Rachid. Regional al-Nahda leader. Born in 1960. Imprisoned 1987, 1991–2002. Interviewed in Sousse, 23 January, 7 February and 2 June, 2014.

Riadh. Regional al-Nahda leader. Born in 1957. In hiding 1987. Interviewed in M'saken, 24 June 2014.

Sahbi. Local al-Nahda leader. Born in 1958. Imprisoned 1983. Interviewed in Chott Meriem, 20 and 21 August 2014.

Saleh. Local al-Nahda member. Born in 1958. Imprisoned 1987, 1991–94. Interviewed in Akouda, 10 and 24 June 2014.

Samia. Local al-Nahda member. Born in 1990. Interviewed in Hammam Sousse, 11 March 2014.

Sayida. Local al-Nahda leader. Born in 1960. Interviewed in Chott Meriem, 21 August 2014.

Tahar. Former al-Nahda member. Born in 1965. Forcibly conscripted 1987, 1989. Interviewed in Sousse, 14 April, 25 August and 16 October 2014.

Tiss, Jawhara. Elected al-Nahda deputy representing Tataouine. Born in 1985. Interviewed in Tunis, 2 July 2013.

Walid. Regional al-Nahda leader. Born in 1963. Imprisoned 1987, 1991–2006. Interviewed in Sousse, 21 April and 30 September 2014; 29 May 2015.

Yahya. Former al-Nahda member. Born in 1952. Imprisoned 1987, 1991–95. Interviewed in Sousse, 27 November 2013.

Youssef. Local al-Nahda leader. Born in 1961. Imprisoned 1993–95. Interviewed in Hammam Sousse, 20 March 2014, 21 May 2015.

Zied. Former al-Nahda member. Born in 1973. Imprisoned 1991–92. Interviewed in Sousse, 3 September 2014.

Zitoun, Lotfi. Senior al-Nahda leader. Interviewed in Tunis, 21 September 2016.

REFERENCES

'544 Shabban Yashrakuna fi Musabaqat Wilayat Susa [544 Young People Participate in a Competition of the Sousse Governorate]'. *al-'Amal*, *Tunis*, 28 August 1977.

Abou El Fadl, Khaled. 'Qur'anic Ethics and Islamic Law'. *Journal of Islamic Ethics* 1:1–2 (2017): 7–28.

AFP. 'Tunisie: La déclaration du successeur'. *Le Monde*, Paris, 8 November 1987.

Ahmad, Mumtaz. 'Islamic Fundamentalism in South Asia: The Jamaat-i-Islami and the Tablighi Jamaat of South Asia'. In *Fundamentalisms Observed*, edited by Martin E. Marty and R. Scott Appleby, 457–530. Chicago, IL/London: University of Chicago Press, 1994.

'Al-Hibi [The Hippy]'. *Al-Ma'rifa*, Tunis, Year 3: No 1 1975, 7–10.

'Al-Nata'ij al-Kamila li-Intikhabat Majalis al-Kulliyyat [The Complete Results for College Council Elections]'. *Al-Fajr*, Tunis, 21 April 1990.

Albrecht, Holger, and Eva Wegner. 'Autocrats and Islamists: Contenders and containment in Egypt and Morocco'. *The Journal of North African Studies* 11:2 (2006): 123–41.

Alexander, Christopher. 'Back from the Democratic Brink: Authoritarianism and Civil Society in Tunisia'. *Middle East Report* 205 (1997): 34–8.

'Opportunities, Organizations, and Ideas: Islamists and Workers in Tunisia and Algeria'. *International Journal of Middle East Studies* 32:4 (2000): 465–90.

Tunisia: Stability and Reform in the Modern Maghreb. Abingdon: Routledge, 2010.

Allani, Alaya. 'The Islamists in Tunisia between Confrontation and Participation: 1980–2008'. *The Journal of North African Studies* 14:2 (2009): 257–72.

'The Post-Revolution Tunisian Constituent Assembly: Controversy over Powers and Prerogatives'. *The Journal of North African Studies* 18:1 (2013): 131–40.

al-Amaduni, Lotfi. 'Safahat min Tarikhu wa-Nidalhu fi Dhikra Rahil al-Ustadh Ali Nuwir [Pages from History and the Struggle in Remembrance of the Late Teacher Ali Nouir]'. *Al-Fajr*, Tunis, 15 April 2016, 12–13.

Aminzade, Ronald R., and Doug McAdam. 'Emotions and Contentious Politics'. In *Silence and Voice in the Study of Contentious Politics*, edited by Ronald R. Aminzade, Jack A. Goldstone, Doug McAdam, Elizabeth J. Perry, William H. Sewell Jr., Sidney Tarrow, and Charles Tilly, 14–50. New York, NY: Cambridge University Press, 2001.

Amnesty International. 'Tunisia: Prolonged Incommunicado Detention and Torture' (London: 4 March 1992).

'Tunisia: Heavy Sentences after Unfair Trials' (London: 19 October 1992).

'Tunisia: Women Victims of Harassment, Torture and Imprisonment' (London: 2 June 1993).

'Tunisia: Repression Thrives on Impunity' (London: 2 November 1995).

'In the Name of Security: Routine Abuses in Tunisia' (London: 23 June 2008).

Anderson, Christopher J., André Blais, Shaun Bowler, Todd Donovan, and Ola Listhaug. *Losers' Consent: Elections and Democratic Legitimacy.* Oxford/New York, NY: Oxford University Press, 2005.

Asad, Talal. *Formations of the Secular: Christianity, Islam, Modernity.* Stanford, CA: Stanford University Press, 2003.

Genealogies of Religion: Discipline and Reasons of Power in Christianity and Islam. Baltimore, MD: Johns Hopkins University Press, 1993.

Ayadi, Abderraouf, Rafik Abdessalem, Imed Abidi, and Ameur Laraïdh. 'Appel de Tunis'. *Tunezine.com*, Tunis, 17 June 2003. www.tunezine.tn/read.php?1,40034,40034 (archived at: www.webcitation.org/6ZleD3Ee9).

Ayari, Michaël. *Le Prix de l'Engagement Politique dans la Tunisie Autoritaire: Gauchistes et islamistes sous Bourguiba et Ben Ali (1957–2011).* Tunis & Paris: Édition Karthala et IRMC, 2016.

al-Azm, Sadik. 'Islamic Fundamentalism Reconsidered: A Critical Outline of Problems, Ideas and Approaches, Part I'. *South Asia Bulletin* XIII:1 & 2 (1993): 93–121.

Badri, E. 'M. Mohamed Ennaceur: Tourisme et industries, le Sahel amorce un nouveau départ sous le signe de l'unité régionale'. *La Presse*, Tunis, 2 March 1973.

Ballard, David. 'An-Nahdha Leader Jebali: Moderate Islamism Is the Future' (US Embassy Tunis via Wikileaks, 6 September 2006), wikileaks.org/cable/2006/09/06TUNIS2298.html (archived at www.webcitation.org/6XIL2jGYL).

Bargu, Banu. *Starve and Immolate: The Politics of Human Weapons*. New York, NY: Columbia University Press, 2014.

Barrouhi, Abdelaziz. 'Le sens des libérations'. *Jeune Afrique*, Paris, 5 March 2006, 44–5.

al-Bawsala. 'Vote sur l'article 167 de la proposition de loi organique relative aux élections et référendums' (Tunis: 30 April 2014), majles.marsad.tn/fr/vote/53613d2912bdaa078ab82503 (archived at: www.webcitation.org/6beouLVrp).

'Vote sur un amendement de l'article 6: Supprimer la liberté de "conscience"' (Tunis: 4 January 2014), majles.marsad.tn/fr/vote/52caefeb12b daa7f9b90f45d (archived at: www.webcitation.org/6bgb39zZ6).

'Vote sur un amendement no. 42 de l'article premier' (Tunis: 4 January 2014), majles.marsad.tn/fr/vote/52c92fa112bdaa7f9b90f423 (archived at: www.web citation.org/6bgaax0KM).

Bayard de Volo, Lorraine, and Edward Schatz. 'From the Inside Out: Ethnographic Methods in Political Research'. *Political Science and Politics* 37:2 (2004): 267–71.

Bayat, Asef. 'Islamism and Social Movement Theory'. *Third World Quarterly* 26:6 (2005): 891–908.

Making Islam Democratic: Social Movements and the Post-Islamist Turn. Stanford, CA: Stanford University Press, 2007.

'Piety, Privilege and Egyptian Youth'. *ISIM Newsletter* 10 (July 2002): 23.

ed. *Post-Islamism: The Changing Faces of Political Islam*. New York, NY: Oxford University Press, 2013.

Beau, Nicolas, and Jean-Pierre Tuquoi. *Notre Ami Ben Ali: L'envers du 'miracle tunisien'*. Paris: La Découverte, 2011.

Belhassen, Souhayr. 'L'islam contestataire en Tunisie'. *Jeune Afrique*, Paris, 14 March 1979, 82–4.

'Un coup à droite, un coup à gauche'. *Jeune Afrique*, Paris, 5 August 1981.

Belhassen, Souhayr, and Abdelaziz Dahmani. '"Sur le Moyen-Orient la Tunisie a su prendre une position d'avant-garde" Une interview de Hedi Nouira, Premier ministre tunisien'. *Jeune Afrique*, Paris, 18 April 1979, 39–41.

Bellin, Eva. 'Civil Society in Formation: Tunisia'. In *Civil Society in the Middle East. Volume 1*, edited by Augustus Richard Norton, 120–47. Leiden, New York, NY/Köln: Brill, 1995.

'Faith in Politics: New Trends in the Study of Religion and Politics'. *World Politics* 60:2 (2008): 315–47.

Ben Ahmad, Al-Asaad. 'We Fought for Freedom Not Sharia Law'. *Al-Ahram Weekly*, Cairo, 5–11 April 2012.

'Ben Ali: "Je veillerai a l'intérêt de la patrie"'. *La Presse*, Tunis, 4 April 1989.

'Ben Ali s'adresse à la Nation: Programme pour une Étape Nouvelle'. *La Presse*, Tunis, 8 November 1989, 4.

Ben Brik, Taoufik. *Une si douce dictature: Chroniques tunisiennes 1991–2000*. Tunis: RMR Editions, 2011.

Ben Dhiaf, Issa. 'Chronique politique Tunisie'. *Annuaire de l'Afrique du Nord XIX* (1980): 577–601.

'Chronique politique Tunisie'. *Annuaire de l'Afrique du Nord XX* (1981): 583–627.

'Chronique Tunisie'. *Annuaire de l'Afrique du Nord XXI* (1982): 655–713.

Ben Younes, Kamel. *al-Islamiyyun wa-l- Ilmaniyyun fi Tunis: Min al-sujun wa-l-idtihad ila tadaddi hukm al-bilad* [*The Islamists and the Secularists in Tunisia: From Prisons and Persecution to the Challenge of Ruling the Country*]. Tunis: Bareq, 2012.

Bermeo, Nancy. 'Democracy and the Lessons of Dictatorship'. *Comparative Politics* 24:3 (1992): 273–91.

Berque, Jacques. *French North Africa: The Maghrib between Two World Wars*. Translated by Jean Stewart. London: Faber & Faber, 1967.

Bessis, Sophie, and François Soudan. 'Mohamed Charfi: Mon combat contre les islamistes'. *Jeune Afrique*, Paris, 30 April 1990, 18–22.

Biernacki, Patrick, and Dan Waldorf. 'Snowball Sampling: Problems and Techniques of Chain Referral Sampling'. *Sociological Methods & Research* 10:2 (1981): 141–63.

Blaise, Lila. 'Interview de Riadh Chaïbi, démissionnaire d'Ennahdha'. *Huffpost-maghreb.com*, Tunis, 9 December 2013.

Bobin, Frédéric. 'Rached Ghannouchi: "Il n'y a plus de justification à l'islam politique en Tunisie"'. *Le Monde*, Paris, 19 May 2016.

Boubekeur, Amel. 'Islamists, Secularists and Old Regime Elites in Tunisia: Bargained Competition'. *Mediterranean Politics* 21:1 (2015): 107–27.

Boughzala, Mohamed, and Azzam Mahjob. 'Chronique économique Tunisie'. *Annuaire de l'Afrique du Nord XIX* (1980): 663–78.

'Bourguiba: Il est inadmissible que l'Université soit transformée en un forum pour des obscurantistes'. *La Presse*, Tunis, 20 February 1987.

Bouslama, Hédi. 'Le Gouvernorat de Sousse en Voie de Developpement: Bulletin économique de la Chambre de Commerce du Centre' (Sousse: Chambre de Commerce du Centre, 1972).

Bras, Jean-Philippe. 'Chronique Tunisie'. *Annuaire de l'Afrique du Nord XXIV* (1985): 697–744.

Brooke, Steven. 'From Medicine to Mobilization: Social Service Provision and the Islamist Reputational Advantage'. *Perspectives on Politics* 15:1 (2017): 42–61.

Browers, Michaelle. 'Rethinking Post-Islamism and the Study of Changes in Islamist Ideology'. In *Rethinking Islamist Politics*, edited by Marc Lynch, 16–19. Washington, DC: Project on Middle East Political Science, 2014.

Brown, Nathan J. 'A Struggle for Power: Islamism and Democracy'. *The Middle East Journal* 69:3 (2015): 463–7.

When Victory Is Not an Option: Islamist Movements in Arab Politics. Ithaca, NY/ London: Cornell University Press, 2012.

Brown, Nathan J., and Michele Dunne. 'Unprecedented Pressures, Uncharted Course for Egypt's Muslim Brotherhood' (Washington, DC: Carnegie Endowment for International Peace, July 2015).

Burgat, François. *Face to Face with Political Islam.* London: IB Tauris, 2003.

The Islamic Movement in North Africa. Translated by William Dowell. Austin, TX: Center for Middle Eastern Studies, University of Texas at Austin, 1993.

Islamism in the Shadow of al-Qaeda. Translated by Patrick Hutchinson. Austin, TX: University of Texas Press, 2008.

Calvert, John. *Sayyid Qutb and the Origins of Radical Islamism.* London: Hurst, 2010.

Camau, Michel, and Vincent Geisser. *Le Syndrome Autoritaire: Politique en Tunisie de Bourguiba à Ben Ali.* Paris: Presses de Sciences Po, 2003.

Cammett, Melani. 'Political Ethnography in Deeply Divided Societies'. *Qualitative Methods* 4:2 (2006): 15–18.

Cammett, Melani, and Pauline Jones Luong. 'Is There an Islamist Political Advantage?' *Annual Review of Political Science* 17 (2014): 187–206.

Carothers, Thomas. 'The End of the Transition Paradigm'. *Journal of Democracy* 13:1 (2002): 5–21.

Case no. 9058, Criminal Circuit Court of Appeal for Sousse, 20 April 1993.

Case no. 12183, Appeal Court of Tunis, 3 October 1981.

Cavatorta, Francesco, and Fabio Merone. 'Moderation through Exclusion? The Journey of the Tunisian Ennahda from Fundamentalist to Conservative Party'. *Democratization* 20:5 (2013): 857–75.

'Post-Islamism, Ideological Evolution and "la *tunisianité* '" of the Tunisian Islamist Party *al-Nahda*'. *Journal of Political Ideologies* 20:1 (2015): 27–42.

Chouikha, Larbi, and Éric Gobe. 'Les organisations de défense des droits de l'Homme dans la formule politique tunisienne: acteurs de l'opposition ou faire-valoir du régime?'. *L'Année du Maghreb* V (2009): 163–82.

Clark, Janine A. *Islam, Charity, and Activism: Middle-Class Networks and Social Welfare in Egypt, Jordan, and Yemen.* Bloomington, IN: Indiana University Press, 2004.

Daifallah, Mohamed. 'Min al-Sirriyya ila al-Mahjar ila al-'Alan [From Secrecy to Exile to Going Public]'. *Al-Fajr*, Tunis, 20 May 2016, 17.

Dalacoura, Katerina. 'Islamism and Neoliberalism in the Aftermath of the 2011 Arab Uprisings: The Freedom and Justice Party in Egypt and Nahda in Tunisia'. In *Neoliberal Governmentality and the Future of the State in the Middle East and North Africa*, edited by Emel Akçali, 61–84. Basingstoke: Palgrave Macmillan, 2016.

Daoud, Zakya. 'Chronique Tunisienne'. *Annuaire de l'Afrique du Nord* XXVIII (1989): 679–712.

Darrag, Amr. 'Politics or Piety? Why the Muslim Brotherhood Engages in Social Service Provision'. In *Rethinking Political Islam*, edited by Shadi

Hamid and William McCants, 218–29. New York, NY: Oxford University Press, 2017.

'Debat sur la tolerance'. *Le Maghreb*, Tunis, 18 July 1981.

'Démission du secrétaire général du bureau régional d'Ennahdha à Sidi Bouzid'. *Business News*, 5 June 2016.

Denoeux, Guilain. 'The Forgotten Swamp: Navigating Political Islam'. *Middle East Policy* IX:2 (2002): 56–81.

Dermech, Abdelkrim. 'Abdellatif El Mekki à La Presse: "Il est temps d'évaluer l'expérience de partenariat au pouvoir avec Nida Tounes"'. *La Presse*, Tunis, 19 March 2017.

Devji, Faisal. 'Islamism as Anti-Politics'. Political Theology Today Blog, 2 August 2013, www.politicaltheology.com/blog/.

Devji, Faisal, and Zaheer Kazmi. 'Introduction'. In *Islam after Liberalism*, edited by Faisal Devji and Zaheer Kazmi, 1–14. London: Hurst, 2017.

Dunn, Michael Collins. 'The An-Nahda Movement in Tunisia: From Renaissance to Revolution'. In *Islamism and Secularism in North Africa*, edited by John Ruedy, 149–64. London: Macmillan, 1994.

Eickelman, Dale, and James Piscatori. *Muslim Politics*, 2nd edn. Princeton, NJ/Oxford: Princeton University Press, 2004.

English, Richard. *Armed Struggle: A History of the IRA*. London: Macmillan, 2003.

Entelis, John P. 'Ideological Change and an Emerging Counter-Culture in Tunisian Politics'. *The Journal of Modern African Studies* 12:4 (1974): 543–68.

'Entre-Nous'. *Tunis Hebdo*, Tunis, 7 January 1980, 3.

Fahem, Abdelkader. 'Un exemple de relations villes—campagne: Sousse et le Sahel tunisien'. *Revue Tunisienne de Sciences Sociales* 15:December (1968).

Feldman, Allen. *Formations of Violence: The Narrative of the Body and Political Terror in Northern Ireland*. Chicago, IL: University of Chicago Press, 1991.

Freer, Courtney. 'Kuwait'. In *Rethinking Political Islam*, edited by Shadi Hamid and William McCants, 132–48. New York, NY: Oxford University Press, 2017.

Frégosi, Franck. 'Bourguiba et la régulation institutionelle de l'islam: les contours audacieux d'un gallicanisme politique à la tunisienne'. In *Habib Bourguiba: La trace et l'héritage*, edited by Michel Camau and Vincent Geisser, 53–67. Paris: Karthala, 2004.

'La régulation institutionelle de l'islam en Tunisie: entre audace moderniste et tutelle étatique' (Paris: Institut Français des Relations Internationales, November 2003), www.sciencespo.fr/ceri/sites/sciencespo.fr.ceri/files/artff.pdf.

al-Furati, Abdellatif. 'Hadith Khass ma' al-Shakyh Rashid al-Ghannushi [A Special Interview with Shaykh Rachid Ghannouchi]'. *Al-Sabah*, Tunis, 17 July 1988, 3.

Gambetta, Diego, and Steffen Hertog. *Engineers of Jihad: The Curious Connection between Violent Extremism and Education*. Princeton, NJ: Princeton University Press, 2016.

Gatti, Roberta, Matteo Morgandi, Rebekka Grun, Stefanie Brodmann, Diego Angel-Urdinola, Juan Manuel Moreno, Daniela Marotta, Marc

Schiffbauer, and Elizabeth Mata Lorenzo. 'Jobs for Shared Prosperity: Time for Action in the Middle East and North Africa' (Washington, DC: World Bank, 2013).

Geisser, Vincent, and Éric Gobe. 'Des fissures dans la 'Maison Tunisie'? Le régime de Ben Ali face aux mobilisations protestataires'. *L'Année du Maghreb II* (2005–06): 353–414.

'La question de 'l'authenticité tunisienne': valeur refuge d'un régime à bout de souffle?' *L'Année du Maghreb III* (2007): 371–408.

'Un si long règne … Le régime de Ben Ali vingt ans après'. *L'Année du Maghreb IV* (2008): 347–81.

Ghannouchi, Rached. 'From Political Islam to Muslim Democracy: The Ennahda Party and the Future of Tunisia'. *Foreign Affairs* 95:5 (2016): 58–67.

'Al-Fajr Musahama fi al-Hall [Al-Fajr is Participating in the Solution]'. *Al-Fajr*, Tunis, 21 April 1990.

al-Hurriyat al-'Amma fi al-Dawla al-Islamiyya [Public Liberties in the Islamic State]. Beirut: Markaz Dirasat al-Wahda al-Arabiyya, 1993.

'Al-Isti'mar Yakhruj min al-Ardh li-Yatasallal al-Ra's [Colonialism left the land to infiltrate the head]'. *al-Ma'rifa*, Tunis, Year 1: No 3 (November–December) 1972, 18–19.

'Al-Thawra al-Iraniyya Thawra Islamiyya [The Iranian Revolution Is an Islamic Revolution]'. *al-Ma'rifa*, Tunis, Year 5: No 3 (February) 1979, 3–5.

'Kalimat al-Shaykh Rashid al-Ghannushi fi Iftitah Ashghal al-Mu'tamar al-'Ashir li-l-Haraka [The Speech of Shaykh Rachid Ghannouchi at the Opening of the Tenth Congress of the Movement]'. *Al-Fajr*, Tunis, 22 May 2016, 5–7.

'Kalimat Ra'is Harakat al-Nahda al-Shaykh Rashid al-Ghannushi Khilal al-Nadwa al-Suhufiyya [The Speech of al-Nahda President Shaykh Rachid al-Ghannouchi at the Press Conference]'. Tunis, 15 August 2013. www.facebook.com/rached.ghannoushi.

'Ma Huwa al-Takhalluf? [What Is backwardness?]'. *al-Ma'rifa*, Tunis, Year 1: No 9 1973, 34–42.

'Mada Misdaq Da'wa Fashal al-Islam al-Siyasi? [How Credible Is the Claim That Political Islam Has Failed?]'. *aljazeera.net*, Doha, 24 October 2013.

Min Tajribat al-Haraka al-Islamiyya fi Tunis [On the Experience of the Islamic Movement in Tunisia]. Beirut: Dar al-Mojtahed, 2011.

'The Participation of Islamists in a Non-Islamic Government'. In *Power-Sharing Islam?*, edited by Azzam Tamimi, 51–63. London: Liberty for Muslim World, 1993.

'Qadat al-Haraka al-Islamiyya al-Mu'asira [The Leaders of the Modern Islamic Movement]'. *al-Ma'rifa*, Tunis, Year 5: No 4 (April) 1979, 13–21.

Speech at an al-Nahda rally in Sousse, 11 October 2014.

El-Ghobashy, Mona. 'The Metamorphosis of the Egyptian Muslim Brothers'. *International Journal of Middle East Studies* 37:3 (2005): 373–95.

Ghorbal, Samy. 'Le Retour du Voile'. *Jeune Afrique*, Paris, 28 July 2003.

Gobe, Éric. 'The Tunisian Bar to the Test of Authoritarianism: Professional and Political Movements in Ben Ali's Tunisia (1990–2007)'. *The Journal of North African Studies* 15:3 (2010): 333–47.

Goodwin, Jeff, James M. Jasper, and Francesca Polletta, eds. *Passionate Politics: Emotions and Social Movements.* Chicago, IL: University of Chicago Press, 2001.

'Gouvernorat de Sousse: Réalisations 1973'. *Bulletin Économique de la Chambre de Commerce du Centre* 64 (July–Aug–Sept 1973).

Gray, Doris H. 'Tunisia after the Uprising: Islamist and Secular Quests for Women's Rights'. *Mediterranean Politics* 17:3 (2012): 285–302.

Gray, Doris H., and Terry Coonan. 'Notes from the Field: Silence Kills! Women and the Transitional Justice Process in Post-Revolutionary Tunisia'. *International Journal of Transitional Justice* 7:2 (2013): 348–57.

Gsouma, Gsouma. 'Mujaz fi Tarikh al-Haraka al-Siyasiyya dhat al-Huwiyya al-ʿArabiyya al-Islamiyya bi-Tunis [A Summary of the History of the Political Movement with an Arab-Islamic identity in Tunisia]'. In *Harakat al-Nahda al-Tunisiyya: Min al-Sujun wa-l-Manafi ila Surrat al-Hukm [The Tunisian al-Nahda Movement: From Prisons and Exile to the Centre of Government]*, edited by Abdedayem Noumi, 11–27. Tunis: Matbaʿa al-Buraq, 2011.

Haenni, Patrick. *L'islam de marché: L'autre révolution conservatrice.* Paris: Éditions du Seuil, 2005.

Hafsia, Jalila. 'Espoir et Renouveau à Sousse, Perle de Culture Enchantée'. *La Presse*, Tunis, 10 April 1979.

Hallaq, Wael B. *The Impossible State: Islam, Politics, and Modernity's Moral Predicament.* New York, NY: Columbia University Press, 2014.

Hamdi, Mohamed Elhachmi. *The Politicisation of Islam: A Case Study of Tunisia.* Boulder, CO/Oxford: Westview Press, 1998.

Hamid, Shadi. 'Arab Islamist Parties: Losing on Purpose?' *Journal of Democracy* 22:1 (2011): 68–80.

Temptations of Power: Islamists and Illiberal Democracy in a New Middle East. New York, NY: Oxford University Press, 2014.

al-Hamrouni, Mohamed. 'Laysa Waridan ʿIndana al-Taraju' ʿan Huquq al-Marʿa wa-Innama al-Matruh Tawsiʿha [For us it is not a question of retracting women's rights, but of expanding them]'. *al-Maoukif*, Tunis, 22 December 2006.

Harakat al-Ittijah al-Islami. 'al-Bayan al-Taʾsisi li-Harakat al-Ittijah al-Islami [The Founding Statement of the Islamic Tendency Movement]'. In *Bayanat Dhikra al-Taʾsis li-Harakat al-Nahda al-Tunisiyya [Statements Commemorating the Foundation of the Tunisian al-Nahda Movement]*, 11–15. Tunis: Harakat al-Nahda, 2012.

'al-Nadwa al-Suhufiyya al-Awwala li-Harakat al-Ittijah al-Islami [The First Press Conference of the Islamic Tendency Movement]'. In *Bayanat Dhikra al-Taʾsis li-Harakat al-Nahda al-Tunisiyya [Statements Commemorating the Foundation of the Tunisian al-Nahda Movement]*, 16–31. Tunis: Harakat al-Nahda, 2012.

'Bayan hawla Tashkil al-Maktab al-Tanfidhi al-Jadid li-Harakat al-Ittijah al-Islami [Statement on the formation of a new Executive Bureau of the Islamic Tendency Movement]' (Tunis: 19 January 1983).

'Ijtima' al-Hay'a al-Ta'sisiyya li-Harakat al-Ittijah al-Islami 31 Mai 1981 [The Meeting of the Founding Organisation of the Islamic Tendency Movement 31 May 1981]'. In *Bayanat Dhikra al-Ta'sis li-Harakat al-Nahda al-Tunisiyya* [*Statements Commemorating the Foundation of the Tunisian al-Nahda Movement*], 8–10. Tunis: Harakat al-Nahda, 2012.

Harakat al-Nahda. *al-Bayan al-Khitami li-l-Mu'tamar al-Tasi' li-Harakat al-Nahda* [*The Concluding Statement of the Ninth Congress of the al-Nahda Movement*]. Tunis: Harakat al-Nahda, 2012.

'al-Bayan al-Khitami li-l-Mu'tamar al-'Amm al-'Ashir li-Harakat al-Nahda [The Concluding Statement of the Tenth General Congress of the al-Nahda Movement]' (Tunis: 25 May 2016), www.webcitation.org/6iVCHE3rH.

'al-Bayan al-Ta'sisi li-Harakat al-Nahda [The Founding Statement of the al-Nahda Movement]' (Tunis: 7 February 2011), www.webcitation.org/6XyfeX2JQ.

'Al-Nizam al-Asasi [The Basic Law]' (Tunis: 21–22 May 2016), www.webcitation.org/6iVBaWIjP.

'al-Qanun al-Asasi li-Harakat al-Nahda [The Basic Law of the al-Nahda Movement]'. In *Bayanat Dhikra al-Ta'sis li-Harakat al-Nahda al-Tunisiyya* [*Statements Commemorating the Foundation of the Tunisian al-Nahda Movement*], 46–53. Tunis: Harakat al-Nahda, 2012.

Barnamaj Harakat al-Nahda: Min ajl Tunis al-Hurriyya wa-l-'Adala wa-l-Tanmiyya [*The Programme of the al-Nahda Movement: For a Tunisia of Freedom, Justice and Development*]. Tunis: Harakat al-Nahda, 2011.

'Bayan al-Dhikra al-Khamisa 'Ashar, Landan fi 6 Juwan 1996. Durus al-Madi wa-Ishkalat al-Hadir wa-Tatallu'at al-Mustaqbal [The Fifteenth Anniversary Statement, London, 6 June 1996. Lessons from the Past, Present Problems and Future Ambitions]'. In *Bayanat Dhikra al-Ta'sis li-Harakat al-Nahda al-Tunisiyya* [*Statements Commemorating the Foundation of the Tunisian al-Nahda Movement*], 57–90. Tunis: Harakat al-Nahda, 2012.

'Bayan Harakat al-Nahda al-Islamiyya ba'd Istiqala al-Sayyid Mohamed al-Ghannouchi [Statement of the Islamic al-Nahda movement after the resignation of Mr Mohamed Ghannouchi]' (Tunis: 27 February 2011), www.webcitation.org/6XygJaY0P.

'Mashru' Dustur al-Jumhuriyya al-Tunisiyya [Draft of the Constitution of the Tunisian Republic]' (Tunis: Harakat al-Nahda, 2012), www.webcitation.org/6YKICg4yC.

'Nata'ij al-Taswit 'ala al-Lawa'ih fi al-Yawm al-Akhir min Ashgal al-Mu'tamar al-'Amm al-'Ashir [Results of the Votes on the Statutes on the Last Day of Work at the Tenth Congress]'. Tunis, 22 May 2016. www.webcitation.org/6ibXXPsQr.

'Shuhada' al-Haraka [The Martyrs of the Movement]'. n.d. www.webcitation.org/6fl0OzT2k.

"Ayyinat min Muraji'at Harakat al-Nahda [Samples of the Reviews of the al-Nahda movement]'. *al-Hiwar.net*, 11 June 2010. www.alhiwar.net/ShowNews.php?Tnd=7329   (archived   at: www.webcitation.org/6fDRJvCnf).

Haugbølle, Rikke Hostrup. 'New Expressions of Islam in Tunisia: an ethnographic approach'. *The Journal of North African Studies* 20:3 (2015): 319–35.

Haugbølle, Rikke Hostrup, and Francesco Cavatorta. 'Beyond Ghannouchi: Islamism and Social Change in Tunisia'. *Middle East Report* 262 (2012): 20–5.

"Vive la grand famille des media tunisiens": Media reform, authoritarian resilience and societal responses in Tunisia'. *The Journal of North African Studies* 17:1 (2012): 97–112.

Haugbolle, Sune. 'Imprisonment, Truth Telling and Historical Memory in Syria'. *Mediterranean Politics* 13:2 (2008): 261–76.

'Hend Chelbi: La femme musulmane doit conserver son authenticité'. *Le Temps*, Tunis, 3 October 1975.

Henry, Clement. 'Tunisia's 'Sweet Little' Regime'. In *Worst of the Worst: Dealing with Repressive and Rogue Nations*, edited by Robert I. Rotberg, 300–23. Washington, DC: Brookings Institution Press, 2007.

Hermassi, Abdelbaki. 'Montée et déclin du mouvement islamiste en Tunisie'. *Confluences Méditerranée* 12:Autumn (1994): 33–50.

'The Rise and Fall of the Islamist Movement in Tunisia'. In *The Islamist Dilemma: The Political Role of Islamist Movements in the Contemporary Arab World*, edited by Laura Guazzone, 105–27. Reading: Ithaca, 1995.

Hermassi, Elbaki. 'The Islamicist Movement and November 7'. In *Tunisia: The Political Economy of Reform*, edited by I. William Zartman, 193–204. Boulder, CO: Lynne Rienner, 1991.

Hermassi, Mohamed Elbaki. 'La société tunisienne au miroir islamiste'. *Maghreb Machrek* 103 (1984): 39–56.

Hibou, Béatrice. *The Force of Obedience: The Political Economy of Repression in Tunisia*. Translated by Andrew Brown. Cambridge: Polity Press, 2011.

Holland, Dorothy, Gretchen Fox, and Vinci Daro. 'Social Movements and Collective Identity: A Decentered, Dialogic View'. *Anthropological Quarterly* 81:1 (2008): 95–126.

Human Rights Watch. 'Tunisia: Long-Term Solitary Confinement of Political Prisoners' (New York, NY: HRW, July 2004).

'Tunisia: Military Courts That Sentenced Islamist Leaders Violated Basic Fair-Trial Norms' (New York, NY: HRW, October 1992).

'Tunisia: Suspension of Associations Arbitrary' (New York, NY: HRW, 13 August 2014).

'Tunisia. Crushing the Person, Crushing a Movement: The solitary confinement of political prisoners' (New York, NY: HRW, April 2005).

'Tunisia's Repressive Laws: The Reform Agenda' (New York, NY: HRW, November 2011).

Ibn Ashur, Muhammed al-Tahir. *Ibn Ashur: Treatise on Maqāṣid al-Shari'ah*. Herndon, VA/London: International Institute of Islamic Thought, 2011.

Ibrahim, Monia. 'Sousse le 16 mai 2004'. *Tunisnews*, 7 August 2004. tunisnews.net/07–08–2004/ (archived at: www.webcitation.org/ 6fO3x2EGy).

'Idrabat Musanida wa ʿItisamat fi al-Jihat [Supportive strikes and sit-ins in the regions]'. *al-Maoukif*, Tunis, 4 November 2005, 6.

INS (Institut National de la Statistique). 'Estimation de la population par commune au 1er janvier 2013' (Tunis: INS, 2013), www.ins.nat.tn.

'Estimation de la population par gouvernorat au 1er janvier 2013' (Tunis: INS, 2013), www.ins.nat.tn.

'Sousse: À travers le Recensement Général de la Population et de l'Habitat 2014' (Tunis: INS, 2014).

'Interview Transcript: Rachid Ghannouchi'. *Financial Times*, London, 18 January 2011. www.ft.com/cms/s/0/24d710a6-22ee-11e0-ad0b-00144feab49a.html.

ISIE (Instance Supérieure Indépendante pour les Élections). 'Taqrir al-Hayʾa al-ʿUlya al-Mustaqilla li-l-Intikhabat hawla al-Intikhabat al-Tashriʿiyya wa-l-Riʾasiyya 2014 [Report of the Independent High Authority for the Elections on the Legislative and Presidential Elections of 2014]' (Tunis: ISIE, March 2015).

Ismail, Salwa. *Rethinking Islamist Politics: Culture, the State and Islamism*. London: IB Tauris, 2006.

al-Jamaoui, Anouar. 'Nurid Hukm al-Balad bi-Tafwid min al-Shaʿb [We Want a Government of the Country with a Popular Mandate]'. *Al-Fajr*, Tunis, 26 October 2012, 8–9.

Jasper, James M. *The Art of Moral Protest: Culture, Biography, and Creativity in Social Movements*. Chicago, IL/London: University of Chicago Press, 1997.

'Emotions and Social Movements: Twenty Years of Theory and Research'. *Annual Review of Sociology* 37:1 (2011): 285–303.

Jebali, Hamadi. 'Bayan wa-Iʿlam [Statement and Notification]'. *Facebook.com*, Sousse, 11 December 2014. www.facebook.com/M.Hamadi.Jebali.

Jelassi, Abdelhamid. *Hisad al-Ghuyyab: al-Yad al-Saghira la Takdhib* [*The Harvest of the Absent: The Small Hand Does Not Lie*]. Tunis: Maktabat Tunis, 2016.

'Qiraʾa ʿAbd al-Hamid al-Jilasi li-l-Waqiʿ baʿda 17 Sana min al-Sijn [Abdelhamid Jelassi's assessment of the facts after seventeen years imprisonment]'. *Assabil Online*, Tunis, 8 December 2007. www.webcitation.org/6XPt3AdE7.

Jones, Linda. 'Portrait of Rashid al-Ghannoushi'. *Middle East Report* 153 (July–August 1988): 19–22.

Jourchi, Salaheddine. 'The State and Identity: The relationship between religion and politics – Tunisia as an example'. *Contemporary Arab Affairs* 6:3 (2013): 358–75.

Julliard, Jean-François, and Hajar Smouni. 'Quand la police tunisienne surveille les journalistes'. *Nawaat*, Tunis, 3 December 2006. nawaat.org/portail/ 2006/12/03/quand-la-police-tunisienne-surveille-les-journalistes/.

Kalyvas, Stathis N. *The Rise of Christian Democracy in Europe*. Ithaca, NY/ London: Cornell University Press, 1996.

Kandil, Hazem. *Inside the Brotherhood*. Cambridge: Polity, 2015.

Kéfi, Ridha. 'La participation des intégristes au processus politique divise l'opposition ... Que faire des islamistes?' *Jeune Afrique*, Paris, 22 January 2006, 40–1.

'La question divise la gauche et l'extrême gauche depuis la libération de nombreux dirigeants d'Ennahdha...Que faire des islamistes?' *Jeune Afrique*, Paris, 7 May 2006, 84–5.

Kepel, Gilles. *Jihad: The Trail of Political Islam*. London: IB Tauris, 2002.

Kerrou, Mohamed. 'La Grande Mosquée de Kairouan: L'imam, la ville et le pouvoir'. *Revue des mondes musulmans et de la Méditerranée* 125:July (2009).

Ketchley, Neil, and Michael Biggs. 'The Educational Contexts of Islamist Activism: Elite Students and Religious Institutions in Egypt'. *Mobilization: An International Quarterly* 22:1 (2017): 57–76.

Khadhraoui, Mongi. "Abd al-Hamid al-Jilasi al-qiyadi fi al-Nahda li-l-Shuruq: Tahaluf al-Nahda wa-l-Nida' ... safqat al-mughaffalin [Al-Nahda leader Abdelhamid Jelassi to al-Chourouk: The Nahda-Nidaa Alliance is ... the deal of the gullible]'. *Al-Chourouk*, Tunis, 22 September 2016.

Khalili, Laleh, and Jillian Schwedler, eds. *Policing and Prisons in the Middle East: Formations of Coercion*. London: Hurst, 2010.

Khan, Wahiduddin. *God Arises*. Riyadh: International Islamic Publishing House, 2005 [1966].

'Khatir: Masjid Yatahawwal ila Shu'ba [Urgent: A mosque is turned into a party office]'. *Al-Fajr*, Tunis, 21 April 1990.

Khiari, Sadri. 'Le Renouveau du Mouvement Democratique Tunisien: Paradoxes et Ambivalences'. In *La Tunisie de Ben Ali: La société contre le régime*, edited by Olfa Lamloum and Bernard Ravenel, 167–96. Paris: L'Harmattan, 2002.

Khiari, Sadri, and Béatrice Hibou. 'La Révolution Tunisienne ne vient pas de nulle part'. *Politique Africaine* 1:121 (March 2011): 23–34.

Kirdiş, Esen. 'Between Movement and Party: Islamic Movements in Morocco and the Decision to Enter Party Politics'. *Politics, Religion & Ideology* 16:1 (2015): 65–86.

Krämer, Gudrun. 'Integration of the Integrists: A comparative Study of Egypt, Jordan and Tunisia'. In *Democracy without Democrats?*, edited by Ghassan Salamé, 200–26. London: IB Tauris, 1994.

Kubick, Jan. 'Ethnography of Politics: Foundations, Applications, Prospects'. In *Political Ethnography: What Immersion Contributes to the Study of Power*, edited by Edward Schatz, 25–52. Chicago, IL: University of Chicago Press, 2009.

Kurzman, Charles. 'Meaning-Making in Social Movements'. *Anthropological Quarterly* 81:1 (2008): 5–15.

'Structural Opportunity and Perceived Opportunity in Social-Movement Theory: The Iranian Revolution of 1979'. *American Sociological Review* 61:1 (1996): 153–170.

Kurzman, Charles, and Didem Türkoğlu. 'Do Muslims Vote Islamic Now?' *Journal of Democracy* 26:4 (2015): 100–9.

'La Commission Bouderbala présente son rapport final'. *Leaders*, Tunis, 4 May 2012.

Ladhari, Zied. Speech at an al-Nahda rally in Hai 9 Avril, Sousse, 15 October 2014.

Televised election broadcast on al-Wataniyya, 8 October 2014.

Lagarde, Dominique, and Camille Le Tallec. 'Tunisie: "Nous avons fait preuve d'un certain laxisme face aux salafistes"'. *L'Express*, Paris, 21 September 2012.

Laraiedh, Ameur. 'Revendications et combat pour les libertés en Tunisie: vers un pacte national de l'opposition'. *Annuaire de l'Afrique du Nord* XII (2003): 329–31.

Larif-Béatrix, Asma. 'Chroniques intérieures: Tunisie'. *Annuaire de l'Afrique du Nord* XXVI (1987): 647–63.

Lawless, Richard. 'Tunisia: History'. In *The Middle East and North Africa 2003*, edited by Joanne Maher, 1050–77. London/New York, NY: Europa Publications, 2003.

'Le coordinateur régional de Nidaa Tounes à Sousse explique les raisons de sa démission'. *AfricanManager.com*, Tunis, 29 December 2013.

'Le reseau Khomeinyst'. *La Presse*, Tunis, 28 March 1987.

'Le scrutin a été tout à fait régulier'. *La Presse*, Tunis, 4 April 1989, 3.

Lönne, Karl-Egon. 'Germany'. In *Political Catholicism in Europe, 1918–1965*, edited by Tom Buchanan and Martin Conway, 156–86. Oxford: Oxford University Press, 1996.

Lourimi, Ajmi. 'al-Islamiyyun wa-l-Sulta fi Tunis [The Islamists and the Regime in Tunisia]'. In *al-Islamiyya fi Tunis [Islamism in Tunisia]*. Dubai: al-Mesbar Studies and Research Center, 2009. www.webcitation.org/6XRNFRIMY.

Lourimi, Ajmi. 'A'tabar anna 18 Uktubir Ahamm Mahatta Siyasiyya [I Consider 18 October the Most Important Political Stage]'. *Mouatinoun*, Tunis, 5 December 2007, 14. www.webcitation.org/6XPtO8SLS.

'Hal Yamlik al-Islamiyyun Mashru'an? [Do the Islamists have a project?]'. *al-'Arab al-Qatariyya*, Doha 2010. www.webcitation.org/6XRhUWbjF.

Lutterbeck, Derek. 'Tool of Rule: The Tunisian Police under Ben Ali'. *The Journal of North African Studies* 20:5 (2015): 813–31.

Lynch, Marc, 'In Uncharted Waters: Islamist Parties Beyond Egypt's Muslim Brotherhood' (Washington, DC: Carnegie Endowment for International Peace, December 2016).

'M. Mzali aux Imams: Protéger les mosquées contre le terrorisme intellectuel'. *La Presse*, Tunis, 31 July 1981.

Magnuson, Douglas. 'Islamic Reform in Contemporary Tunisia: Unity and Diversity'. In *Tunisia: The Political Economy of Reform*, edited by I. William Zartman, 169–92. Boulder, CO: Lynne Rienner, 1991.

Mahmood, Saba. *Politics of Piety: The Islamic Revival and the Feminist Subject*. Princeton, NJ: Princeton University Press, 2005.

Makhlouf, Afifa. Speech at an al-Nahda rally in Zaouiat Sousse, 17 October 2014.

March, Andrew F. 'Geneaologies of Sovereignty in Islamic Political Theology'. *Social Research* 80:1 (2013): 293–320.

Marks, Monica L. 'Convince, Coerce, or Compromise? Ennahda's Approach to Tunisia's Constitution' (Doha: Brookings Doha Center, February 2014).

Marouki, Manoubi. 'Tunisie: débat sur la démocratisation. Les huits propositions de l'opposition'. *Jeune Afrique*, Paris, 21–27 November 1990, 32–3.

Marzouki, Nadia. 'From Resistance to Governance: The Category of Civility in the Political Theory of Tunisian Islamists'. In *The Making of the Tunisian Revolution: Contexts, Architects, Prospects*, edited by Nouri Gana, 207–23. Edinburgh: Edinburgh University Press, 2013.

Masbah, Mohammed. 'His Majesty's Islamists: The Moroccan Experience' (Beirut: Carnegie Middle East Center, 23 March 2015).

Masoud, Tarek. *Counting Islam: Religion, Class, and Elections in Egypt*. New York, NY: Cambridge University Press, 2014.

Masri, Safwan M. *Tunisia: An Arab Anomaly*. New York, NY: Columbia University Press, 2017.

McAdam, Doug, John D. McCarthy, and Mayer N. Zald, eds. *Comparative Perspectives on Social Movements: Political Opportunities, Mobilizing Structures, and Cultural Framings*. Cambridge: Cambridge University Press, 1996.

McAdam, Doug, Sidney G. Tarrow, and Charles Tilly. *Dynamics of Contention*. Cambridge: Cambridge University Press, 2001.

McCarthy, Rory. 'Protecting the Sacred: Tunisia's Islamist Movement Ennahdha and the Challenge of Free Speech'. *British Journal of Middle Eastern Studies* 42:4 (2015): 447–64.

'Re-Thinking Secularism in Post-Independence Tunisia'. *The Journal of North African Studies* 19:5 (2014): 733–50.

Meddeb, Hamza. '*Peripheral Vision: How Europe Can Help Preserve Tunisia's Fragile Democracy*' (London: European Council on Foreign Relations, January 2017).

'*The Streets, the Ballot Box and Consensus: High-Stakes Elections in Tunisia*' (Oslo: Norwegian Peacebuilding Resource Centre, 2014).

Mellakh, Habib. *Chroniques du Manoubistan*. Tunis: Cérès Éditions, 2013.

Merone, Fabio. 'Enduring Class Struggle in Tunisia: The Fight for Identity beyond Political Islam'. *British Journal of Middle Eastern Studies* 42:1 (2015): 74–87.

al-Mhiri, Faouzi. Speech at an al-Nahda rally in Hammam Sousse, 18 October 2014.

Micaud, Charles, Leon Carl Brown, and Clement Henry Moore. *Tunisia: The Politics of Modernisation*. London: Pall Mall Press, 1964.

Milton-Edwards, Beverley, and Stephen Farrell. *Hamas: The Islamic Resistance Movement*. Cambridge: Polity, 2010.

Monastiri, Taoufik. 'Tunisie: Chronique Sociale et Culturelle'. *Annuaire de l'Afrique du Nord XI* (1972): 429–43.

Montgomery Watt, William. *Islamic Fundamentalism and Modernity*. Abingdon: Routledge, 2013.

Moore, Clement Henry. *Tunisia since Independence: The Dynamics of One-Party Government*. Berkeley, CA: University of California Press, 1965.

Moore, Clement Henry, and Robert Springborg. *Globalization and the Politics of Economic Development in the Middle East*. Cambridge/New York, NY: Cambridge University Press, 2001.

Murphy, Emma. *Economic and Political Change in Tunisia: From Bourguiba to Ben Ali*. Basingstoke: Macmillan, 1999.

Naccache, Gilbert. *Cristal*. Tunis: Les Éditions Mots Passants, 2011 [1982].

al-Naqati, Khawla. 'Awlawiyyatna fi al-Marhala al-Qadima [Our Priorities in the Coming Stage]'. *Al-Fajr*, Tunis, 3 October 2014, 8–9.

'Ma Zilna fi Marhala Intiqaliyya [We are Still in a Transitional Stage]'. *Al-Fajr*, Tunis, 6 November 2015, 7.

''Abd al-Hamid al-Jilasi kama Lam Yatahaddath min Qabl [Abdelhamid Jelassi as he has never spoken before]'. *Al-Fajr*, Tunis, 15 April 2016, 8–9.

Nashif, Esmail. *Palestinian Political Prisoners: Identity and Community*. Abingdon/New York, NY: Routledge, 2008.

Nasr, Seyyed Hossein, ed. *The Study Quran: A New Translation and Commentary*. New York: HarperOne, 2015.

Neier, Aryeh. 'Confining Dissent: The Political Prison'. In *The Oxford History of the Prison: The Practice of Punishment in Western Society*, edited by Norval Morris and David J Rothman, 391–426. New York, NY/Oxford: Oxford University Press, 1995.

Netterstrøm, Kasper Ly. 'The Islamists' Compromise in Tunisia'. *Journal of Democracy* 26:4 (2015): 110–24.

'The Nobel Peace Prize for 2015' (Oslo: The Norwegian Nobel Committee, 10 October 2015), www.nobelprize.org/nobel_prizes/peace/laureates/2015/press.html.

'Notre voie vers la démocratie' (Tunis: Collectif du 18 octobre pour les droits et les libertés en Tunisie, 23 November 2007).

Osman, Tarek. *Islamism: What It Means for the Middle East and the West*. New Haven, CT/London: Yale University Press, 2016.

Ould Mammar, Nacer. 'Face à la crise, Leoni Tunisie Groupe se replie sur ses bases'. *Kapitalis*, 2012, 2 August 2012.

Ounissi, Sayida. 'Ennahda from Within: Islamists or 'Muslim Democrats'?'. In *Rethinking Political Islam*, edited by Shadi Hamid and William McCants, 230–43. New York, NY: Oxford University Press, 2016.

Pace, Michelle, and Francesco Cavatorta. 'The Arab Uprisings in Theoretical Perspective – An Introduction'. *Mediterranean Politics* 17:2 (2012): 125–38.

Pargeter, Alison. 'Radicalisation in Tunisia'. In *Islamist Radicalisation in North Africa: Politics and Process*, edited by George Joffé, 71–94. Abingdon/New York, NY: Routledge, 2012.

Pickard, Duncan. 'Al-Nahda: Moderation and Compromise in Tunisia's Constitutional Bargain'. In *Political and Constitutional Transitions in North Africa: Actors and Factors*, edited by Justin O. Frosini and Francesco Biagi, 4–32. London/New York, NY: Routledge, 2015.

'Proclamation du Pacte Nationale: Une étape éminente dans l'histoire de la Tunisie'. *La Presse*, Tunis, 8 November 1988.

Qutb, Muhammad. 'Mudhakkirat al-Du'aa [A Reminder for the Preachers]'. *al-Ma'rifa*, Tunis, Year 2: No 10 (June) 1975, 34–9.

'Raf' Iltibas [A Clarification]'. *Al-Sabah*, Tunis, 14 October 1993.

'Ramadan: Les cafés et les commerces de restauration fermeront durant le jour'. *La Presse*, Tunis, 4 July 1981.

'Reflets de la vie quotidienne'. *Jeune Afrique*, Paris, 20 February 1976.

'Loi no. 59–154 du 7 novembre 1959, relative aux associations', issued by Republic of Tunisia. Tunis, 1959.

'Loi no. 72–38 du 27 avril 1972, portant création d'un régime particulier pour les industries produisant pour l'exportation', issued by Republic of Tunisia. Tunis, 1972.

'Loi no. 87–70 du 26 novembre 1987, portant modification de certains articles du code de procédure pénale', issued by Republic of Tunisia. Tunis, 1987.

'Loi no. 87–79 du 29 décembre 1987, portant suppression de la cour de sûreté de l'État', issued by Republic of Tunisia. Tunis, 1987.

'Loi no. 2003–75 du 10 décembre 2003, relative au soutien des efforts internationaux de lutte contre le terrorism et à la répression du blanchiment d'argent', issued by Republic of Tunisia. Tunis, 2003.

'Loi organique no. 88–32 du mai 1988 organisant les partis politiques', issued by Republic of Tunisia. Tunis, 1988.

Robbins, Michael. 'Tunisia Five Years after the Revolution: Findings from the Arab Barometer' (Arab Barometer, 15 May 2016).

Rock-Singer, Aaron. 'A Pious Public: Islamic Magazines and Revival in Egypt, 1976–1981'. *British Journal of Middle Eastern Studies* 42:4 (2015): 427–46.

Rollinde, Marguerite. 'Les émeutes en Tunisie: un défi à l'État?'. In *Émeutes et mouvements sociaux au Maghreb: Perspective comparée*, edited by Didier Le Saout and Marguerite Rollinde. Paris: Karthala, 1999.

Rouis, Jaleleddine. *al-Khasa'is al-Tanzimiyya wa-l-Haykaliyya li-l-Haraka al-Islamiyya fi Tunis—al-'Amal al-Jama'i [Organisational and Structural Characteristics of the Islamist Movement in Tunisia—Collective Action]*. Tunis: Manshurat Karem al-Sharif, 2014.

Roy, Olivier. *The Failure of Political Islam*. Translated by Carol Volk. London: IB Tauris, 1994.

  Globalised Islam: The Search for a New Ummah. London: Hurst, 2004.

'Political Islam after the Arab Spring'. *Foreign Affairs* 96:6 (2017): 127–32.

'The Transformation of the Arab World'. *Journal of Democracy* 23:3 (2012): 5–18.

Rudebeck, Lars. 'Developmental Pressure and Political Limits: A Tunisian Example'. *The Journal of Modern African Studies* 8:2 (1970): 173–98.

Sadiki, Larbi. 'Political Liberalization in Bin Ali's Tunisia: Façade Democracy'. *Democratization* 9:4 (2002): 122–41.

Samti, Farah, and Carlotta Gall. 'Tunisia Attack Kills at Least 38 at Beach Resort Hotel'. *New York Times*, New York, NY, 26 June 2015.

Schmitter, Philippe C. 'Twenty-Five Years, Fifteen Findings'. *Journal of Democracy* 21:1 (2010): 17–28.

Schwedler, Jillian. 'Can Islamists Become Moderates? Rethinking the Inclusion-Moderation Hypothesis'. *World Politics* 63:2 (2011): 347–76.

Faith in Moderation: Islamist Parties in Jordan and Yemen. Cambridge: Cambridge University Press, 2006.

'A Paradox of Democracy? Islamist Participation in Elections'. *Middle East Report* 209 (1998): 25–9.

Scott, James C. *Weapons of the Weak: Everyday Forms of Peasant Resistance.* New Haven, CT/London: Yale University Press, 1985.

Sdiri, Abdelwahab. *Dans cinq ans il n'y aura plus de Coran: Un prisonnier tunisien témoigne.* Translated by Luiza Toscane. Paris: Éditions Paris-Méditerranée, 2003.

Shahin, Emad Eldin. *Political Ascent: Contemporary Islamic Movements in North Africa.* Boulder, CO: Westview, 1997.

Slama, Abdul Qadir. 'Al-Iftitahiyya [The Editorial]'. *al-Ma'rifa*, Year 1: No 1 (September) 1972, 1.

Smith, Christian. 'Correcting a Curious Neglect, or Bringing Religion Back In'. In *Disruptive Religion: The Force of Faith in Social-Movement Activism*, edited by Christian Smith, 1–25. New York NY/London: Routledge, 1996.

Soli, Evie, and Fabio Merone. 'Tunisia: The Islamic Associative System as a Social Counter-Power'. *openDemocracy*, London, 23 October 2013.

Solidarité tunisienne, and Comité de défense des prisonniers politiques en Tunisie. *Les prisonniers à caractère spécial ou la tragédie des prisonniers politiques en Tunisie.* Aubervilliers: Solidarité tunisienne, 2003.

Soudan, François. 'Tunisie: La stratégie des islamistes'. *Jeune Afrique*, Paris, 19 April 1989, 36–8.

Soufan Group. 'Foreign Fighters: An Updated Assessment of the Flow of Foreign Fighters into Syria and Iraq' (New York, NY: The Soufan Group, December 2015).

'Sousse terrorist attack has caused closure of 17 hotels, 35 per cent drop in tourists (official)'. *Agence Tunis Afrique Press*, Tunis, 25 June 2016.

'Sousse: Poursuite du procès des syndicalistes impliqués dans les événements du 26 janvier'. *L'Action*, Tunis, 2 August 1978.

'Sousse: Projection du film "Le Message"'. *Le Temps*, Tunis, 7 January 1978.

Spiegel, Avi Max. 'Morocco'. In *Rethinking Political Islam*, edited by Shadi Hamid and William McCants, 54–72. New York, NY: Oxford University Press, 2017.

Young Islam: The New Politics of Religion in Morocco and the Arab World. Princeton, NJ/Oxford: Princeton University Press, 2015.

Sraieb, Noureddine. 'Tunisie – Chronique Intérieure 1993'. *Annuaire de l'Afrique du Nord* XXXII (1993): 591–643.

Starrett, Gregory. *Putting Islam to Work: Education, Politics, and Religious Tranformation in Egypt.* Berkeley and Los Angeles, CA/London: University of California Press, 1998.

Stepan, Alfred. 'Tunisia's Transition and the Twin Tolerations'. *Journal of Democracy* 23:2 (2012): 89–103.

Stepan, Alfred, and Juan J. Linz. 'Democratization Theory and the "Arab Spring"'. *Journal of Democracy* 24:2 (2013): 15–30.

Stroobants, Jean-Pierre. 'Vie et mort des assassins de Massoud'. *Le Monde*, Paris, 19 April 2005.

'Tabarra' [A Declaration of Innocence]'. *Al-Sabah*, Tunis, 17 March 1993.
'Tabarra' wa-Iltizam [A Declaration of Innocence and Commitment]'. *Al-Sabah*, Tunis, 14 September 1993.
Tamimi, Azzam. *Rachid Ghannouchi: A Democrat within Islamism*. Oxford: Oxford University Press, 2001.
Tarrow, Sidney. *Power in Movement: Social Movements and Contentious Politics*. Cambridge and New York, NY: Cambridge University Press, 2011.
Tenfelde, Klaus. 'Civil Society and The Middle Classes in Nineteenth-Century Germany'. In *Civil Society before Democracy: Lessons from Nineteenth-Century Europe*, edited by Nancy Bermeo and Philip Nord, 83–108. Lanham, MD: Rowman & Littlefield, 2000.
Tessler, Mark. 'Political Change and the Islamic Revival in Tunisia'. *The Maghreb Review* 5:1 (1980): 8–19.
Tezcür, Günes Murat. 'The Moderation Theory Revisited: The Case of Islamic Political Actors'. *Party Politics* 16:1 (2010): 69–88.
Tibi, Bassam. *Islamism and Islam*. New Haven, CT/London: Yale University Press, 2012.
Tilly, Charles. *The Contentious French*. Cambridge, MA: Belknap Press, 1986.
Tilly, Charles, and Sidney Tarrow. *Contentious Politics*, 2nd edn. Oxford: Oxford University Press, 2015.
'Tous les résultats des législatives'. *La Presse*, Tunis, 4 April 1989, 4–5.
Tripp, Charles. *The Power and the People: Paths of Resistance in the Middle East*. Cambridge: Cambridge University Press, 2013.
Tuğal, Cihan. 'Islamism in Turkey: Beyond Instrument and Meaning'. *Economy and Society* 31:1 (2002): 85–111.
'Transforming Everyday Life: Islamism and Social Movement Theory'. *Theory and Society* 38:5 (2009): 423–58.
'Tunisie: le procès des intégristes. Les islamistes du MTI menacent de réagir "face à la tyrannie"'. *Le Monde*, Paris, 11 September 1987.
'Tunisie: le procès des islamistes. L'avocat général requiert la peine de mort'. *Le Monde*, Paris, 15 September 1987.
'Tunisie: ouverture du procès d'Amina'. *Le Monde*, Paris, 30 May 2013.
al-Turki, Nadia. 'al-Jebali fi Mudhakkirathu li-l-Sharq al-Awsat: Kuntu shabban masisan bidun tawajjuh Islami [Jebali in his Recollections to Asharq al-Awsat: I was a politicized young man without an Islamist orientation]'. *Asharq al-Awsat*, London, 7 July 2014.
UPI (United Press International). 'M. Mzali à l'agence UPI: Tous les Tunisiens présentent un front uni contre l'osbcurantisme et l'intolérance'. *La Presse*, Tunis, 18 July 1981.
Usher, Graham. 'The Reawakening of Nahda in Tunisia'. *Middle East Research and Information Project*, Washington, DC, 30 April 2011. www.merip.org/mero/mero043011.
Volpi, Frédéric. *Political Islam Observed*. London: Hurst, 2010.
Volpi, Frédéric, and Ewan Stein. 'Islamism and the State after the Arab Uprisings: Between People Power and State Power'. *Democratization* 22:2 (2015): 276–93.

Walmsley, Roy. *World Prison Population List*, 6th edn (London: International Centre for Prison Studies, King's College, 2005).

Waltz, Susan. 'Islamist Appeal in Tunisia'. *Middle East Journal* 40:4 (1986): 651–70.

'Wazir al-Shu'un al-Diniyya li-l-Shuruq: Harisuna 'ala al-Tasaddi li-Zawahir al-Ta'ifiyya [Minister for Religious Affairs tells al-Chourouk: We are keen to address the phenomenon of sectarianism]'. *al-Chourouk*, Tunis, 4 January 2006.

Welchman, Lynn. 'Trying Times in Tunis: Notes from a Purposeful Observer'. In *Narratives of Truth in Islamic Law*, edited by Baudouin Dupret, Barbara Drieskens and Annelies Moors, 177–95. London: IB Tauris, 2008.

White, Gregory. *A Comparative Political Economy of Tunisia and Morocco: On the Outside of Europe Looking In*. New York, NY: State University of New York Press, 2001.

White, Jenny. *Islamist Mobilization in Turkey: A Study in Vernacular Politics*. Seattle, WA/London: University of Washington Press, 2002.

Wickham, Carrie Rosefsky. *Mobilizing Islam: Religion, Activism, and Political Change in Egypt*. New York, NY: Columbia University Press, 2002.

The Muslim Brotherhood: Evolution of an Islamist Movement. Princeton, NJ/Oxford: Princeton University Press, 2013.

Willis, Michael J. 'Between *alternance* and the *Makhzen*: At-Tawhid wa Al-Islah's entry into Moroccan politics'. *The Journal of North African Studies* 4:3 (1999): 45–80.

'Morocco's Islamists and the Legislative Elections of 2002: The Strange Case of the Party that Did Not Want to Win'. *Mediterranean Politics* 9:1 (2004): 53–81.

Politics and Power in the Maghreb: Algeria, Tunisia and Morocco from Independence to the Arab Spring. London: Hurst, 2012.

'Revolt for Dignity: Tunisia's Revolution and Civil Resistance'. In *Civil Resistance in the Arab Spring: Triumphs and Disasters*, edited by Adam Roberts, Michael J. Willis, Rory McCarthy and Timothy Garton Ash, 30–52. Oxford: Oxford University Press, 2016.

Wolcott, Harry F. *Ethnography: A Way of Seeing*. Lanham, MD/Plymouth: AltaMira Press, 2008.

Wolf, Anne. *Political Islam in Tunisia: The History of Ennahda*. London: Hurst, 2017.

Wolford, Wendy. *This Land Is Ours Now: Social Mobilization and the Meanings of Land in Brazil*. Durham, NC: Duke University Press, 2010.

World Bank. 'The Unfinished Revolution: Bringing Opportunity, Good Jobs And Greater Wealth To All Tunisians' (Washington, DC: World Bank, May 2014).

Yuval-Davis, Nira. 'Belonging and the Politics of Belonging'. *Patterns of Prejudice* 40:3 (2006): 197–214.

Zartman, I. William. 'The Conduct of Political Reform: The Path toward Democracy'. In *Tunisia: The Political Economy of Reform*, edited by I. William Zartman, 9–28. Boulder, CO: Lynne Rienner, 1991.

Zeghal, Malika. 'Competing Ways of Life: Islamism, Secularism and Public Order in the Tunisian Transition'. *Constellations* 20:2 (2013): 254–74.

'Public Institutions of Religious Education in Egypt and Tunisia'. In *Trajectories of Education in the Arab World: Legacies and Challenges*, edited by Osama Abi-Mershed, 111–24. Abingdon: Routledge, 2010.

Zemni, Sami. 'The Extraordinary Politics of the Tunisian Revolution: The Process of Constitution Making'. *Mediterranean Politics* 20:1 (2015): 1–17.

Zghal, Abdelkader. 'Les Effets de la Modernisation de l'Agriculture sur la Stratification Sociale dans les Campagnes Tunisiennes'. *Cahiers Internationaux de Sociologie* 38 (1965).

'The New Strategy of the Movement of the Islamic Way: Manipulation or Expression of Political Culture'?. In *Tunisia: The Political Economy of Reform*, edited by I. William Zartman, 205–17. Boulder, CO: Lynne Rienner, 1991.

'The Reactivation of Tradition in a Post-Traditional Society'. *Daedalus* 102:1 (1973): 225–37.

Zitoun, Lotfi. 'Lutfi Zaytun: Al-Nahda al-Jadid ... 'Almana am Tunasa? [Lotfi Zeitoun: The New Nahda ... Secularizing or Tunisianizing?]'. *al-Jadid*, Tunis, 29 March 2016. www.webcitation.org/6gPotjooe.

Index

Books in the Series